Uncle John's
BATHROOM READER®

PLUNGES INTO TEXAS

Uncle John's
BATHROOM
READER®

PLUNGES
INTO
TEXAS

Foreword by William Dylan Powell

The Bathroom Readers'
Hysterical Society

San Diego, CA

iv

UNCLE JOHN'S
BATHROOM READER
PLUNGES INTO TEXAS

For information, write
The Bathroom Readers' Hysterical Society
Portable Press
5880 Oberlin Drive, San Diego, CA 92121
e-mail: unclejohn@advmkt.com

Library of Congress Cataloging-in-Publication Data

Uncle John's bathroom reader plunges into Texas / The Bathroom
Readers' Hysterical Society ; foreword by William Dylan Powell.
    p. cm.
ISBN 1-59223-112-8 (trade paper)
1. Texas--Miscellanea. 2. Texas--Humor. I. Title: Plunges into
Texas. II. Bathroom Readers' Hysterical Institute (Ashland, Or.)

F386.6.U53 2004
976.4'002--dc22

                                                    2004050547

Printed in the United States of America
First printing: May 2004
Second printing: July 2005

05 06 07 08 09   10 9 8 7 6 5 4 3 2

v

Project Team:
Amy Briggs, Project Editor

Allen Orso, Publisher
JoAnn Padgett, Director, Editorial and Production
Stephanie Spadaccini, Copy Editor
Michael Brunsfeld (brunsfeldo@comcast.net), Cover Design
Amanda Wilson, Interior Design and Composition
Vince Archuletta, Interior Artwork
Georgine Lidell, Inventory Manager

Recipe for "Deep-Fried Rattlesnake" on page 238 is taken from *Small Game Cooking Care*, (F&N 2-7) Texas Agricultural Extension Services, The Texas A&M University System. Reproduced with permission.

CONTENTS

THANK YOU
<u>HYSTERICAL SCHOLARS!</u>

*The Bathroom Readers' Hysterical Society sincerely thanks the
following people who contributed selections to this work.*

Brian Boone

Myles Callum

Jennifer Carlisle

Jeff Cheek

Clay Griffith

Kathryn Grogman

Gordon Javna

Lea Markson

Art Montague

Geoffrey Myers

Joseph O'Connell

Bethanne Kelly Patrick

Debbie Pawlak

William Dylan Powell

John Scalzi

Stephanie Spadaccini

Sarah Thom

Christi Young

FOREWORD

Texas! Few words spark such a roaring fire of imagery, imagination, and inspiration.

From cattle trails and black gold to Enron and NASA, the name is known from London to Laos. Tell a taxi driver anywhere on the planet that you're from the United States and you're just an American. Tell them you're from Texas and you're in for a hailstorm of questions and comments ranging from cattle to gun control to Anna Nicole Smith to the TV show *Dallas*. It's more than a location—it's a legend. And whether you hang your hat in Houston like me, raise cattle in the Panhandle, or are just passing through, this land between the Red River and Rio Grande holds something that will astound you; almost too much to keep up with, in fact!

That's where Uncle John comes in. The *Uncle John's Bathroom Reader* series and Texas are a perfect fit: both are too big to ignore and too interesting to forget. This carefully crafted collection of amazing facts and figures and legends and lore gives locals the insight they're thirsting for and lets visitors in on the Texas they don't often read about in other books. Only Uncle John could take the king-size tales and tidbits of Texas and pack them into an easily digestible digest that's as easy to read on the trail as it is in the homestead.

To make it happen, members of Uncle John's Texas team traipsed all across the state from the Big Thicket to the Big Bend so you could enjoy its most amazing facts—and all from the comforts of your Lone Star sanctuary. Deep in the heart of this latest Uncle John's installment, you'll find tales and trivia on all things Texas including:

- Urban legends gone Texan
- Hidden barbecue hotspots
- The inspiration for *Lonesome Dove*
- Legal issues that surround dining on roadkill

- Classic football rivalries
- And much more!

If this is your first time to crack an Uncle John's cover, I'd like to issue you an especially warm howdy. You're now part of an underground movement dedicated to using the peace and quiet of los baños to squeeze some smarts into your cabeza—rather than just sitting there doing nada. If you're a long-time Uncle John compadre, you'll be glad you didn't miss this Texas version: just another part of a tradition of rustling up the best in rest-stop reading!

If you're from Oklahoma . . . well . . . sorry there aren't more pictures.

Make note of this book's smooth pages and unbent back because in a month it will be as weathered and worn as a West Texas ranch-hand. So hang up your Stetson, put the Cowboys game on TiVo, and let your wranglers roam free-range while you flip the page and . . .

Plunge into the great state of Texas!

William Dylan Powell
Houston, Texas, U.S.A.

PREFACE

Greetings Y'all!

    If you have this book in your hands (which you must, if you're reading this)—I envy you for you're about to embark on a larger-than-life journey through the land of the big, the bad, the beefy and the bodacious—the land where the old and new West converge (drum roll, please): the great state of Texas!

    The first in our new book series dedicated to the fifty states, ***Uncle John's Bathroom Reader Plunges into Texas*** has been written for Texians, Texicans, native-born and transplanted Texans, and anyone with a big appreciation for the legendary Lone Star State. The good folks at the Bathroom Readers' Hysterical Society, along with special contributors native to Texas (as well as those who just wish they were), worked hard and long on this inaugural edition. It even has a map for those of us who don't know where "Marfa" is.

    So saddle up, sit down, and kick off your boots to enjoy some quality reading about:

- San Antonio's Toilet Seat Museum
- The Cut-throat World of Texas Cheerleading
- Texas Jukebox: The Songs of Texas
- The Dirty Low Down on Rattlers
- Distinctive College Traditions
- The True and the False of Janis Joplin
- The Real Dirt on Rodeo Lingo
- Cowboys, Cattle, and Cabernet
- The Land of Thousand Tornadoes, and so much more.

Enough of my jabbering on, or as Frank Dobie said, "The way to spoil a story is to talk about it rather than tell it." So let's get on with our **Plunge into Texas!**

As always—go with the flow . . .

Uncle Al
Publisher

THE GRAND THRONES OF SAN ANTONE

Michelangelo had the Sistine Chapel ceiling; Leonardo had the walls of Santa Maria delle Grazie; Rembrandt had his canvases. And Barney Smith has his toilet seats.

Eighty-one-year-old Barney Smith has spent the past 35 years expressing his creative vision on approximately 700 toilet seat lids. As the collection has grown, he has turned his overflowing garage into the admission-free Texas Toilet Seat Museum, which attracts about 1,000 San Antonio visitors per year.

STILL LIFE WITH TOILET SEAT

Smith's association with toilet seats is long-standing (or you could say, sitting). He spent the first part of his adult life as a master plumber, concentrating purely on the toilet's more practical uses. However, upon retiring from that trade, the artist in Barney Smith was free to give vent to his creative urges.

Barney Smith found his new calling by accident—in one of those divinely ordained collisions of circumstance and creativity. He'd returned from a hunting trip with his father and was looking for a way to display the antlers of the deer he'd bagged. Being something of a pack rat, Smith scrounged through his stuff and happened upon a discarded toilet seat. It was the perfect size and shape; he mounted the deer horns onto it and, as they say, the rest is (art) history.

A BARNEY SMITH ORIGINAL

Smith is very particular about his "canvas." Not just any seat will do. He spurns lids made of wood or plastic, preferring instead the ones made of pressed sawdust and glue. And like the Renaissance artists of old, lucky Barney has a patron: a plumbing supply company has generously donated most of seats (although Barney prefers to call them "plaques") he's transformed into art over the years.

THE ARTIST AT WORK

Each plaque has a specific theme, commemorating special events in Barney's personal life, like the one inspired by his own eye surgery, complete with photographs and eye patches. Or social issues, like his "Stop Drugs, Say No," which features a genuine marijuana leaf embedded in it. (Its reverse side includes a note from the San Antonio Police Department giving Smith permission to own and display the pot leaf "for educational purposes.")

His work has memorialized deceased pets, chronicled vacations, and celebrated personal milestones. And as his star has risen (he has appeared on the *Today Show*, *The Early Show*, and *Montel Williams*, and been featured in *National Geographic*) people from all over the world have sent him objects to incorporate into his work.

Smith estimates that it takes him about 20 hours to go from toilet seat to work of art; he paints, etches, carves, as well as glues and embeds objects into the plaques. Each one is special to him, and he has refused repeated offers from would-be buyers.

UNFINISHED MASTERPIECE

When asked, Barney has said that he's unable to select one as a personal favorite. But if there's one that might be called his obsession it's the plaque that commemorates his wife Velma's gallstone surgery, which includes her IV, ID bracelet, and a photo of her on a gurney—but not her actual gallstones. She had to draw the line somewhere! Velma has hidden the removed stones somewhere in their house, and has refused to divulge their location. So far—search as he might—Barney Smith has been unable to find them.

* * * * *

In 2004, the first house built in Dallas, an historic log cabin, will be looking for a new address in order to make way for a parking garage. In 1841, Dallas founder John Neely Bryan built his cabin on the banks of the Trinity River. As his city has grown, his cabin has had to make way for expansion several times, although no one is certain how many times the cabin has moved.

Texan "Dooley" Wilson, the piano player Sam in *Casablanca*, couldn't play the piano.

TEXAS BASICS

Think you know the Lone Star State? Then belly up pardner, grab a pencil, and test your T.Q, Texas Quotient that is.

1. What is the state capital of Texas? (C'mon now, this is a gimme!)
   A. Austin
   B. Houston
   C. Dallas
   D. San Antonio

2. Okay then, so what's the largest city in Texas?
   A. Austin
   B. Houston
   C. Dallas
   D. San Antonio

3. There are 254 counties in Texas alone. Which one of these is not one of them?
   A. Deaf Smith County
   B. Loving County
   C. Castro County
   D. Boone County

4. Which is the largest river wholly contained in Texas?
   A. Red River
   B. Brazos River
   C. Canadian River
   D. Colorado River

5. If you were a'counting, how many species and subspecies of poisonous snakes would you find in Texas?
   A. 100
   B. 57
   C. 16
   D. 5

6. Texas is certainly a land of extremes, and the weather is no exception. Can you guess the hottest and coldest recorded temperatures in the Lone Star State?
    A. 120 degrees F and -23 degrees F
    B. 140 degrees F and -10 degrees F
    C. 115 degrees F and -15 degrees F
    D. 100 degrees F and 0 degrees F

7. Texas towns are known for their distinctive names. Can you pick out the one made up by Uncle John?
    A. Tolette
    B. Point Blank
    C. Whatchamacallit
    D. Cut and Shoot

8. Nearly all of Texas's 254 counties derive more revenue from cattle than any other agricultural commodity. Can you guess how many cattle and calves were inventoried in Texas in 2003?
    A. 14,000,000 head
    B. 100,000,000 head
    C. 10,000,000 head
    D. 30,000,000 head

9. Calling all leadfoots! What is the maximum daytime speed for cars and light trucks traveling down the Texas highways?
    A. 90 mph
    B. 70 mph
    C. 65 mph
    D. 55 mph

10. Everyone wants to live down Texas way, so it's no shock that Texas is the second most populous state in the Union. According to the last U.S. census, how many people make Texas their home?
    A. 33 million
    B. 12 million
    C. 8.4 million
    D. 20 million

Answers on page 301.

SIX FLAGS OVER TEXAS

It isn't just an amusement park.

At one time or another, six different Western nations planted their flags on the landmass that is now called Texas. Which ones were they? In chronological order:

Claimant: Spain

Held Claim to Texas:
1519–1685; 1690–1821

Flag: Spain had a number of flags, but this is the one that's usually flown as one of the six flags. The upper and lower horizontal stripes are red and the inside field is yellow. The castle and lion symbolize the arms of Castile and Leon, two ancient Spanish kingdoms.

History: Spain claimed Texas as early as 1519, when the coastline was mapped. Spain kept its claim on the area (despite the incursion of the French, which we'll get to in just a second) for 300 years, which makes the Spanish flag the one that flew the longest over Texas, so far.

Claimant: France

Held Claim to Texas: 1685–1690

Flag: A field of white with alternating rows of golden fleur-de-lis (these look like clubs on playing cards or the emblems for the New Orleans Saints if you're an NFL fan.) The fleur (French for "flower") has long been associated with all things *français*.

History: Short and nasty. The French were already in Louisiana, so they figured, what the heck, why not try for Texas? Despite the prior Spanish claims to the land, the pushy French planted their flag upon sweet Texas soil; explorer René-Robert Cavelier, Sieur de La Salle, founded an outpost known as Fort St. Louis (in what is now Victoria County, Texas) in 1685 with 200 other pushy Frenchmen. After five years of disease, famine, and attacks by Native Americans, there were only fifteen left. La Salle himself was murdered in 1687. Spain regained control and kept it for more than a century.

Frognot, based on a Texas place of that name, was "a Dallas-based alternative groove funk band."

Claimant: Mexico

Held Claim to Texas: 1821–1836

Flag: A tricolor field with green to the left, red to the right, and white in the center. Although the symbolism has changed over the years, green stood for independence, white for faith (specifically of the Catholic persuasion) and red for unity; later green stood for hope, white for purity, and red for the blood of heroes (there are still other interpretations as well). In the center of the flag is Mexico's coat of arms: an eagle on a prickly pear cactus, eating a snake. The image refers to a myth in which the Aztec people were commanded by the god Huitzilopochtli to build a city where they saw such a scene. And they did, too, right where Mexico City stands today.

History: Mexico declared its independence from Spain in 1821 but had a rough time maintaining their North American territory. Part of the problem was that so many of those irritating Americans kept crossing the border to settle there: 20,000 of them by 1832. By 1835 Texas had formed its own provisional government and in early 1836 it declared itself independent from Mexico, a move that was made official in April of '36, when Sam Houston captured Mexican leader Santa Anna at the San Jacinto River. And just like that, Mexico got the boot.

Thomas Preston, also known as "Amarillo Slim" the world-famous gambler, hails from Texas.

Claimant: Texas

Held Claim to Texas: 1836–1845

Flag: Every Texan knows it: To the left, a blue vertical stripe with a lone white star in the center; the remainder of the flag is equally divided between two horizontal stripes: white on top, red on the bottom. But did you know that, while Texas won its independence from Mexico in 1836, this familiar banner didn't become the Texan national flag until 1839? For three years *another* flag flew over Texas, a golden star centered on an azure-blue field. The flag was designed by David Burnet, the interim president of Texas in 1836.

History: Texans are proud of the fact that the state was once an independent country, and of their flag (although the rumor that Texas is the only state allowed to fly its flag at the same height as the U.S. flag is just that—a rumor). Be that as it may, the Republic of Texas had a rough go of it during its decade of independence, mostly financial. From the very start, some Texans were angling for annexation by the U.S. And interestingly enough, the U.S. wasn't in a huge rush to do it, since both Presidents Jackson and Van Buren passed on the chance to bring Texas into the fold. Eventually, in 1845, the Republic was annexed—a move that precipitated the Mexican-American War in 1846, in which the U.S. definitively got title to Texas, as well as what would become New Mexico, Arizona, California, Utah, Nevada, and parts of Colorado.

There are seaworthy replicas of the Niña, Pinta, and Santa Maria in Corpus Christi.

Claimant: The United States of America

Held Claim to Texas: 1845–1861; 1865–Present Day

Flag: This one should look familiar: the field of thirteen alternating stripes of red and white, symbolizing the original thirteen colonies of the United States; the rectangle with the white stars representing the number of states in the union. Texas was the 28th state, and so with its induction, the U.S. flag had 28 stars, arrayed in four horizontal rows of seven stars.

History: Texas was the last slave state admitted to the Union (West Virginia, which seceded from Virginia, was admitted to the Union in 1863 on the condition that slaves in the state were to be emancipated on a schedule). The slavery issue, among others, inclined Texas to secede from the U.S. with other Southern states to join the Confederate States of America in 1861. This meant that within the space of 40 years, Texas was under the control of four separate countries: Mexico, Texas, the U.S.A. and the C.S.A. Anyway, that whole C.S.A. thing ended badly, as most Americans know, but Texas's second marriage to the U.S. has been going strong for 140 years.

Stephen F. Austin and Santa Anna belonged to the same freemasonry lodge in Mexico City.

Claimant: The Confederate States of America

Held Claim to Texas: 1861–1865

Flag: The "Southern Cross" flag that many people consider the "Confederate flag" was not actually the Confederacy's national flag, it was its Naval Jack. The C.S.A. flag, known as the "Stars and Bars" had a design more similar to the Union Stars and Stripes. The similarities between two were significant enough to cause confusion on the battlefield—yipes! The number of the stars on the flag also ranged from seven to thirteen, depending on the C.S.A.'s optimism about acquiring states under Union control (the "Southern Cross" features thirteen stars). The Confederacy went through two more iterations of its flag before the Civil War ended in 1865.

History: Of the six nations that flew flags over Texas, the C.S.A. flew its flag for the briefest amount of time. Nor was the transfer to the C.S.A. a painless one for Texas: Sam Houston, governor of Texas in 1861, vehemently opposed secession and refused to pledge his allegiance to the C.S.A., a move that prompted his removal from office. During the Civil War, not only did Texas have to deal with attacks by the Union troops, but also raids by Native Americans and the Mexicans.

After the end of the Civil War, Texas returned to the Union fold and has flown the Stars and Stripes ever since.

BIG SCREEN TEXANS

They're cool, they're Texans, and you can catch them the big screen.

RENEE ZELLWEGER
Born in: Katy, Texas
Big break: Tom Cruise's love interest in *Jerry McGuire*.
Famous for: *Bridget Jones's Diary*, *Chicago*, *Cold Mountain*
Did you know: Her father was born in Switzerland and raised in Australia; her mother was born and raised in Norway. Renee is the second University of Texas graduate to win an Oscar.

TOMMY LEE JONES
Born in: San Saba, Texas
Big break: Cast on Broadway shortly after college.
Famous for: *The Fugitive*, *Batman Forever*, *Men in Black*
Did you know: Brainy Mr. Jones attended Harvard where he roomed with future Vice President Al Gore.

SISSY SPACEK
Born in: Quitman, Texas
Big break: Cast opposite Martin Sheen in *Badlands*
Famous for: *Carrie*, *Coal Miner's Daughter*, *In the Bedroom*
Did you know: Before she struck it big, Sissy lived in New York City with her cousin, actor Rip Torn. She was a folk singer and even recorded a record under the name "Rainbo."

OWEN AND LUKE WILSON
Born in: Dallas, Texas
Big Break: Owen co-wrote *Bottle Rocket*, an independent film that starred both Luke and him.
Famous for: (Owen) *Shanghai Noon* (Luke) *Old School*
Did you know: Owen was expelled from Dallas's St. Mark's Academy in the tenth grade, which inspired his *Rushmore* screenplay. Younger brother Luke stayed at St. Mark's, where he still holds five all-time track-and-field records.

In Texas, the wool-mill town of Eldorado is pronounced el-doe-RAY-doe.

OFFICIALLY IN TEXAS

Every state has a state bird, flower, and motto. But in typical Texas style, the legislature has gone and designated an official "just about anything you can think of" to represent all the truly wonderful and diverse things that make up Texas.

State Dinosaur	Pleurocoelus
State Dish	Chili
State Fabric	Cotton
State Fish	Guadalupe Bass
State Flying Mammal	Mexican Free-Tailed Bat
State Folk Dance	Square Dance
State Gem	Texas Blue Topaz
State Gemstone Cut	Lone Star Cut
State Grass	Sideoats Grama
State Insect	Monarch Butterfly
State Motto	"Friendship"
State Musical Instrument	Guitar
State Pepper	Jalapeño
State Plant	Prickly Pear Cactus
State Shell	Lightning Whelk
State Shrub	Crape Myrtle
State Snack	Tortilla Chips and Salsa
State Song	"Texas, Our Texas"
State Stone	Petrified Palmwood

Dancer Cyd Charisse (real name: Tula Ellice Finklea) was born in Amarillo on March 8, 1921.

LITTLE-KNOWN TEXAS FIRSTS

You may know that the first word spoken from the moon was "Houston," but did you know that Texas is the home of a few other fabled firsts that you probably thought happened somewhere else? Read on.

FIRST FLYING SAUCER

The term "flying saucer" dates back to a Texan named John Martin who, in Grayson County, just south of the Red River, went out hunting on January 25, 1878, hoping to see some deer or rabbits. Instead, he was stunned to see "a dark object high in the northern sky."

According to an article in the *Denison Daily News*, Martin ". . . first noticed it appeared to be about the size of an orange, after which it continued to grow larger . . . When directly over him it was about the size of a large saucer and was evidently at great height." And thus the "flying saucer" was first reported.

Idaho pilot Kenneth Arnold is often given credit for coining the term in the late 1940s.

FIRST AMERICAN THANKSGIVING

Massachusetts? Never heard of it. The real first Thanksgiving celebration took place in Texas. In 1540, Francisco Vázquez de Coronado of Spain was appointed to explore North America and seek out the "Quivira," a legendary city of gold. The expedition turned out to be a disaster—and a bad career move for everyone involved. The only gold Coronado found was in the West Texas sunset, and he lived the rest of his life as a desk jockey in Mexico City. (Yes, they had desks in the 16th century.)

But along the way, Coronado *did* find the first Thanksgiving celebration. On May 23, 1541, running low on both food and morale, Coronado and his men happened upon a band of Tejas Indians in Palo Duro Canyon (southeast of Amarillo), who gladly gave them both grub and a good time. A grateful Coronado declared it a day of giving thanks for this bounty in the new country. In 1959, the Texas Society Daughters of the American Colonists dedicated a plaque to the canyon, designating it as the place where the "first Thanksgiving feast" took place. And that makes it official.

FIRST QUIZ SHOW

This is long before *Jeopardy!* and *Who Wants to Be a Millionaire*. The world's first quiz show was the brainchild of Parks Johnson, a Houstonian who sold advertising for local radio station KTRH (still on the air). Starting in November 1932, Johnson would stand in front of Houston's Rice Hotel and—live, on the air—ask trivia questions to passersby.

The show, *Vox Pop* (as in "vox populi," meaning "the voice of the people"), didn't really take off until one stormy night when Johnson, a marketing-savvy kind of guy, offered a dollar to anyone who would brave the weather and come out to participate in his question-and-answer game. Hopeful contestants flocked to the scene and the ratings soared. Johnson sold the show to a number of networks including CBS and NBC, eventually bringing *Vox Pop* to New York, Paris, and London.

* * * * *

CARTOON KING

Fredrick Bean Avery was perhaps better known by his nickname: "Tex." Born in Taylor, Texas, Tex Avery was a true pioneer of cartoon animation. Avery's Texas-sized sense of humor and boundless imagination made his creations all the more memorable.

First at Warner Brothers, he is credited with creating Porky Pig, Daffy Duck, and in developing the wiseacre Bugs Bunny. After leaving Warner for MGM, Avery did some of his best known and loved work. The deadpan Droopy Dog and sexy Red Hot Riding Hood are among his most famous characters. For a few good laughs, check out these Avery classics: *Bad Luck Blackie*, *King Size Canary*, and *Droopy's Good Deed*.

RIDE 'EM, COWBOY!

Yee-haw! Uncle John's guide to the main events at a Texas rodeo.

Chances are if you go to a Texas rodeo, you're bound to see some roping and riding. In the meantime, you can beef up your knowledge with this quick and dirty summary of rodeo's biggest attractions.

CALF AND STEER ROPING
In the olden days, cowboys had to rope a sick calf to give it medicine, but nowadays it's done for sport, too. Here's how it works. The cowboy begins on horseback and chases a calf that's been given a head start. The cowboy has to rope the calf, flank it (imagine a mini-version of cow tipping), tie three of the calf's legs together, and remount the horse. If the calf doesn't kick its way to freedom within six seconds, the cowboy has successfully completed the event.

Steer roping is calf roping, but on a larger scale. In fact, it's on *too* large a scale, which is why this event is rarely performed—most arenas aren't big enough . . . even in Texas. For this event you have to cross the border into Oklahoma to the Lazy E Arena, where the National Steer Roping Finals are held each November.

TEAM ROPING
This is a two-man job. One cowboy is the "header" whose job is to rope the steer's head. The other cowboy is the "heeler" who must rope the steer's—you guessed it—heels or feet. The event ends when the steer is roped and both riders' horses are facing each other. Giddy-up!

STEER WRESTLING
In this corner, the challenger, weighing in at 195 pounds. In the opposite corner, the defending champion, at 855 pounds. It's man versus beast. The steer is given a head start and runs in a straight line while driven by a "hazer," a rider on horseback. The cowboy or "bulldogger" rides a horse to catch up to the galloping steer, leans over to grab onto the steer's horns. Then he slides completely off his horse to leverage his weight, slow down the steer,

---

and throw it on its side. The clock stops when the cow is completely tipped with all four hooves pointing the same direction. Billed as the fastest event in rodeo, the current world record is 2.4 seconds!

SADDLE BRONC RIDING

In this event, all a cowboy has to do is stay on the horse for eight seconds. Easy? You try it. The rider starts with his feet over the horse's shoulders, which makes it easier for the horse to throw the rider. With one hand only, the rider then holds onto a thick rein attached to the horse's halter while the horse basically goes nuts and tries to toss the rider. The idea is to aim for a smooth ride in rhythm with the horse's movements. Not so easy. The rider is disqualified if his free hand touches anything (including himself), if he drops the rein, or if a foot falls from a stirrup. So, now that you know the rules, find the softest saddle money can buy, throw it on the bronc's back, and go for it cowboy!

BAREBACK RIDING

This event is like the saddle bronc ride, only sans saddle. Some say this is most physically demanding event in the rodeo. The handhold, called "rigging," is made of leather and secured atop the base of the horse's neck (also known as "withers"). The rider holds onto the rigging with one hand and tries to stay on the horse for the eight seconds. As with the other rides, the free hand must not touch anything or the rider will be disqualified.

BULL RIDING

In the rodeo they save the best for last, and that's no bull! Well, actually, it is bull. This is the most popular event of the rodeo. It's just like riding a bronco bareback except the bull is hundreds of pounds heavier, has a meaner disposition, and a pair of very sharp, very pointy horns. If the rider manages to stay on the bull for eight seconds without his free hand touching anything, or without being trampled or gored, then that cowboy will get applause and live to see another prairie sunset. Coordination, balance, strength, and flexibility all factor in, but mental toughness is probably a bull rider's most prized asset.

For more on rodeo, see "Rodeo Lingo" on page 91, "Who Started It?" on page 184, and "Horse, Cow and the Hoosegow" on page 279.

There are 16 major military installations in Texas.

HOTTER 'N A BURNIN' STUMP

Whether five-alarm or just smoke-alarm, there's nothing like a bowl of Texas chili to fill a belly up!

If you know beans about chili, allow us to tell you something really important: Texas chili has no beans. Not a one. Maybe in other states you'll find a bean or two. But in Texas, chili is just a fiery molten stew made of beef, onions, tomatoes, spices, and lots and lots of chili peppers. Everybody has a special recipe, but no true Texan would add a legume to the mix.

CONSIDER THE SAUCE

Chili's past is a little bit shady since nobody quite knows who invented it or when. Some say it was invented by cattle drivers and trail hands during long cattle drives. Others speculate that chili's origins go much farther back in time to the Mayans, Aztecs, and Incas. Still others give credit to Canary Islanders who started immigrating to the San Antonio region as early as 1723. They were known for concocting tasty dishes using local peppers, meat, onions, and most important of all, cumin.

And let's not forget the Chili Queens of San Antonio, a group of ladies who, legend has it, earned that moniker when they stirred up and sold vats of the meaty goo on street corners and in front of the famed Alamo in the mid-nineteenth century. No matter who you thank for it, there's no denying the melting-pot influence of a variety of cultures on this hot and spicy dish.

HOT STUFF

Even the field of chili technology is a heated battleground. The invention of chili powder enabled cooks to streamline their recipes a bit, but just who invented chili powder also remains a mystery. We do know that chili powder is indeed a Texan invention, but was it German immigrant, Willie Gebhardt, who moved to San Antonio near the turn of the century and registered his Eagle Brand Chili Powder? Or was it Fort Worth grocer DeWitt Clinton

---

The largest, Fort Hood, is located in Killeen in central Texas.

Pendery's own blend of spices that was the first true chili powder?

Either way, chili's popularity grew and grew during the late nineteenth century. It first hit the global stage at the 1893 World's Fair in Chicago, where a booth offered San Antonio Chili for all to taste.

TOP CHILI DOG

One of the most famous chili contests is the Chilympiad, a festival that began in 1969 in San Marcos, Texas. Every year during the second week of September, competitors bring their chili recipes out for battle. All chili has to be made from scratch and all contestants have to be male. Luckily, the gals have their own women-only contest in Luckenbach called Hell Hath No Fury Like A Woman Scorned. Winners of both festivals automatically qualify for the World's Championship Chili Cookoff, held every year in Terlingua, Texas.

The World Championship is held during the first weekend in October. Men and women compete for a $25,000 grand prize and the title of world champion. A number of colorful characters have won this contest, but their recipes have even more colorful names:

- Warning Shot Chili - Runs for Your Life (2002)
- Road Meat Chili (1991)
- Tarantula Jack's Thundering Herd Buffalo Tail Chili (1989)
- Shotgun Willie Chili (1985) (named after Willie Nelson)
- Bottom of The Barrel Gang Ram Tough Chili (1984)
- Capitol Punishment (1980)

THE REST OF US

If "Capitol Punishment" and "Warning Shot Chili" are world champions, then what are toned-down recipes called? Maybe "Slap on the Wrist" or "Water Pistol Chili" would be appropriate recipe names for those among us with tender stomachs.

The largest roundup of wild mustangs in Texas was staged about 1878.

GAME-TIME TRADITIONS AT TEXAS UNIVERSITIES

Check out these major Texas universities and their game-time football traditions.

Texans *love* their football—especially when their alma mater hits the field. And each school has its own unique traditions to help give the fans something to cheer, or jeer, about.

HOOK 'EM HORNS!
UNIVERSITY OF TEXAS AT AUSTIN

1. *The Torchlight Parade*
This annual event ramps up the fans for the big game against the University of Oklahoma at the Red River Shootout in Dallas. Sponsored by the alumni association, Texas Exes, the tradition dates back to 1916 when it was originally held prior to a Thanksgiving Day game against Texas A&M.

2. *The Hex Rally*
This tradition was started in 1941 when a palm reader was asked to put a curse on the Texas A&M team to help break a University of Texas losing streak. It worked, and now it's an annual event. Each night before their Thanksgiving Day game against A&M, Longhorn fans gather at UT's main building to hex their opponents.

3. *Old Smokey*
To get the crowd pumped up, the official University of Texas cannon, Old Smokey, fires off at halftime, after a Texas touchdown, and when the game is over. The cannon has been traditionally fired by a "spirit" group known as the Texas Cowboys.

A herd of 1,000 horses was captured to fill an order from the Argentine government.

4. *Alpha Phi Omega Texas Flag*

The Alpha Rho Chapter of Alpha Phi Omega, a service fraternity at University of Texas, owns the three largest Texas flags in the world. During the pre-game activities in Austin, the game-time flag is marched out onto the field, where it blocks out an impressive amount of turf. It's also marched at the annual Texas-Oklahoma game at the Cotton Bowl in Dallas.

5. *Socializing*

Every football game is a chance to socialize, but UT fans have it down to an art form. The fact that campus is only two short miles from Austin's famous Sixth Street means that a home game is often just the first in a series of the evening's social events before a long night of visiting the live music scene, restaurants, and piano bars of Texas's capital.

GO TECH!
TEXAS TECH UNIVERSITY, LUBBOCK

1. *The Masked Rider*

Started on a dare in 1936, this tradition involves an unknown masked man circling the football field on a horse. The men who rode were first called "ghost riders" because their identities were kept secret, even to other students. The tradition was made official on January 1, 1954, at the Gator Bowl in Jacksonville, Florida, when just as the team was about to meet Auburn University, Tech student Joe Kirk Fulton donned a black cape and unexpectedly charged a horse in front of the team on the field. Today the Masked Rider leads the team into the game and circles the stadium accompanied by cannon fire when a Tech touchdown is scored.

2. *The Wrapping of Soapsuds*

At the entrance of Texas Tech University sits a 3,200 pound statue of Will Rogers on his favorite horse, Soapsuds, riding into the West Texas sunset, permanently positioned so that the horse's rear faces Texas A&M. During a home game, the statue and its base are wrapped in red crepe paper by a student group called the Saddle Tramps. During national tragedies, the Saddle Tramps wrap the horse and rider in black.

The wreck of the USS *Hatteras* lies in 60 feet of water about 20 miles south of Galveston.

3. Victory Bells

The victory bells that hang over the east tower of the Administration Building were a gift from the class of 1936. That year, the students were told that if they beat Texas Christian University, they could ring the 1,200-pound bells all night long. They did, but almost nobody in Lubbock could sleep a wink that night with a bell nearing the size of the Liberty Bell clanging away. From then on, it was agreed that a half-hour of bell ringing would suffice.

4. Tortilla Toss

This recent tradition is passionately discouraged—and officially prohibited by University officials. Tech football fans spin tortillas by the thousands on their fingertips and fling them into the air. The gesture started in the late 1980s when someone from a rival school said Lubbock was "good for nothin' but tortillas." The field has been so thick with flying flour frisbees at times that yardage penalties have been assessed against the team.

GIG 'EM AGGIES!
TEXAS A&M UNIVERSITY, COLLEGE STATION

1. The Twelfth Man

In a tradition known as "The Twelfth Man," every spectator at an A&M football game stands the entire time. The tradition dates back to the late 1920s at the Dixie Classic football game in Dallas when Texas A&M was playing Kentucky's Centre College. There'd been a number of injuries, so A&M coach Dana Bible asked E. King Gill, there as a spectator in the press box, to join the game. He suited up and stood at the ready for the whole game, just waiting to be called in. He didn't make it into the game, but now spectators all stand in tribute to him.

2. Aggie Bonfire

Every year since 1909, when their game against the rival University of Texas rolls around, the students of Texas A&M construct a huge bonfire representing their burning desire to win the game. The fire's design, construction, and maintenance personnel are called "red pots" because of the red hardhats they wear. The event was banned from campus in 1999, when some students were

It was sunk in an engagement with the Confederate raider CSS *Alabama*.

tragically killed because their pile of logs collapsed during construction. The student body has since taken the event off-campus.

3. Midnight Yell
Held the night before a home game, and Thursdays before an away game, students are led in old army songs, the A&M fight song, and speeches declaring their opponents' impending doom on the football field. At the end, each participant kisses his or her date. Those who don't have dates are supposed to light a cigarette lighter—the idea being that two dateless people could find each other in the crowd.

4. Maroon Out
A recent addition, this involves the fans wearing maroon T-shirts to wash out the opposing team's colors in the stands. While that's sort of every college team's goal, the Aggies take it to the extreme. Prior to a 1998 game versus Nebraska, Aggies created a national shortage of maroon T-shirts. Each year, one game is chosen for the Maroon Out—its victims thus far including Notre Dame, Texas, and Oklahoma.

5. Sportsmanship
In what can only be called a collegiate freak of nature among state universities, you will exclusively find only well-groomed, and well-mannered "good sports" in the stands at A&M. Visitors to College Station frequently comment that there's nary a scruffy ne'er-do-well in the bunch. As opposed to conventional college environments, peer pressure among Texas A&M students actually discourages drinking, cussing, and fighting at football games.

For more on college football in Texas, turn to "Always an Aggie? Lifetime Longhorn?" on page 182.

The earliest Texas pottery, related to a tradition known as Tchefuncte, dates back to c. 500–100 BC.

ISN'T SHE LOVELY?

Beauty pageants are serious business in Texas—especially in the smaller towns. Check out these small-town titles and their 15 minutes of down-home fame.

QUEEN CITRIANA, MISSION

Queen Citriana is the Rio Grande Valley's most coveted small-town beauty title, and her coronation is the high light of the Texas Citrus Fiesta. The contestants wear antebellum gowns themed to the principal agricultural products of their hometowns (oranges, grapefruits, etc.). During the product style review, the ladies model outfits made from the actual fruits, vegetables, or flowers which, according to the Chamber of Commerce, have been cleverly manipulated by contestants and at times, according to officials, "pulverized, dehydrated, blended or microwaved."

MISS CRAB LEGS, CRYSTAL BEACH

Every Mother's Day, thousands of crab lovers scuttle over to the Texas Crab Festival on the Bolivar Peninsula, a key event of which is the Miss Crab Legs contest. The quest for cuties is divided into categories from "Sand Fiddler" (babies) to "Miss" (girls 13 to 21). According to the commissioners, the contestants are judged based on "personality, cuteness, and crab festival spirit," and will do anything from gymnastics to throwing candy to curry favor with the crowd. Not all contestants go home with a title, but none of them go home hungry (as long as they like crab legs).

OLD TIME BEAUTY, OZONA

The Ozona Chamber of Commerce starts its Fourth of July celebration early, with a pretty amazing (for Texas) spectacle. On the evening of July 3, everyone turns out to eat old-fashioned home-made ice cream and watch the Old Time Beauty Pageant in which men model old-fashioned swimsuits.

Rattlesnake Canyon in southwestern Val Verde County has pictographs dating to prehistoric times.

WATERMELON THUMP QUEEN, LULING

Every June, Texans descend on the small Central Texas town of Luling for its annual Watermelon Thump and the prestigious crowning of the Watermelon Thump Queen. Once the queen is crowned (and puts on her sequined watermelon-themed gown) she presides over all the festivities and mingles with her court of 40,000 melon-hungry subjects. Being royalty and all, she's not encouraged to participate in the seed-spitting contest.

MISS QUITO, CLUTE

Under the watchful eyes of Willie-Man-Chew, the world's largest mosquito (26 feet tall and wearing a cowboy hat, of course), the Great Texas Mosquito Festival holds foot races, a cook-off (fajitas, not mosquitoes), a Mosquito-Calling Contest, the Xtreme Karaoke Finals, and, oh, yes, the reason we brought you here—the Miss Quito Beauty Pageant. The organizers, who Willie affectionately calls his "Swat Team," invite you to drop by this next July.

MISS GOAT BBQ, ELECTRA

Held in early May, during this Texas-Oklahoma border town's annual Electra Goat BBQ Cook-Off, the Miss Goat BBQ is one of Electra's most important events. Officially sanctioned by the Lone Star Barbecue Society, the pageant gives beauty contestants the chance to participate in the "cow patty plop." A 100-square grid is laid out on a field and participants can buy a square for $20.00 a pop. If you're lucky enough to have a cow defile your square, then you can win $1,000. But, the Miss Goat BBQ contest could cause a scheduling conflict and difficult career choices concerning the Miss Crab Legs contest, which is usually held on the same day.

QUEEN YAM, GILMER

Held in the fall since 1935, the four-day-long East Texas Yamboree—celebrating, you guessed it, the yam—brings folks in from all over the state. The queen is crowned in "royal cere-monies" over the course of two nights, amidst the event-packed festival's other activities, which include a bass-fishing tournament, barn dance, yam-decorating contest for kids, and an air show. The lucky Queen Yam gets to star in her own high-profile parade, along with the usual gang of Shriners, boy and girl scouts, and high school marching bands. As American as sweet potato pie.

Sam Houston's home is on the campus of Sam Houston State University in Huntsville.

DIRTY, LOW-DOWN RATTLESNAKES

Nothing fires the imagination like the Western Diamondback rattlesnake. Macho Texans hunt them, stuff them, mount them, eat them, and wear their skins as hatbands, belts, and cowboy boots.

ALL THAT SLITHERS
Texas has more species and subspecies of snakes than any other state in the Union; they can be found in every Texas county. Of the more than 100 species and subspecies, 16 are poisonous—the list includes copperheads, coral snakes, cotton-mouths (water moccasins that get their name from the whiteness inside their open mouths), and most notably, rattlesnakes.

VITAL STATISTICS, VITAL INFORMATION
The Western Diamondback rattlesnake (*Crotalus atrox*, to scientists) lives in almost any Texan environment: rocks, caves, brush, cactus, mesquite, and arid or semiarid regions, but—and note this well—is especially partial to junk piles, woodpiles, and trash.

They can grow more than seven feet long and live as long as 25 to 30 years. They don't just slither along the ground either: they also climb trees and swim. The diamondback belongs to the pit viper family, a snake that has heat-sensitive "pits" near its eyes and nose, that enable it to target warm-blooded prey such as rodents and other small mammals—or, when disturbed or surprised, people. There are about 8,000 reported pit viper bites every year in the United States.

Bites are extremely painful and can be fatal. The Western Diamondback is responsible for more human deaths than any other snake in the United States In Texas, two to three deaths every year can be attributed to rattlesnake bites. A rattler's venom is a powerful anticoagulant, which thins the blood, and contains enzymes that digest nearby tissue.

SHAKE IT, BABY!
A rattlesnake is distinguished by its rattle, which consists of a light horny material that grows much like fingernails. Every time

the snake sheds its skin (about two or three times a year), new rattles are added at the base of the tail. But you can't tell a rattlesnake's age by the length of its rattle because, as with fingernails, the ends sometimes break off.

Scientists think that the rattle developed as a means of intimidating enemies. A rattlesnake will rattle before striking, but not necessarily if it's surprised or frightened.

Rattles vibrate at 40 to 60 cycles per second, which is faster than the human eye can perceive. Many people think that the sound of a rattlesnake's rattle is unmistakable, but in fact, it can be mistaken for the sound of a buzzing insect, such as a cicada.

Several other snakes vibrate their tails when alarmed, but only the rattlesnake possesses true rattles. The ratsnake and the bullsnake, two species of nonpoisonous snakes that often share rattlesnakes' habitats, are very clever at imitating rattlers to warn off predators. When they shake their tails around dead leaves and debris, it's nearly impossible to tell the difference. When in doubt, stay away.

DON'T BE A SUCKER

Being bitten by a rattlesnake is a staple of Western movie plots. The hero shows his courage and resourcefulness by using his trusty knife to make an x-shaped incision over the bite and then by sucking out the venom. This practice has led to a number of jokes involving snakebites on various parts of the anatomy, with the punch line, "You want me to *what?*"

But you can't believe everything you see in the movies. For instance, an incision near the wound can introduce serious infection, and venom can be absorbed through the mouth.

The recommended treatment includes washing the affected area with soap and water, wrapping a bandage above the bite (but not so tight as to cut off blood circulation), and seeking immediate medical care for treatment with antivenin. The victim should try to remain calm, since activity only speeds up absorption of the venom.

LOW-DOWN, DIRTY FACTOIDS

• Rattlesnakes can't hear the sound of their own rattles.

• Fangs are hinged so they fold back into the mouth when not in use.

• Fangs are hollow and deliver venom like a hypodermic needle.

• Rattlesnakes aren't immune to their own venom. A rattlesnake has been known to bite itself and die from the bite. (Hey, nobody ever accused them of being geniuses.)

• About 25 percent of rattlesnake bites are "dry," meaning that they contain no poison.

• Recently dead snakes can still have the reflex to bite, and their fangs can still contain venom.

• Some bites don't show expected two-fang punctures. They can even look like a single scratch or abrasion.

• A rattlesnake can lift its head off the ground 20 inches when striking. Its head and tail characteristically incline at 45-degree angles.

• Rattlesnakes bear live young.

• Although they hunt alone, rattlesnakes tend to live in groups of 200 to 300, and sometimes as many as a thousand.

For more on rattlesnakes, see "Yet Another White Meat" on page 236.

Galveston County's Bolivar Lighthouse appeared on TV in the 1970 drama *My Sweet Charlie.*

TRAIPSING THROUGH TEXAS

The cowboy boot right yonder is crammed with the names of 34 Texas towns and cities, reading across, down, and diagonally. Your job is to track them down in the grid. Once you've found them all, the leftover letters will reveal a tidbit about a few more Texas cities that have something in common.

ALBANY	MULESHOE
ALICE	ODESSA
ATHENS	ORANGE
BOSTON	OZONA
COLORADO	PADUCAH
COLUMBUS	PALESTINE
COMANCHE	PANHANDLE
DICKENS	PECOS
EDNA	PITTSBURG
EL PASO	RICHMOND
ELDORADO	SAN ANTONIO
FLOYDADA	SAN DIEGO
HONDO	SEMINOLE
KERMIT	SEYMOUR
MARFA	VEGA
MATADOR	WACO
MEMPHIS	
MIAMI	

Answers on page 304.

```
              S  O  M  E  O  T  H
           R  U  O  M  Y  E  S  F  E
           O  D  A  R  O  D  L  E  R
           D  C  P  E  C  O  S  I  C
           A  K  T  A  Y  I  E  O  E
           T  S  E  D  D  A  L  L  L
           A  O  A  R  R  U  P  E  D
           M  D  E  B  M  A  C  P  N
           A  E  N  B  S  I  R  A  A
           T  S  U  O  L  O  T  L  H
           H  S  S  A  M  W  N  E  N
           E  A  A  I  L  H  F  S  A
           N  N  N  I  H  B  C  T  P
           S  A  D  P  E  P  A  I  L
           D  N  I  M  A  I  M  N  R           B
           R  T  E  O  W  A  E  E  Y           O
           T  O  G  K  R  H  L  N  M     R  Z  S
        S  H  N  O  F  C  O  L  O  R  A  D  O  C  A  W
     B  S  O  I  A  N  N  I  V  I  N     L  N  L
  U  E  T  N  O  A  I     V  D  G  E        A
  R  L  S  E  D  M  M     A  E  N  D        D
G  U  O  B  R  O  E        O  W  G  N
M  B  N  W  C  S           O  O  D  A
```

His mother, Florence, started it with a $60 loan in 1905. It now has annual sales of about $2 billion.

TEXAS JUKEBOX

The stories behind some of Texas's greatest hits.

Once you learn the facts about a few Texas songs, you'll be able to belt out the tunes Texas style—loud and proud!

FROM LARGEST TO BOLDEST

The official state song of Texas is "Texas, Our Texas," music by William J. Marsh and lyrics by Marsh and Gladys Yoakum Wright of Fort Worth. The state legislature officially adopted it in 1929 after it won a state song competition. It goes something like this:

> Texas, Our Texas! All hail the mighty State!
>
> Texas, Our Texas! So wonderful so great!
>
> Boldest and grandest, withstanding ev'ry test
>
> O Empire wide and glorious, you stand supremely blest.

But wait. That third line used to read "largest and grandest," but after Alaska became the forty-ninth state in 1959, Texas wasn't the biggest state anymore. Despite the loss, Marsh swapped "largest" for "boldest." Just try to take *that* one away from Texas!

THE OTHER ROSE OF TEXAS

"The Yellow Rose of Texas" gets all the good press, but what about the beautiful "San Antonio Rose"?

> Deep within my heart lies a melody,
>
> A song of old San Antone,
>
> Where in dreams I live with a memory
>
> My rose, my rose of San Antone

Bob Wills, the "King of Western Swing" and front man for the Texas Playboys, penned the song. It was first released as an instrumental; the lyrics weren't recorded till 1940. Since then, it's been covered by the likes of John Denver, Patsy Cline, Willie

---

There are 11 creeks or streams in Texas called Honey Creek.

Nelson, and Elvis Presley. Rumor has it that the *Apollo 12* astronauts sang it as they looked back on Earth from the Moon.

CLAP! CLAP! CLAP! CLAP!
June Hershey and Don Swander wrote the lyrics and music for this hand-slapping song back in 1941.

> The stars at night are big and bright
>
> (Clap! Clap! Clap! Clap!)
>
> Deep in the heart of Texas

A popular standby for most of the twentieth century, the song got big play in 1985 in the movie *Pee-Wee's Big Adventure*. The plot went like this: Pee-Wee's bike was stolen and a psychic told him it was being hidden away in the basement of the Alamo. So Pee-Wee raced off to Texas and phoned his girlfriend Dottie once he arrived, but she didn't believe him. To prove he was really in Texas, Pee-Wee belted out "The stars at night are big and bright!" to which the people walking on the street emphatically replied "(Clap! Clap! Clap! Clap!) Deep in the heart of Texas!"

By the way, we wouldn't recommend looking for much of anything in the basement of the Alamo, since it doesn't have one.

GOING STRAIT TO TENNESSEE
If all your exes live in Texas, should you move to Tennessee? That's what proud Texan George Strait recommended in his 1988 Grammy-nominated song, "All My Exes Live in Texas".

> All my exes live in Texas,
>
> And Texas is a place I'd dearly love to be.
>
> But all my exes live in Texas
>
> And that's why I hang my hat in Tennessee.

During the 1980s and 1990s, Strait had 26 number-one hits on the country music charts. Not bad for a young farmhand from Poteet, Texas. With Merle Haggard as one of his musical influences, Strait gave his music a true country feel with honky-tonk roots and steel guitar riffs. He does a nice job of making you feel sorry for the narrator of this song; Texas being such a big place, that guy must have *a lot* of exes.

There's a town named Honey Creek in Texas too.

STATE BIRD: THE NORTHERN MOCKINGBIRD

Senate Concurrent Resolution No. 8, 40th Legislature, Regular Session (1927)

MOCK. Yeah!

ING. Yeah!

BIRD. Yeah!

YEAH. Yeah!

So much more than a James Taylor-Carly Simon duet, the mockingbird is a proud symbol of Texas. Despite a rather dowdy appearance—drab gray feathers and white patches on its wings—the northern mockingbird makes up for what it lacks in looks with its beautiful voice. Without a call to call its own, the mockingbird does what it's named for: imitates other birds (or whatever else it hears, like a dog's bark or a whistle). Some scientists think that the more sounds a male mockingbird can imitate, the more females he'll attract. The bird's official name also reflects its talent, *Mimus* (to mimic) *polyglottos* (many-tongued). Just call him the Rich Little of the animal kingdom.

MARRIED, WITH CHILDREN

The bird averages ten inches in length and weighs in at less than two ounces, with a fourteen-inch wingspan. Dinners consist of delicacies like insects, berries, and snails. Anyway, no matter how many females a male attracted in his younger days, when he finds that special one, he keeps her—mockingbirds mate for life. They share the duties of building cuplike nests in the spring to house their three to five blue-green brown-spotted egg-children that hatch in about twelve days, and are ready to leave the nest at two weeks old.

Houston is the fourth-largest U.S. city after New York, Los Angeles, and Chicago.

NO PLACE LIKE HOME

They're small but tough—and passionate protectors of their home. They don't think twice about attacking a hawk, cat, or human being if they feel threatened.

Back in 1926, the Texas Federation of Women's Clubs campaigned to make the northern mockingbird the official state bird of Texas. The following year, the legislature declared that: " . . . [the northern mockingbird] is found in all parts of the State, in winter and in summer, in the city and in the country, on the prairies and in the woods and hills, and is a singer of distinctive type, a fighter for the protection of his home, falling, if need be, in its defense, like any true Texan . . ." And as any true Texan knows, no one could ask for more.

* * * * *

SATISFIED APPETITES

Texas's Chicken Ranch, in La Grange, Fayette County, was made famous by the Broadway musical *The Best Little Whorehouse in Texas*. It was perhaps the oldest continuously running brothel in the nation. But how'd it get that odd name? In 1905, Miss Jessie Williams (born Faye Stewart) bought two buildings and eleven acres outside of the city limits of La Grange. This became the location of what would become the Chicken Ranch. As the Great Depression hit, Miss Jessie was forced to lower her prices. Customers were not so plentiful and the girls grew hungry. So Miss Jessie began the "poultry standard" of charging "one chicken for one screw." Soon chickens were everywhere, the establishment became known as the Chicken Ranch, and full bellies and satisfied customers abounded.

Singer-songwriter Kris Kristofferson was born June 22, 1936, in Brownsville, Texas.

GHOSTLY GALS
OF TEXAS

*Some people think Texas is the closest thing to heaven.
Here are the stories of three late, lamented ladies who still won't
leave, even after death.*

Who: Josephina "Chipita" Rodriguez
Where: San Patricio, Texas
What: Appears on dark nights sporting a noose round her neck.
When: Starting in 1863
Why: Chipita owned a small inn on the banks of the Aransas
River. When her father left to fight for Texan independence (and
eventually to be killed), one of those men of poor character came
upon her inn and took advantage of pretty Chipita. The man
stayed long enough to be considered her common-law husband,
until she had his baby—at which time he abandoned her. After
that, she lived quietly and kept to herself.

One day in 1863, a weary traveler named John Savage arrived
to rent a dusty cot and get a cheap meal. He was carrying $600 in
gold. According to legend, after Savage had eaten and lay down,
she went for her usual evening walk. When she returned, she saw
a man standing over Savage's murdered body. As the story goes,
the moonlight brightened his face to reveal him as Chipita's son,
Juan Silvera.

To the sheriff, it looked like robbery. Savage's body had been
found near Chipita's place and she was the last to see him alive—
there was even some blood right there on her porch. Chipita was
tried, convicted, and jailed. She told nobody the true events until
she entrusted her secret to a close friend just before she was
hanged on November 13, 1863. Since then she's been seen roam-
ing the countryside near San Patricio—the noose still dangling
from her neck. They say she appears each time a woman is wrong-
fully accused of a crime on Texas soil.

Who: Rebecca "Miss Bettie" Brown
Where: Galveston, Texas
What: Appears in the old Ashton Villa mansion, playing the piano, watching over the house, and generally messing with everything.
When: Starting in the 1980s
Why: Miss Bettie was the daughter of James Brown (no, not *that* James Brown), one of Texas's most successful businessmen. Brown had made his money in hardware, and lots of it by the looks of the thick-walled, three-story Victorian Italianate mansion he built in 1859.

His daughter looked after the household, entertained guests, and broke the heart of many a young man. She lived like a princess, and took tremendous pride in her home, which survived the great hurricane of 1900—even as neighboring homes were being carried away in the currents.

After Bettie died, the home passed through several hands. The Shriners bought it in the 1920s and used it as an office for four decades. Today, beautifully restored, it belongs to the Galveston Historical Foundation. Only somebody forgot to tell Miss Bettie. Rumor has it that Miss Bettie lived such a grand life there, she just can't let go. Visitors report seeing her playing the piano, walking the stairway and halls, and making the occasional appearance in "The Gold Room," where her personal effects are on display. If you're not spooked yet, get this: one of the beds upstairs remains wrinkled and slept-in no matter how many times a day it is made.

Who: "The Houston Bride"
Where: Austin, Texas
What: Appears wearing a wedding dress and carrying a handgun—sometimes going into the ladies' restroom of the Driskill Hotel.
When: Starting around 1991
Why: In 1990, a beautiful socialite from Houston was devastated when her fiancé (the skunk!) called their wedding off at the last minute. Bitter, embarrassed, and angry, she needed some time alone and went to Austin—to Room 29 of the luxurious Driskill Hotel to be specific—to get her head together. She spent a week on a shopping spree, maxing out her nongroom's credit cards. Guests reported seeing her arms laden with packages as she walked daily from the elevator to Room 29, until the hotel maids noticed

she hadn't appeared for a few days. They checked her room and discovered her dead body in the bathtub; the jilted bride shot herself with a pistol and used a pillow to hide the noise.

Today, visitors to the Driskill claim to see the Houston Bride walking the hallways—dressed in her wedding gown and holding her trusty handgun. She has also been seen in the ladies' restroom, peering into the stalls! Two women reported seeing a pretty young lady carrying an armload of packages to Room 29 when they returned late one night from Sixth Street. Nothing overly odd about that, except it was two in the morning. "Where had she gone shopping at such an hour?" they wondered. The ladies mentioned her to the manager, who was concerned since that room was supposed to be under renovation.

The next morning he opened up the room. No normal guest could have occupied it the night before. Its walls were lined with plastic. It had no bed, and a disconnected sink surrounded by tools and spare parts sat in the middle of the floor. The air was unseasonably cold.

* * * * *

LUCKY BREAK?

A 60-year-old Houston man must have been carrying a four-leaf clover one night in 2004. As he walked home from work that evening, he was struck and injured by a slow moving train. Apparently, he was supposed to be wearing two hearing aids, but only wore one, and did not hear the train approaching. Then, as if being hit by a train weren't enough, as he was being loaded into an ambulance, a car slammed into it. Another ambulance made it to the scene and successfully took the man to the hospital. He was lucky to escape with only cuts, bruises, and a broken finger.

The now-vanished town of Zulch, Texas, was on the headwaters of Kickapoo Creek.

TEN THINGS YOU DIDN'T KNOW YOU DIDN'T KNOW ABOUT *DALLAS*

Yes, you know who shot J.R. (Kristin), but how about these ten tidbits of Texas soap opera trivia? We'll bet the ranch (Southfork) you don't!

From April 2, 1978 through May 3, 1991 and across 357 episodes (not counting the three made-for-TV movies), Americans from Seattle to Miami made *Dallas* their night-time drama destination. Over 13 seasons, the saga of the Ewing family and its struggle for control of the Ewing Oil empire—and especially the dirty dealings of that consummate cad, J. R. Ewing—kept TV watchers' tongues wagging. But even if you kept track of all the plot twists and turns, from the multiple marriages to the shootings to that entire season that was "just a dream," there's still more you didn't know. We've got the dirt from deep in the heart of Texas.

1. THE SHOCKING START TO THE *DALLAS* DYNASTY!
Dallas got its start when the series was developed for an actress named Linda, who was supposed to play the role of Pamela Ewing. Does this mean that *Dallas* star Linda Gray, who wound up playing Sue Ellen Ewing, was considered for the Pamela role (which was filled by Victoria Principal)? No, because the "Linda" for which the series was initially developed was . . . Linda Evans, who would of course go on to take the role of Krystle Carrington that *other* massively successful nighttime soap opera, *Dynasty*.

2. THAT OTHER EWING BOY
Week in and week out, Ewing siblings J.R. and Bobby were front and center, but there was another Ewing brother as well: Gary, the

middle sibling. Some series would have eventually trotted Gary out as a plot device, probably in season five or so, just to keep things fresh, but not the makers of *Dallas*: They had other plans for Gary, namely, that he was the centerpiece of the *Dallas* spin-off series *Knots Landing*, which was filled with as many ridiculous plot twists and turns as its parent series (only in California, not Texas). This spin-off plan was a smart move, because *Knots Landing* lasted nearly as long as its parent series: 344 episodes, that ran from 1979 through 1993. However, while *Dallas* landed in the top ten of the Nielsens for every year of its run except its last two, *Knots Landing* cracked the top ten only once: the 1984-85 season, when it ranked ninth, proving it's tough to top Southfork for nighttime soap intrigue.

3. SPEAKING OF SOUTHFORK
Have a hankerin' to visit the Southfork Ranch? Well, it's located twenty miles north of Dallas in Parker, Texas. Now touted as an event and conference center, Southfork is open daily so anyone can live it up Ewing style! But the house that became famous as Southfork wasn't the first Ewing residence to bear the name. When Dallas first aired as a five-part miniseries, it used a different big, white mansion to house the squabbling oil barons. According to UltimateDallas.com, the first ranch has since burned down. If we didn't know better, we'd swear it was a plot twist.

4. THE SCI-FI CONNECTION
Several writers who toiled in the *Dallas* stable would later go on to write significant science fiction films or television series. (Maybe that explains the whole "dream season" thing.) Most notable among them is Jonathan Hales, who would cowrite the screenplay to *Star Wars Episode II: Attack of the Clones* with George Lucas (he was tapped for that gig because of his time as a writer on Lucas's *Young Indiana Jones Chronicles* television series). Other writers with a *Dallas*/sci-fi connection: D. C. Fontana, who wrote "Encounter at Farpoint," the series premiere of *Star Trek: The Next Generation*, and Bryce Zabel, who created and wrote for the sci-fi series *M.A.N.T.I.S*, *Dark Skies*, and *Crow: Stairway to Heaven*.

Only a church now remains of the town of Zigzag, Texas.

5. WHAT I REALLY WANT TO DO IS DIRECT
Numerous members of the *Dallas* acting troupe also spent time
behind the camera as directors for the series, including Larry
Hagman, Patrick Duffy, Linda Gray, and Steve Kanaly. When
Gray expressed interest in directing, the producers turned her
down, which made her think about leaving the show entirely. But
she got her chance to direct when Hagman interceded on her
behalf.

6. THINK LOVELY THOUGHTS
Larry Hagman is the son of Mary Martin, best known for playing
Peter Pan on stages around the world (the name he was born with
was Larry Martin Hageman). When "Ellie Ewing" Barbara Bel
Geddes left the show in 1984, the producers offered the role to
Martin, which would have meant she would have been playing
the role of her son's character's mother. Martin turned it down,
and the role went to Donna Reed instead.

7. OSCAR COMES TO SOUTHFORK
Donna Reed, who played Ellie Ewing for one season, won an
Oscar for her role in *From Here to Eternity* in 1953. But she wasn't
the only Oscar winner to spend time in Dallas. George Chakiris,
who played "Nicholas" in the 1985-86 season, won a Best
Supporting Actor Oscar for *West Side Story* in 1961. And Joel
Grey, who had a memorably sinister guest shot in the final episode
of the series, was the 1972 Best Supporting Actor winner for his
role as the Emcee in *Cabaret* (a role he originated on Broadway,
and for which he also received a Tony award).

8. THE DONNA REED SHOW
Donna Reed's single year as Ellie Ewing was apparently not a very
happy one. Early in the year, when Patrick "Bobby Ewing" Duffy
jokingly asked if he could call Reed "mama," Larry Hagman was
allegedly heard to mutter "she isn't *my* mama" and stalked off (in
later interviews Hagman declared he had "loved" Reed). Reed also
believed the producers were intentionally giving her character little to do and photographing her in harsh light to make her look
older and less attractive. When Reed was fired from the part in
1985 (Bel Geddes wanted to return to the role), she was in the first

year of a three-year contract. She sued to get her contractually obligated cash and got it all.

9. THE SCORECARD

You probably know that the character of J. R. Ewing was a womanizing cad, but how many women did he sleep with over the thirteen-year run of the series and the made-for-TV movies that followed? According to the UltimateDallas.com: a grand total of 29, followed by Cliff Barnes with 15, Ray Krebbs with 10, and Bobby Ewing (that slacker) with 9. Among the female characters, the most promiscuous was Charlene Tilton's Lucy, with 9 notches in her belt, followed closely by Sue Ellen, with 8.

10. WHO KEEPS SHOOTING J.R.?

The 1980 cliffhanger episode of *Dallas* in which antihero J. R. Ewing gets shot is a landmark in TV history (as is its follow-up episode, which became the most-watched television episode then to date). But it's worth noting that it wasn't the first or last time J.R. took a slug on the show. He ate lead 4 other times: in the first season, during a hunting trip; in the 1986–1987 season he was shot by character B. D. Calhoun (played by the appropriately named Hunter von Leer); in the next season's final episode by Sue Ellen, and then in the 1998 *Dallas* TV movie *War of the Ewings* by Peter Ellington (actor Philip Anglim). Then there's the matter of the last episode of the series, where J.R. is seen putting a gun to his head. The next scene is an exterior shot of Southfork. A shot rings out, but the audience doesn't see what happens this time around. Darn cliffhangers.

* * * * *

"Texas does not, like any other region, simply have indigenous dishes. It proclaims them. It congratulates you, on your arrival, at having escaped from the slop pails of the other 49 states."

—Alistair Cooke

WILLIE NELSON: THE FIVE-SONG BIOGRAPHY

Can five songs truly express the five-decade career of this Texas legend? Let's find out!

Willie Nelson's music is a little bit like Texas itself: sometimes spare and uncompromising, eclectic and varied, but always with an independent spirit. From the Texas native's first regional hit in 1956, Nelson has kept the Texas twang where it belongs, at the heart of country music.

SONG #1: "CRAZY"

One of the ironies of Willie Nelson's career is that one of the most willful and idiosyncratic voices in both country and popular music found his first fame writing songs for other artists. Willie had been playing music since he was a child—both he and his sister Bobby picked up musical instruments as a way of dealing with the death of their father and their abandonment by their mother. At age 23, Nelson had a modest local hit in Texas with his 1956 cover of Lloyd Price's "Lumberjack." But local fame as a musician wasn't enough for Nelson. In 1960 he decided to take a chance on Nashville, and drove into the town in a Buick that died nearly as soon as it crossed the city limits.

Fortunately for Nelson, the expiring car was not a metaphor for his career. Nelson quickly landed a songwriting contract with Pamper Music, headed by Hal Smith and Ray Price (who took Nelson's "Night Life" for his own and gave Nelson a gig playing bass in his band). Within two years, Nelson had written some of the biggest hits in country music: "Hello Walls," which Faron Young used to grab the number one spot on the country charts for nine weeks; "Funny How Time Slips Away," for Billy Walker; and most memorably, "Crazy" for the fabulous Patsy Cline, which not only became a country classic but which was also a crossover hit, lodging itself in the national top-ten charts and becoming the most popular jukebox song in America.

During this time Nelson wasn't doing too shabbily himself: a recording contract with Liberty Records yielded two top-ten hits, "Willingly" and "Touch Me," both in 1962.

SONG #2: "BLUE EYES CRYING IN THE RAIN"

Ah, but just when things were going so well! Two things happened: Liberty Records shut down its country division, and Nelson found himself at greater and greater odds with the strings-coated "Nashville Sound." Despite a gig at the Grand Ol' Opry, Nelson's singing career eventually sputtered to a halt in the early 1970s. Willie became so disgusted with the music industry that he ditched it entirely and headed back to Austin, Texas, where the chart-topping hitmaker tried his hand at . . . pig farming. Talk about "Crazy." Pigs didn't help Willie get music out of his blood, so Nelson tried again—but this time from his Texas home and on his terms. And his terms were like a hard Texas summer: stark and unadorned country music without strings or a comfort zone. It was "outlaw country."

Nelson shocked Columbia Records in 1975 when he delivered *Red-Headed Stranger*, which was so acoustically bare that it seemed skeletal (it featured Willie on guitar and sister Bobby on piano). But the album was a smash hit, as was the album's unlikely single, a mournful and austere take on Roy Acuff's "Blue Eyes Crying in the Rain." Nelson rode the success of *Stranger* back into the national limelight, teaming up with fellow Texan and musical outlaw Waylon Jennings in 1978 with the very successful *Waylon and Willie* album, and even throwing a gleeful curveball in the same year with *Stardust*, a genre-taunting album that mixed musical standards and pop hits done (mostly) in stripped-down outlaw style.

SONG #3: "ON THE ROAD AGAIN"

The hits kept coming during the late 1970s and early 1980s. Nelson's persona now stretched from Texas to Hollywood— Nelson took a featured role in the Robert Redford hit *The Electric Horseman* in 1979 and in 1980 was the star of his own hit movie, *Honeysuckle Rose*. *Rose* was also the film that launched what would become Nelson's signature tune, the well-nigh-inescapable "On

---

The 1890 census showed 11,523,117 chickens on Texas farms.

the Road Again," the ultimate paean to nonstop touring. America loved it and clamored for more. Nelson kept serving it up—but again always on his own terms. For example, he dared fans to follow him in 1984 when he teamed up with Latin superstar Julio Iglesias for the pop hit "To All The Girls I've Loved Before."

And sure enough they followed, although undoubtedly some of them wondered what the heck became of the Outlaw Willie they used to know and love. But around this time Willie Nelson salvaged his credibility in the heartland by becoming one of the driving forces behind Farm Aid, the now-annual benefit concert that raised money for, and awareness of, family farmers in the U.S.A.; to date the organization has disbursed over $17 million in grants for farm-related issues. He also teamed up with Jennings, Johnny Cash, and Kris Kristofferson to form the popular outlaw supergroup, the Highwaymen. So fans found it easy forgive Willie for mixing up his musical stylings now and then.

SONG #4: "WHO'LL BUY MY MEMORIES?"

But in 1990, Nelson ran afoul of an organization that was *not* willing to overlook his transgressions—his financial ones at least: the IRS. While the outlaw life had been good to Willie, the IRS calculated that the country icon owed them a gobsmackingly huge sum of $16 million. Outlaw or not, the Red-Headed Stranger was going to pay. In addition to cashing out nearly every possession he owned, Nelson handed over two albums worth of songs, which were sold on television as *The IRS Tapes: Who'll Buy My Memories*, which included the plaintive, wistful and—considering most of his property was up for grabs—all-too-appropriate title tune. (These days Nelson gets mileage out of joking about his tax disaster days; one of the most popular commercials of the 2004 Super Bowl was one from tax preparer H&R Block, which featured a Willie Nelson Tax Advice Doll as a cautionary tale.)

Through the sales of his stuff, the album, and contributions from friends and fans, Nelson settled up with the IRS in 1993 and celebrated with *Across the Borderline*, a radio-friendly, superstar-laden return effort produced by Don Was (who had previously revived the careers of both Roy Orbison and George Harrison). The album brought him back into the public eye and also found him willing to go for the unusual rather than the comfortable (for example, a somber version of Peter Gabriel's "Don't Give Up," sung with Sinead O'Connor).

SONG #5: "THE RAINBOW CONNECTION"

Since the mid-1990s, Nelson has aggressively confounded the expectations of anyone who assumed he would rest on his laurels as a music icon. Instead, Nelson has spent the last several albums cashing in on his rock-solid musical credibility to spin out explorations in several musical genres, from atmospheric electric folk (1996's *Teatro*, produced Daniel Lanois, best known for producing U2 and Bob Dylan), to straight-up blues (2000's *Milk Cow Blues*, featuring some smoky versions of "Crazy" and "Funny How Time Slips Away"), jazz (1999's *Night and Day*) and even kid's music: 2001's *The Rainbow Connection*, which features a truly delightful take on the song made famous in *The Muppet Movie*.

Let's just say it takes a musician comfortable with his legacy to seriously cover a tune originally performed by cloth-covered hands. But that's Willie Nelson for you: his music, his terms. It's just like a Texas outlaw to make his own rules—and make them stick.

* * * * *

WISDOM FROM WILLIE

"I was doomed by the time I was 7. I had been told that if you smoke cigarettes and drink beer, you're going to hell. And by 7, I was gone."

"There are more serious problems in life than financial ones, and I've had a lot of those. I've been broke before, and will be again. Heartbroke? That's serious. Lose a few bucks? That's not."

"When I started counting my blessings, my whole life turned around."

"As long as I got my guitar, I'll be fine."

STEAK YOURSELF TO A FREE MEAL

Think you can handle the Big Texan Steak Ranch challenge?

BELLY UP TO THE STEAK
Billboards leading to the Big Texan Steak Ranch, in Amarillo, offer a "Free 72-oz. steak!" Now everybody knows there's no such thing as a free lunch, but the Big Texan will happily give it to you, provided you can clean your plate. For a $50 fee, anyone can try their hand at consuming an entire 72-ounce steak dinner. Contestants have one hour, that's 60 minutes to eat the equivalent of 4 1/2 sixteen-ounce steaks (or 4 1/2 pounds of meat). In addition, you also have to finish a shrimp cocktail, salad, baked potato, and dinner roll that come with the Texas-size top sirloin (yep, all in that same 60 minutes). A few ground rules:

- Don't leave the table for any reason once you start eating.
- Cut your own meat. Aside from cheering you on, no one can assist you with your meal.
- Try your best not to boot. If you get sick, the contest is over, period.
- If you don't finish the meal, you're not allowed to share it.

The Big Texan doesn't offer this meal on their menu. If they did, it would retail for about $200.00!

THE BIG TEXAN HALL OF FAME
Of the more than 28,600 people who've tried, more than 4,780 hearty eaters have succeeded since the challenge began in 1960. The overall odds against your doing it are 6 to 1. Out of the four to five women who try annually, about half succeed, so the win rate is a bit higher for the ladies.

Winners get their names in the Steak Eater's Hall of Fame. Some standouts include professional wrestler, Klondike Bill, who finished two 72 ouncers in the allotted time. A pitcher for the Cincinnati Reds is rumored to have downed the entire meal in just over 9 minutes. The oldest person to finish it all, she was a 69-year-old grandmother. The youngest person was an 11-year-old boy. That boy's got a real good future in eatin'.

The motto of Mary Kay Cosmetics, headquartered in Dallas, is "Fake it till you make it."

HOLY HIROHITO, BATMAN!

Not too many people know about one of America's most bizarre wartime experiments. Nor about the major role that Texas played in it.

During World War II, the U.S. government went to great lengths researching new weapons for all theaters of the war, but one of the most unusual experiments involved dropping loads of armed bats over the cities of Japan. That's right. Bats.

BURNING DOWN THE HOUSE

With time-delayed incendiary devices clipped to their little kamikaze bodies, the bats would descend upon the city *en masse* and do what bats do best—hide in and around trees, homes, buildings, and bridges. The theory behind this mammalian air force was that since Japanese architecture of the time consisted of wood and paper, the cities would incinerate but with little loss of civilian life. Property and morale would be destroyed, but there would still be time to evacuate. Not a bad plan—unless, of course, you're a bat.

A FEW GOOD BATS

A dentist from Pennsylvania had conceived the idea, originally known as "Adams's Plan." Government bureaucracy wasn't immediately receptive, but the simple logic of the idea proved too strong to overlook. The search for a few good bats was on. All kinds of bats were drafted for the project, but the leading candidates deemed best fit for this mission flourished at Ney Cave, near Bandera, Texas. In 1943, the Navy leased four caves in the area, and Bandera became the unofficial headquarters of America's martial bat research, the greatest hope for immediate relief on the Pacific front. Military scientists and bat experts came from across the country and, when not hanging out at the honky-tonks and rodeos, experimented with how best to get bats to deliver bombs.

THE BANDERA PROJECT

Extensive testing was conducted using various weighted "dummy bombs," clips, and methodologies. After two million dollars had been spent on bat research, a full-scale bat bomb test raid was planned for August 1944. But before an all-out demonstration could be mounted, the project was scrapped. Researchers and soldiers were devastated. "Why?" they wanted to know, "when they were so close?" Government officials cited difficulties with the timeline, but that didn't keep rumors from spreading of a rival experiment with greater killing potential that beat them to the punch (and more funding). On July 16, 1945, the world's first nuclear test explosion—code-named Trinity—took place near Alamogordo, New Mexico.

* * * * *

TO THE BAT BRIDGE!

The Congress Avenue Bridge in Austin has long been a favorite stop for bats migrating from central Mexico; deep crevices underneath the roadbed are the perfect environment for bats to roost when they come north in mid-March to give birth. Upwards of 1.5 million bats make the Congress Avenue Bridge their home from March to November, creating the largest urban bat colony in North America.

Huge crowds of people gather nightly to witness huge crowds of bats' emerging at dusk from underneath the bridge. The *Austin American-Statesman* has generously made their parking lot and grassy campus available to the watchers. Visitors are warned not to attempt to handle the bats, as they may be carriers of diseases such as rabies. And, for reasons that should be obvious, spectators are advised to wear hats or bring umbrellas, regardless of the weather.

Midwife practice has always been legal in Texas.

TEXAS
<u>TORNADO QUIZ</u>

*Texas has had more recorded tornadoes than any other U.S. state, with
an average of 153 funnels plopping out of the sky each year. So it's no
wonder that Texans talk a lot about tornadoes. But is it all just hot air?
Take our little true-or-false quiz and see.*

J ust answer true or false:

Tornadoes can pluck the feathers right off a chicken!
False. If a tornado in Pampa, Texas, once moved a 30,000-pound
piece of equipment (that's around 7,500 chickens), it's a safe bet that
the chickens and their feathers would blow away together before any
plucking could occur. It's true that tornadoes can cause chickens to
lose their feathers, but only because chickens molt as a natural
response to stress. And if you've seen a tornado, you know stress.

Trailer parks attract tornadoes.
False. Nonsense. The reason you hear so many stories about tornadoes destroying trailer homes is that these homes are simply not
built to withstand violent weather. Winds of around 60 miles per
hour can level a mobile home. Experts typically recommend that
mobile home dwellers forget the usual advice about finding the
safest room in the house and just get out! Fast!

Opening your windows will keep your roof from blowing off.
Technically true, but we wouldn't bother. Experts say that for this trick
to work you have to know the tornado's exact angle of approach and
open the right windows—otherwise, you can cause *more* damage. It's
not likely you'll have the time to make the correct calculations—the
smarter move would be to use that valuable time to seek cover.

Under a highway overpass is a good place to seek shelter.
False, False, False. Actually, an overpass makes you a sitting (and
ducking) target for flying debris such as, oh, say, a pick-up truck
parked nearby and pieces of your own home's crown molding. Plus,
overpasses create a wind-tunnel effect that can actually shoot you out
into the air—and possibly land you miles away. Forget the overpasses
and head to a major structure (or a ditch in a worst-case scenario).

Rolling Stone was a Texas paper produced in 1894–95 by William Sydney Porter, a.k.a. O. Henry.

You can build a tornado-proof safe room in your house.
True. Texas Tech University's Wind Science and Engineering
Research Center reports that you can actually build a tornado safe
room in your house at a reasonable cost: as little as $2,000. The
catch is that you have to design it while building the house. While
these rooms may protect you from most tornadoes, in the cases of
the largest tornadoes, everything above ground disappears—period.

Texas tornadoes rotate counter-clockwise.
True. Most Texas tornadoes rotate counter-clockwise as a result of
the Coriolis Effect, rotational forces generated as the Earth spins.
Tornadoes spin counter-clockwise in the Northern Hemisphere
and clockwise in the Southern Hemisphere. The same is not true
of your toilet, by the way. The direction a toilet flushes depends
on its design. Texas toilets would flush the same direction in
Argentina, where tornadoes do spin in the opposite direction.

Large stores and shopping malls are safe tornado shelters.
False! They may appear extremely safe because of their size and
seeming stability, but structures such as shopping malls, grocery
stores, or the "Home Labyrinth-style" hardware store are especially
susceptible to roof damage—or collapse—during severe winds. If
you're stuck in one during a tornado, take cover in a restroom.
Avoid these buildings during a tornado watch, even if Nordstrom
is having a sale or you badly need beer for the big game.

The tornado in *The Wizard of Oz* was animated.
False. MGM Special Effects Coordinator Arnold Gillespie created
the 1938 movie's surprisingly realistic tornado by building a 35-
foot long woven-cloth sock. Compressed air, powdered black dust,
cotton, wind machines and a yellow-black smoke made from sulfur
and carbon (which made the crew ill for days) coalesced to make
it amazingly real for around $15,000. The 1996 Warner Brothers
film *Twister* cost $92 million to produce.

Over 50 tornadoes have struck Texas in a single day.
You bet your basement it's true. On September 20, 1967, a record-
setting 67 tornadoes hit the state during a single day. Stemming
from hurricane Beulah, whose winds reached almost 140 mph, 115
known tornadoes touched down in Texas between September 19
and September 23, 1967. That year also marked the greatest
number of tornadoes touching down in a year: a whopping 232.

One legend has it that Pecos Bill died laughing at dudes who called themselves cowboys.

THE TEXAS UNDERGROUND

What's mysterious, chilling, and thousands of years in the making? No, not the construction on Interstate 45—it's the thousands of cool caves hidden deep in the heart of Texas. Grab a flashlight as we explore these dark and undisturbed habitats, home to enigmatic fossils, bats, and the occasional Austin computer programmer.

Serious scientific study of Texas caves began around 1900, but people have been using Texas caves for food and shelter for over 10,000 years. Most Texas caves are Cretaceous period karst formations, that is, limestone regions with underground streams, sinkholes, and caverns.

Modern study has yielded some cool archaeological finds: cave paintings, and weird fossils and animal specimens, from the now extinct Colombian Mammoth to the very much alive—and creepy—eyeless scorpion.

Here are eight of the "show caves" in Texas; caves that don't require years of experience or yogalike contortions to enjoy. You'll find it hard to decide which one to visit first.

CASCADE CAVERNS
Located in Boerne (pronounced BURN-EE), the tour of these brilliant rooms, passages, and rock formations climaxes with a view of the breathtaking 100-foot waterfall that gave Cascade Caverns its name. One of the earliest visitors was a mastodon, whose bones are still in the caverns today. It's a cool 68 degrees inside. Outside, 100 acres of park make for a great picnic before or after the tour. A new leisurely, well-lit 45-minute tour starts every half-hour.

THE CAVE WITH NO NAME
A contest to find a name for this cave (also in Boerne) was won by a schoolchild who said, "It was too beautiful to have a name." And so it is. The hour-long, 66-degree tour covers six rooms with awesome stalactites and stalagmites, waves of strange, delicate formations, and hypnotizing prehistoric architecture.

1982: Tommy Tune of Houston wins his third Tony for directing the Broadway musical *Nine*.

CAVERNS OF SONORA

Located roughly between San Antonio and Midland just outside the small town of Sonora, these caverns have something for everyone. In the 1920s two teenagers, a brother and sister, explored the cave using only candles and twine to find their way in and out. The pros took over in the 1950s and the caverns were opened to the public in 1960. The unusual rock formations include a famous one that looks like a butterfly. General tours leave constantly: the Horseshoe Lake tour (an hour and fifteen minutes) and the Crystal Palace tour (an hour and forty-five minutes). The Discovery Challenge tour is more . . . (how can we say this?) challenging. It requires reservations and genuine spelunking equipment, which is provided by the management.

INNER SPACE CAVERN

Billed as Texas's most accessible cavern, it was discovered in 1963 when highway workers were drilling to put in an overpass 20 miles north of Austin. Eventually, a team of explorers uncovered dazzling rooms with towering ceiling heights, unusual formations that grow sideways as opposed to up and down—and a multitude of life. A variety of tours ranging from an hour and fifteen minutes to an hour and thirty-five minutes (complete with flashlights) are available.

KICKAPOO CAVERN STATE PARK

Kickapoo Cavern State Park isn't for the casual spelunker; tours are by appointment only. If you decide to take the plunge, you'll have to sign a waiver and bring plenty of water (no wusses allowed). Twenty-two miles northwest of Brackettville, the park has over a dozen caves, but only two are open to the public: Kickapoo Cavern and Stuart Bat Cave. Kickapoo is famous for its 80-foot twin, crystalline calcite columns, the largest in Texas; Stuart Cave offers bat fans a chance to watch as tens of thousands of Brazilian free-tailed bats swoop out of the cave at night to search for dinner.

LONGHORN CAVERN

With a temperature of 65 degrees and a layer of tool-friendly flint lying around, it's no wonder the local Comanches used the site as their base starting about 400 years ago. Later, the cavern was reputedly used as a hideout by legendary Texas outlaw Sam Bass. Now, lots of interesting rooms and caverns, including an area of calcite crystals known as Crystal City, make for an exciting tour. General tours start hourly, but don't forget to check out the customized kind: the Wild Cave tour and Geological tour, for instance.

NATURAL BRIDGE CAVERNS
Convenient to San Antonio, the largest-known cavern in Texas was discovered in 1960 by a group of students from St. Thomas University in San Antonio. Early excavation uncovered an arrowhead from over 5,000 BC. The largest room is the Hall of Mountain Kings—nearly the size of a football field and 100 feet high. Other, no less amazing, rooms include Sherwood Forest, Pluto's Anteroom, and the Castle of the White Giants. Along with the usual tours, the caverns offer the Adventure Tour (complete with caving equipment) and "Caroling in the Caverns," a special Christmas show.

WONDER WORLD
In the Central Texas town of San Marcos, the too-cutely named Wonder World was the first Texas cave to open its maw to the public in 1903. Wonder Cave sits on the Balcones Fault Zone, where an earthquake millions of years ago split Texas's Edwards Plateau and the Gulf Coastal Plains; the area is believed to be the line that separated the North and South American continents. The cave was discovered in the late 1800s by an ex-cowboy drilling for water. It has six rooms, an observation tower, and lots of non-cave attractions, including a wildlife park, Anti-Gravity House, and the Mexico World Market.

Adopting Cherokee ways, Sam Houston married Tiana Rogers, an Indian woman of mixed blood.

53

LEARN THE TEXICON

Planning a visit to the Lone Star State? If so, you might find these translations helpful when conversing with the natives.

Ahm
Contraction of "I" and "am," as in "*Ahm* hungry."

Ahmo
A notice of intention, as "*Ahmo* hit you upside the head if you don't quit that."

Biggo
Large or extreme, as in "He's nothin' but a *biggo* drunk."

Binness
Personal concern, as in "It's none-a yer goldarn *binness* where Ahm goin'!"

Fixinta
Intending to, as in "Ahm *fixinta* go to the movies."

Gace
What makes a car run, as in "You got enough *gace* in your truck to git there?"

Hair yew
A common greeting in Texas, as in "Mornin', darlin', *hair yew* today?"

Idjit
Someone who's not too sharp, as in "That boy's an *idjit*!"

Ite
The number that follows "seb'n."

Jeet
A question about a person's previous meal, as in, "Hey, *jeet* yet? Ahm hungry."

Erastus "Deaf" Smith and his scouts spied on the Mexicans during the Texas Revolution.

Putnear
Almost, as in "Ah was so tard ah *putnear* fell asleep."

Sketty
A dish served with meatballs at an Italian restaurant.

Tard
Sleepy. See Putnear.

Wan
An alcoholic beverage, as in "Sangria *wan* is tasty."

Worm Drowning
More commonly referred to as "fishing."

Y'all
A right friendly way to address a group or a single person, as in "Hey *y'all*."
"All *y'all*" is a commonly accepted plural form, as in "All *y'all* better come 'ere."

* * * * *

YANKEE GO HOME

"In Texas, the difference between a Yankee and a damn Yankee is that the Yankee has the sense to stay where he belongs."
—*Old Texas Saying*

A visiting Yankee stopped in to buy a cigar, and the Texas tobacconist handed him a foot-long cigar. "This is huge!" the Yankee exclaimed. The tobacconist politely explained that everything is bigger in Texas. Next the Yankee went to a bar and ordered a beer. The bartender presented him with a gallon jug of brew. The Yankee exclaims, "This is enormous!" while the barkeep reminds him that everything is bigger in Texas. Feeling a little tipsy from all the cigar smoke and beer, the Yankee staggers back to his hotel, where he takes a wrong turn, stumbles and falls into the pool. Sputtering and splashing wildly, he yells: "Help! Get me outta here quick before someone flushes this thing!"

REMEMBER THE TOMALAMO!

A fierce rivalry that can be summed up by the bumper sticker: "Keep Colorado Beautiful: Put a Texan on a Bus."

Part of Colorado (today its most densely populated area) was originally part of the Republic of Texas. Is it any wonder that Texans like to drop by every once in a while to visit the old homestead, do a little skiing, and maybe buy some real estate?

THEY CAME, THEY SAW, THEY BOUGHT A CHALET

During Colorado's ski season, Texans drop big bucks on lift tickets and big parcels of land. But money can't buy love, especially when the money comes from across the border.

The stereotype is that Coloradans feel that Texas tourists are loud, drink too much, wear funny hats, ski like cattle, can't drive on snowy mountain roads, think the world revolves around Texas, brag like it was an Olympic sport, and are constantly trying to "develop" Colorado land in the hopes of raking in obscene profits. Those generalizations are silly, of course. In truth, many Texans don't drink at all.

SUNDAY, BLOODY (MARY) SUNDAY

Texas-Colorado tensions reportedly came to a boil in 1982, in the small Colorado town of Twin Lakes (about 150 miles southwest of Denver) where, at a local bar called The Placer Bar and Grill, a bunch of local ranch hands had an argument (the content of which is lost to posterity) with a group of Texan tourists. Demanding gentlemanly satisfaction from this perceived affront, they challenged the Texans to a snowball fight the next day at high noon. Since it was early fall, the gentlemen had a major problem—no snow. Hmm. Tomatoes would have to do. The next day the Texans were pummeled into drippy defeat at the hands of the native Colorado population. The Placer Bar and Grill declared a rematch for the next year. And so it was in 1982, the tradition of the great Tomato War between Texas tourists and Colorado natives was born.

Baylor was founded by the Baptist Church in 1845.

DEFENDING THE TOMALAMO

Having a near-biological aversion to losing any kind of contest, the Texans reportedly brought plenty of friends the second year, and won. Over the years, the contest grew more complex. Armed with plastic sacks of tomatoes, the Coloradans would go on the offensive and the Texans would retreat into a fort flying the Lone Star flag known as the Tomalamo. The rules were that if a contestant was hit above the waist, it was considered a kill. The initial fight often lasted hours, followed by a shoot-out the next day between finalists. Eventually, having the home-tomato advantage, the Colorado offensive would win most of the time. But more than a few times the Coloradans were outnumbered.

Never afraid to use the best tools at their disposal, one year the Texans descended on the battlefield via helicopter. Another time, somebody arrived via parachute. And on one chilling occasion, a beautiful Texan woman reportedly began to undress on the battlefield—shocking the Colorado contingency so badly that they were quickly decimated. And all the while, peace protestors on the sidelines help hand-painted signs reading "Hell No, We Won't Throw."

Sadly for some, the contest has cooled in recent years, probably in large part due to reduced Texas travel to Colorado in favor of fresher ski destinations such as Canada, Utah, and Montana. As one Texas skier reported in the *Denver Post* in December 2003: "Been there, done that."

* * * * *

CRIMINAL LAST WORDS

"Four sixes to beat!"—John Wesley Hardin
Texas outlaw, killed in 1895 while playing dice in a bar.

"Let me go, the world is bobbing around me." —Sam Bass
Texas outlaw, killed 1878.

"I'm going down with my six-guns."—Joel Collins
Texas outlaw and member of Sam Bass's gang, killed 1871.

The first oil well on land owned by the University of Texas was drilled in 1923.

A TALE OF
TWO TWISTERS

*The tiny burg of Jarrell figured the worst was over when a 1989
tornado blew through town. But eight years later the winds blew in
again—and took a much greater toll.*

E ven though more tornadoes have been recorded in Texas
than in any other state, the odds are high against a tornado
striking in the same place twice. But there's always an
exception.

TWISTER NUMBER ONE
Jarrell is a small town in central Texas on the Blackland Prairies,
where tornadoes are fairly common. In 1989, the population was
just over 700 people. Tornadoes had brushed by before, but none
had ever struck it directly. They had a close call in 1987, but the
only major damage was to a barn.

Jarrell's luck began to change when it started raining in the
predawn hours of May 17, 1989. Then the winds began to howl.
At 4:02 a.m. the clocks stopped when a tornado ripped through
town at speeds topping 200 mph, leaving a seven-mile swath of
damage in its wake. In all, 108 houses, businesses, or barns were
leveled at a total loss of $3 million. The debris littered the fields
and closed down Interstate 35 to travelers journeying between
Dallas and Austin. Thirty-one people walked away with injuries
and one life was lost. Still, the folks in Jarrell breathed a sigh of
relief because they knew it could have been worse.

DID SOMEONE SAY WORSE?
Eight years later, Jarrell's fortunes took an even stronger downward
turn. On May 27, 1997, a storm arose in the afternoon. The skies
darkened, and officials grew worried enough to send children
home from school for the rest of the day. Rain, hail, and high
winds all threatened cars trying to make it home to safety. Power
was out from Jarrell to Austin, 40 miles north.

The well was dubbed Santa Rita, after a patron saint of the impossible.

TWISTER NUMBER TWO

A cold blast of air whipped across Texas from the north and banged up against a bank of warm air near Jarrell. Experts have compared the collision to a dynamite explosion. Far deadlier than the 1989 storm, this big slow monster ambled through town at a speed of 5 to 10 mph while its interior winds raged at around 260 mph. Tornadoes usually move at speeds closer to 35 mph, but this beast just plodded along, giving itself plenty of time to wreak more havoc. Overall, this tornado took from eleven to eighteen minutes to travel just one mile through Jarrell's neighborhoods. It changed directions twice, but finally turned sharply into a residential area. Fifty houses were reduced to shreds. Twenty-seven Jarrell residents died, 13 of whom were children.

A PERFECT STORM

The most powerful of its kind ever reported in a 33-county area, the 1997 storm ranked as an F5 on the Fujita Scale (or F-Scale), the "Richter Scale" equivalent for tornadoes; scientists measure the amount and intensity of wind damage to come up with this rating and also to infer the top wind speeds in the tornado. An F5 is the rarest and most destructive storm, with winds at least 261 mph, so rare that only .005 percent (about 1 out of 200) of tornadoes is powerful enough to be classified as one.

THE AFTERMATH

The town pulled together and rebuilt again. Some generous folks donated $1.7 million to the cause. Despite the loss of eight athletes, the Jarrell football team took to the field in the fall. The town planted 27 red oak trees in a memorial to the storm's victims in 1998. Since then, the population has grown to 1,200.

Experts said the chance of such a deadly tornado happening in any year was less than 1 percent. The odds of a tornado hitting the same town three times? No one dares guess, but a lot of new homes in Jarrell have underground storm shelters. They're not taking any chances.

The Colt revolver, a six-shooter patented in 1836, is used today by the Texas Rangers.

MORE THAN YOU EVER WANTED TO KNOW ABOUT <u>ARMADILLOS</u>

They look like no other animal on earth: kind of like a short-eared rabbit that's been partly eaten by a horseshoe crab. Some people think they're cute. Other people think they're delicious.

The nine-banded armadillo (*Dasypus novemcinctus*) is the official Texas small mammal; the word *armadillo* is from Spanish for "armed one." Here's a variety of things you can do with them.

HOW MUCH IS THAT ARMADILLO IN THE WINDOW?
The care and feeding of pet armadillos can be complicated, so pay attention.

- First check local armadillo ownership ordinances before purchasing one as a pet.
- The rumors about armadillos spreading leprosy have been greatly exaggerated. True, they're more susceptible to it than other creatures, but not so for armadillos bred in captivity. To actually contract the disease you'd have to eat an armadillo—raw.
- Give your possums-on-the-half-shell plenty of space and keep them warm (Like fellow Texan Lance Armstrong, they have no hair or body fat). It's best to keep them outside, though they need a lot of space and can't tolerate cold temperatures.
- Don't forget to pamper your armadillo. Docile and timid, they like to sleep up to 18 hours a day. They also like to be scratched softly. Whether they like to be scratched while asleep depends on the 'dillo.

• Kiss your carpet goodbye. Armadillos are diggers whether on grassland or your $79 per square yard wool carpet. Provide a surface they can dig at, or they may damage their claws trying to dig into hard, manmade surfaces.

ARMADILLO ALFRESCO

Their proficiency at digging can make hosting an armadillo on your land a frustrating experience. The bug population may take a nosedive, but the number of holes on your property will certainly shoot up. If an armadillo moves unwanted into your backyard, remember to be nice—they don't bite, won't bother you, and only want food and shelter. If you want to run them off, then here are some humane options:

• Sprinkle mothballs around a flowerbed or garden to keep armadillos out—they hate the smell.
• Build a fence buried at least one foot deep to keep them out.
• Remove them from under your house by luring them out with earthworms (a favorite 'dillo treat), then fill in their holes—mothballs or chain-link fencing can keep them from coming back.
• Remember that armadillos suck up insects like tornadoes suck up double wides. So do consider what bothers you more: bugs or holes.
• Oh, and when they curl themselves up, don't stick your finger between the bands of armor or you'll be a nine-fingered human being.

STILL LIFE WITH ARMADILLO

Whether you've got a stuffed and mounted specimen or a few desktop curios made from armadillo shell, here's how to keep your 'dillo-based objets d'art from going to pot—should that actually be your goal:

• Keep stuffed armadillos and armadillo-made items out of direct sunlight, which will fade them.
• Avoid placing these objects where your dog can reach them. For some reason, dogs think they're as much fun as an old shoe.
• Clean them with a dry, soft cloth or feather duster.
• Keep stuffed armadillos—and anything else made from armadillo—in a dry place.

Miss Ima Hogg, the "First Lady of Texas," was a beloved philanthropist and patron of the arts.

• Think for a minute before you give anyone a stuffed armadillo. What are the odds they'll "regift" it back to you next year?

AND ON HIS FARM HE HAD AN ARMADILLO

Corporate layoff? New college grad? Have the overwhelming urge to go into business for yourself? Armadillo husbandry might be the career you've been looking for:

• Think in fours. Armadillos always have babies in groups of four—and always the same sex. The same cell splits into four, even sharing the same placenta.
• Pen your animals in something solid. If you use netting, they can climb up the side, fall off, and injure themselves.
• Let the males mark their territories by scenting. If you keep cleaning off their scent, they will keep marking it—possibly until they die of dehydration in the attempt to keep up with you.
• Beware of panthers. Florida panthers (who don't just live in the Sunshine State) especially love to eat armadillo and will gobble up your herd in a heartbeat.
• Get a day job. Unless you're planning to spend time as a third-world street vendor, don't plan on turning your shrewd armadillo deals into a real living.

ARMADILLO SCAMPI, ARMADILLO GUMBO, ARMADILLO CHILI . . .

"But they're so cute!" Well, some people actually can—and do— eat them. If you're an armadillo fancier, remember these handy cooking tips:

• Thoroughly cook the armadillo meat until there's absolutely no doubt in your mind that it's safe to eat.
• Try armadillo meat in chili for the ultimate taste of Texas.
• Consider armadillo meatballs the next time you cook pasta; for an extra Texas treat, serve it with a Texas Merlot.
• Bake an armadillo-meat pie with onions, Texas veggies, and brown gravy for cold winter nights.
• Try your hand as a saucier; lots of terrific armadillo recipes for traditional sauce piquant are available online.

Have fun with your 'dillo no matter what you do with it!

THE YELLOW ROSE OF TEXAS

This story comes to us straight from the pages of Uncle John's Bathroom Reader Plunges into Great Lives. *It was so darn good, we brought it along on the plunge into Texas.*

The first known copy of the song "The Yellow Rose of Texas" was written around 1836; the composer signed it with just three initials. Based on the verses, history's best guess is that he was a black soldier from Tennessee. But who was the Yellow Rose? The original lyrics make it clear that she was a woman of color. At that time, "yellow" was used to describe a person of mixed black and white ancestry, a mulatto. The word "rose" could describe any beautiful woman. The answer to the mystery of the "Yellow Rose" may lie in the title of a second version of the song, "Emily, The Maid of Morgan's Point."

DEEP IN THE MESS OF TEXAS

In early 1836, Texas was in a heap of trouble. The Mexican army under General Antonio Lopez de Santa Anna was sweeping across the state crushing the rebellious Texans bent on independence for their state. On March 6, 1836, the fortress at the Alamo fell, along with all its defenders. Three weeks later, at Goliad, the Mexican army rounded up the Texans who'd surrendered under a white flag and executed them by firing squad.

The new Texas government was on the run. By April 21, the remnants of the Texas army under Sam Houston faced the much larger Mexican army under Santa Anna on the plains of San Jacinto for what became the final showdown.

Mexico was about to lose Texas forever—but Santa Anna had more important things to pursue. A beautiful woman was waiting for him in his tent—time for a siesta.

ALL THE COMFORTS

General Santa Anna, the so-called "Napoleon of the West," was a man of lust and luxury. He had a wife in Mexico, but he loved women and was never lonely for long. He even entered into a marriage ceremony with a San Antonio girl during the siege of the

The famous Gilley's honky-tonk in Pasadena was demolished in 1990 after being damaged by fire.

Alamo so that he could enjoy her womanly comforts with the blessings of her family—before moving on to the next señorita. He traveled with a three-room silk tent, carpets, champagne, chocolates, a piano, and his own supply of opium. The Napoleon of the West was addicted to more than women.

THE GAL WHO GAVE HER ALL FOR TEXAS
The woman in Santa Anna's tent at San Jacinto was Emily D. West, a free mulatto woman, not from Texas, but from Connecticut. Here's what we know about her: in October 1835, she was working at a hotel in New Washington, Texas (probably as a chambermaid). On April 16, 1836, a Mexican cavalry unit raided New Washington, looted and plundered the town and the hotel, and took captives, including Emily. She and the others were dragged off to the plains of San Jacinto. Whether Emily was attracted to General Santa Anna and willingly became his battlefield mistress or whether she was one of the unwilling spoils of war will never be known.

What is known is that on that fateful afternoon of April 21, 1836, with the armies of Texas and Mexico facing each other, General Santa Anna ordered a siesta and retreated to his tent to spend some quality time with Miss Emily.

Legend has it that on the morning before the battle, Sam Houston climbed a tree to spy into the enemy camp and saw Emily preparing a champagne breakfast for Santa Anna. He remarked: "I hope that girl makes him neglect his business and keeps him in bed all day."

THE BRIEF BATTLE OF SAN JACINTO
The Texans attacked at 3:30 in the afternoon; by 3:50 it was over. More than 1,300 Mexicans were either killed or captured. The Texans lost nine men. Santa Anna escaped in the confusion but was captured the following day hiding in a swamp wearing a private's uniform he'd taken off a dead soldier.

DEEP IN THE HEART OF NEW YORK
The beautiful Emily survived the battle. Her story and the song circulated through minstrel shows, barrooms, and around the campfires of the frontier. But Emily had had enough of Texas. She left in March 1837 on a ship bound for New York. From there she vanished from history—but never from song.

Carol Burnett—comedienne and actress—was born on April 26, 1936, in San Antonio.

CITRUS MAXIMUS

The story of one Texas man's love affair with a citrus fruit.

The first-known reference to oranges was in China around 500 BC. From there, oranges wended their way westward through India, Persia, and eventually to Spain, orange central to the world. From Spain the orange found its way to Texas, when an eighteenth-century Spaniard planted seven Spanish orange trees in Hidalgo County at Edinburgh's Laguna Seca Ranch. And there they sat, just waiting for the birth of their greatest fan, Jeff McKissack.

MR. MCKISSACK MEETS HIS MATCH

Georgia-born Jeff McKissack had led a fairly interesting life before his arrival in Texas in the late 1940s. He'd shaken the hand of Thomas Edison, studied at Columbia University, and had been a soldier in World War II. But one of his most formative experiences was trucking oranges to and from Florida during the Great Depression. He had a thing for oranges; he considered the orange an unbeatable source of energy and would talk even a Texan's ear off about the orange's salutary effects.

Settling in Houston, Texas, he went to work at the post office, but he never forgot his love of oranges. McKissack bought two adjacent lots in Houston's Eastside neighborhood and opened a nursery—which seemed to be doing well, until one day he announced he was going out of business—and gave away all his plants. He then published a book entitled *How to Live 100 Years and Still Be Spry* in which he promoted good nutrition (including oranges, of course), exercise, and having a hobby. And like a lot of middle-aged men, he sought his next big adventure. One day in 1956, his squirt of inspiration came; he would build a Texas-sized artistic tribute to the orange!

IF YOU BUILD IT . . .

For the next 20 years, McKissack collected building materials from "found sources" such as demolition and construction sites—everything from wheels to roof tiles to all sorts of decorative objects. With this material he built "The Orange Show," his 3,000-square-foot tribute to "the perfect food" and one of the most impressive examples of folk art in the Southwest. When he wasn't at his job at the post office (from which he retired in 1966), he collected and constructed a little bit at a time. His whimsical designs and decorations included sculptures, mosaics, amphitheaters, a wishing well, a pond, and several upper decks—all in a mazelike layout.

McKissack had big plans for The Orange Show. "You could take 100,000 architects and 100,000 engineers and all of them put together couldn't conceive of a show like this," he once stated matter-of-factly. He thought it: "the most beautiful show on earth, the most colorful show in harmony and the most unique," and pictured it drawing a bigger crowd than Houston's Astrodome, which seated around 50,000 at a time. Finally, after decades of sweat, imagination and oversight, McKissack threw open his doors on May 9, 1979. His dream had come true.

... THEY WILL COME, WON'T THEY?
Unfortunately, the big crowds and nationwide interest McKissack envisioned never materialized. His artistically expressed theories of how to live a healthy life—through hard work, good nutrition, and oranges couldn't compete with three-martini lunches, lavish parties, and Astroworld's high-tech roller coasters. The Orange Show didn't go out of business, but McKissack was crushed that more people didn't take an interest; he withdrew from society and died of a stroke only months after the grand opening.

THE SHOW MUST GO ON
The unique art and architecture of The Orange Show were on track to be demolished and cleared off the property until a small group of fans pooled their cash and founded The Orange Show Foundation. The foundation not only maintains The Orange Show, but also sponsors a number of other attractions and events including the Art Car Festival, Beer Can House, and numerous area concerts and projects. *Texas Monthly* magazine said: "The Orange Show may not be the 'biggest thing to hit Houston since the domed stadium' as McKissack predicted, but it has certainly

galvanized the arts community in a way no museum or gallery has." The magazine also called this folk art tour one of the "Top 50 Things Every Texan Should Do."

TODAY'S ORANGE

Jeff McKissack would be proud. Orange juice is vastly popular in the U.S.; Americans consume more than 2.5 times more orange juice than its nearest competitor, apple juice. And more people visit The Orange Show than ever before—thousands each year. The Orange Show Foundation is now known as The Orange Show Center for Visionary Art, and serves as one of the city's artistic engines, kept alive by grants from the National Endowment for the Arts, the Texas Commission on the Arts, and the City of Houston.

How sweet.

* * * * *

A REAL SHINER

Texas is known for its tall, cool Shiner Bocks brewed at the Spoetzl Brewery in the little town of Shiner (population 2,070). The Spoetzl Brewery is the second oldest and last independent brewery in Texas. It has been making beer for almost 100 years—Spoetzl got started in 1909. Famous for Shiner Bock, Spoetzl also bottles a mean Winter Ale, sunny Hefeweizen, and golden Blonde. There's also Shiner Light for those of you watching your waistline. So if you're ever in Shiner (about eighty miles southeast of Austin), stop by the brewery to take a tour and see where they make almost 5,600 cases of beer per day.

Pioneering rock 'n' roll legend Buddy Holly was born in Lubbock, Texas, on September 7, 1936.

WOULDN'T YOU LIKE TO BE A "WACO" TOO?

One more claim to Texas fame. A short, sweet soft drink success story.

The Place: Waco, Texas. The Year: 1885. When he wasn't filling prescriptions at Morrison's Old Corner Drug Store, pharmacist and medical doctor Charles Alderton doubled as a soda jerk, serving up carbonated beverages at the drugstore's soda fountain.

JUST WHAT THE DR ORDERED

The young pharmacist loved those soda fountain smells: cherry, vanilla, lemon, raspberry, and all the other flavors that were popular in those pre-Pepsi days. He thought a soft drink flavored like that combo of smells would be a hit, so he tried various formulas, all the while keeping a log of all his experiments. Eventually, he came up with an unusual, almost indescribable combination of syrups and fruity extracts. The customers loved it so of course the storeowner, Wade Morrison, was thrilled!

Soon "Shoot me a Waco" was the favorite soda fountain order.

SO MISUNDERSTOOD

But "Waco" wasn't good enough. Alderton and Morrison experimented with names for the concoction (at the same time experimenting with other soft drink flavors with names like "ZuZu" and "Celery Champagne." It's a good thing they kept trying.)

As the popularity of the fruity soft drink grew, Morrison eventually settled on the name, "Dr. Pepper." The official company history credits the name as honoring Dr. Charles Pepper of Rural Retreat, Virginia because he gave Morrison his first job. The unofficial lore is that Dr. Pepper's daughter was Morrison's first love. Whether Morrison was thinking of a job or a girl, the "doctor" name caught on at a time when soft drinks were often touted for their supposed medicinal qualities. (Dr Pepper's early advertising promoted it as a brain tonic, a cure for hangover, an antidote to nicotine, and an aphrodisiac.)

He was born Charles Hardin Holley.

THE GREATEST THING SINCE SLICED BREAD
In 1904, Dr. Pepper (billed as a "health drink") was offered to the 20 million visitors to the St. Louis World's Fair. There it became a rising star along with other now-classic foods introduced at the fair: hamburgers and hot dogs served on buns, the ice cream cone, peanut butter, and sliced bread.

EXCUSE ME, DID YOU DROP SOMETHING?
Today Dr Pepper, the oldest major soft drink in America, ranks sixth on the current list of best-selling carbonated soft drinks; the top non-cola trademark brand. By the way, if you're ever in Waco, you can pay homage to the great inventor at the Dr Pepper museum that's housed in the 1906 Artesian Manufacturing and Bottling Company building.

And no, Uncle John's proofreaders are not sleeping on the job! There is no period after the "Dr" in "Dr Pepper" anymore. The company dropped the period from its trademark in the 1950s.

* * * * *

SUPER SODA SLOGANS
A few key slogans throughout the years for Dr Pepper, a true Texas taste sensation:

The King of Beverages

Drink a bite to eat at 10, 2, and 4

The Friendly Pepper-Upper

The Most Misunderstood Soft Drink

The Most Original Soft Drink Ever in the Whole Wide World

Be a Pepper

Be You

The first European exploration of the Texas coastline was in 1519.

WE DON'T NEED
NO EDUCATION

*Your mother may have warned you that if you dropped out of school
you'd never amount to anything. It's a good thing she never told
that to these Texas millionaires.*

MICHAEL DELL: COMPUTER GIANT

Michael Dell was precocious. At the age of eight, West Houston-born Dell sent away for his high school equivalency exam. At twelve, while his friends quibbled over baseball cards, he organized a stamp auction via mail and walked away with a couple thousand bucks. At sixteen, he started a newspaper subscription business and earned enough money to buy a BMW off the showroom floor. He dropped out of University of Texas as a freshman, to sell custom-made computers directly to the public (you may have heard of them—Dell computers?). Today his net worth is around $11.2 billion.

HOWARD HUGHES:
MOVIE PRODUCER, AVIATOR, ECCENTRIC

Even back in Hughes's day, Rice University was one of the most exclusive schools in the South. When his father died in 1923, Hughes flushed his Rice futures, and with the millions he'd inherited, became a film producer—eventually cranking out the original *Scarface* and *Hell's Angels*. He loved airplanes, too, and broke quite a few airspeed records. He even constructed and flew a giant seaplane made entirely of wood, the *Spruce Goose* (which was actually made of birch, not spruce). Either way, it was too heavy to fly more than once. Hughes also helped the CIA secretly recover a sunken Russian submarine in 1974.

Hughes spent the last portion of his life in a reclusive state. He moved from hotel penthouse to hotel penthouse. He bought Las Vegas's Desert Inn after the management threatened to evict him. Few people actually saw him during this period of his life, but rumors abounded that he wore Kleenex boxes for shoes and stored his urine in jars. (What would Uncle John think!) When he died on a plane between Los Angeles and Houston in 1976, officials had to use his fingerprints to identify him since so few people knew what he looked like. But there were plenty who knew what he was worth. After his death, 400 heirs and more than 40 wills skulked out of the woodwork for a shot at his billions.

JOAN CRAWFORD: DRAMA QUEEN

Born Lucille LeSueur in San Antonio, Texas (the pseudonym "Joan Crawford" was the winner of a nationwide publicity contest run by MGM), Crawford tanked as a student. A sixth-grade drop-out, she still managed to get into Missouri's Stephens College, but she already knew she wanted to be a professional entertainer. So she dropped out of Stephens and eventually landed a dance gig in Chicago, then a contract with MGM where she got her start in silent pictures and went on to make almost 80 films and become a Hollywood legend. When her fourth husband, the chairman of the board of Pepsi-Cola, died, Crawford took a seat on the board of directors—much to the chagrin of the suits who ran the place. She was also the "Mommie" in question in the tell-all biography *Mommie Dearest*, written by her daughter Christina.

WALTER CRONKITE:
"THE MOST TRUSTED MAN IN AMERICA"

Young Houstonian Walter Cronkite ran for freshman class president when he arrived at the University of Texas in 1933 (he lost). While at school, he split his time between jobs at the university's newspaper and the state capitol, where he was employed as a copyboy and junior journalist. In 1935, he quit school altogether to work for the *Houston Post*. When World War II broke out he went to Europe for the United Press to cover everything from the Normandy invasion to the Nuremberg trials. He joined CBS in 1950 and cocreated and anchored the CBS Evening News from 1962 to 1981. An editorial that he wrote in 1968 advocating a negotiated settlement in Vietnam is considered a milestone in American journalism.

STEVIE RAY VAUGHAN: BLUES GUITARIST EXTRAORDINAIRE

Born in the Dallas suburb of Oak Cliff in 1954, Vaughan started playing guitar when he was eleven. By the time he was in high school, he was playing every night—all through the night until sunrise—at a number of Dallas nightclubs. During his sophomore year, he transferred to a gifted arts program for talented musicians at Southern Methodist University, but finally quit school altogether and moved to Austin looking for his break—sometimes sleeping on pool tables and collecting bottles to survive. His gamble paid off. He went on to become a Texas music icon, cut a half-dozen critically acclaimed albums, and win numerous industry awards including four Grammies. He died, too young, in 1990 when a helicopter he was on crashed into a hill during bad weather.

BEN HOGAN: A GOLF PRO'S CINDERELLA STORY

Born in 1912 in Stephenville, Texas, Ben Hogan's family moved to Fort Worth when he was nine years old. Three years later, young Ben went to work as a caddy at Fort Worth's Glen Garden Country Club. A competitor at heart, Ben decided to become a pro golfer and dropped out of high school in 1929 to pursue his career. For the first few years, he wasn't very good. He went broke, twice, but kept on playing. During one particularly bad stretch, he was down to his last hundred dollars when the tires were stolen right off his car. That was the last straw—Hogan told his wife that he was quitting and would find "a real job," but she convinced him to stick with golf. Lucky for him, too, because by 1940, he was golf's leading money-winner. And for decades, he was a dogleg demon—winning 63 major victories and nine major tournaments. He started the Ben Hogan Company, a manufacturer of golf clubs and accessories, and was inducted into the World Golf Hall of Fame in 1974.

The geographic center of Texas is 15 miles northeast of Brady.

STATE NATIVE PEPPER: CHILTEPIN

House Concurrent Resolution No. 82, 75th Legislature, Regular Session (1997)

Cooks use this little red devil to liven up salsas, soups, and stews. Wanting to claim this hot dish as their own, Texans adopted the chiltepin as their official native pepper in 1997. The word "chiltepin" (pronounced CHIL-TUH-PEEN) roughly translates from the Aztec language to "flea chile," because of its bite. The "mother of all peppers," the chiltepin is found mainly in the wild, though some farmers and gardeners grow it domestically. The hearty plants last anywhere from 25 to 35 years and can reach six feet in height. Frost-resistant, the plants bear white flowers, which then turn into tiny round red peppers. The whole process from flower to pepper takes about 90 days.

ONE HOT LITTLE NUMBER

One single chiltepin plant yields anywhere from fifty to a hundred little berrylike peppers. But don't let their diminutive looks fool you—chiltepins pack a mean punch. So mean, in fact, that the ancient Tarahumara Indians of Mexico firmly believed that the chiltepin protected them against evil. According to their folklore, if a man refused to eat one, it was proof that he was a bad 'un. Nowadays, the most common legend is that Texas parents have replaced soap with the chiltepin in the fight against "potty mouths."

Scientists think that the wild chiltepin has been around for close to 10,000 years and is most likely the original hot pepper from whence all hot peppers come. A transplant, you might say, from Bolivia and southern Brazil, the fruit was probably carried throughout South and Central America, as well as the southern border of North America, by birds. Even today, the birds love these little peppers. Texas's own state bird, the Northern Mockingbird, dines on them almost exclusively when the chiltepins are in season.

THE SOUTH TEXAS DIET?

And people like them too. Chiltepins are used in fresh and dried forms. A spicy favorite in soups and chilies, the most amazing aspect of this little red pepper is that it has been shown to fire up the human metabolism by as much as twenty-five percent, which as we all know, can translate to weight loss. Watch out all you low-carb diets, the chiltepin might be the next big thing!

* * * * *

CALL HIM TEX

Woodard Maurice Ritter, better known as Tex, was born on January 12, 1905 in Murvaul, Texas, a small town in Panola County. The youngest of six kids, Tex grew up with a love of music. By 1929, he was singing on Texas radio and then found his way to New York where he sang in the Madison Square Garden Rodeo and starred in one of New York's first western radio programs, "The Lone Star Rangers." Ritter eventually made it to Hollywood where he appeared in over eighty movies. In 1942, Capitol Records signed Tex up to sing for them. His hits included "You Are My Sunshine," "(I've Got Spurs That) Jingle Jangle Jingle," and "Deck of Cards." Best remembered for his rich voice, his devotion to country western music, and his work to preserve its heritage, Ritter was undoubtedly a true hero and proud son of Texas. Want to know more? Then hop on over to the Tex Ritter Museum in Carthage, Texas.

Mirabeau B. Lamar was the Republic of Texas's second president (1838–1841).

LAS CIUDADES DE TEJAS*

Spain played a big part in shaping today's Texas. Just look at a map and you can easily see the Spanish influence. Ever wonder what those Texas towns' names mean? Us too.

En Español: Amarillo
In English: Yellow
The Reason? Spanish settlers thought the nearby creek looked yellow; its early houses were painted yellow, too.

En Español: Bandera
In English: Flag
The Reason? The town is named after nearby Bandera Pass, which got its name either from an early Spanish landowner or the site of a battle between Spaniards and the natives.

En Español: Bovina
In English: Bovine
The Reason? It was called Bull Town first; when it was renamed, the residents thought it sounded more elegant in Spanish so they changed it.

En Español: Corpus Christi
In English: Body of Christ
The Reason? The Spanish explorers who first discovered the nearby Corpus Christi Bay from Europe were devout Catholics.

En Español: Cuero
In English: Leather or hide
The Reason? Cuero was named after a nearby creek where Native Americans killed wild cattle that got stuck in its mud.

En Español: Del Rio
In English: Of the River
The Reason? The city sits where the Rio Grande and San Felipe Creek come together.

George "Spanky" McFarland of the *Our Gang* film series was born October 2, 1928, in Fort Worth.

En Español:	El Paso
In English:	The Pass
The Reason?	Originally named: "El Paso Del Norte," because it provided a north-south passage from the southern part of "New Spain."

En Español:	Hondo
In English:	Deep
The Reason?	And nearby Hondo Creek is pretty darn deep.

En Español:	Lamesa
In English:	The Table
The Reason?	If you've driven through there, you'll know. If not, the town is just plain flat. The name is actually the two words, "la" and "mesa," put together.

En Español:	Lampasas
In English:	Water Lily
The Reason?	Lampasas was named for the beautiful lilies in a nearby stream.

En Español:	Laredo
In English:	Laredo
The Reason?	The city's founder, Tomás Sánchez de la Barrera y Garza, named it in honor of his commanding officer's hometown of Laredo, Spain.

En Español:	Llano
In English:	Level
The Reason?	It's named after the nearby Llano River, a tributary of the Colorado River.

En Español:	Ozona
In English:	Ozone
The Reason?	It was named for all the open space or "ozone."

En Español:	Port Lavaca
In English:	The Cow
The Reason?	Originally just "La Vaca," the area has been home to cows for hundreds of years.

He is the only *Our Gang* member to have a star on Hollywood's Walk of Fame.

En Español:	Refugio
In English:	Shelter
The Reason?	In 1795, the Spanish moved an elaborate mission, Nuestra Señora del Refugio Mission, to what was then an Indian campground.

En Español:	Salado
In English:	Salty
The Reason?	It was named after the Salado Creek, a creek that flows across a giant salt formation that stretches from Big Bend to Kansas.

En Español:	San Antonio
In English:	St. Anthony
The Reason?	The city is named after St. Anthony of Padua (an Italian, by the way), known to Catholics as the "finder of lost articles."

En Español:	Sierra Blanca
In English:	White Mountain
The Reason?	The city is near Sierra Blanca Mountain, the biggest of the three mountains in the Sierra Blanca Range.

En Español:	Terlingua
In English:	Three Tongues
The Reason?	The word is actually a corruption of the words "tres lenguas." Some say it's because Terlingua Creek splits into three branches.

En Español:	Victoria
In English:	Victory
The Reason?	It was originally called Guadalupe Victoria (Our Lady of Guadalupe Triumphant), after an honorary name granted to the first president of Mexico.

*By the way, the title of this piece translates to "The Cities of Texas."
But be careful to spell "Tejas" with a capital "T" because "Las ciudades
de tejas" means "The cities of roofing tiles." Not the same thing at all.*

COWBOYS, CATTLE, AND CABERNET

Belly up to the bar for a glass of Texas wine.

The accents may be more Fort Worth than France. But wine-making—introduced to Texas by Franciscan monks in the 1600s—was wetting Texan lips for a hundred years before Californians started their "wining."

VINO EN ESPAÑA NUEVA

The Spanish first laid eyes on Texas soil in 1519 when Álvarez de Pineda was searching the Gulf Coast for riches. Over the next 300 years, Spain endowed Texas with the groundwork of its culture, including vineyards.

The Spanish scattered their missions across what they called New Spain in an attempt to settle the land and promote Christianity to Native Americans (who already had both land and their own established religion, but that's another story). At least the Spanish brought something new to drink. In 1682, Franciscan monks built a mission near present-day El Paso, and established a vineyard to make wine for religious ceremonies, medicinal purpose, and just plain satisfaction with dinner.

Soon the valley around El Paso was awash with vineyards. The Spanish even exported Texas wine back to Spain. As the years rolled by, most Anglo settlers were unfamiliar with wine-making and therefore did not promote the endeavor. But the German and Italian immigrants who flooded into Texas in the 1800s, seeking cheap land and a change of scenery, brought with them a rich winemaking (and drinking) culture.

TODAY'S TEXAS WINE LIST

Six regions in Texas comprise the majority of Texas winemaking: the High Plains near Lubbock, the Hill Country near Austin, the Davis Mountains, Fredericksburg, Escondido Valley, and the hills west of Dallas/Fort Worth. Cabernet Sauvignon is a favorite among Texas winemakers, as are other red varieties such as Merlot, Pinot

Some of Texas's ghost towns are called Bug Tussle, Big Lump, Gay Hill, and Who'd Thought It.

Noir, Zinfandel, Red Cabernet, and Barbara. The white wine list includes Riesling, Chenin Blanc, Chardonnay, and Sauvignon Blancs that would satisfy even the snootiest of wine snobs.

MERCI BEAUCOUP, MONSIEUR MUNSON

If not for a Texas vintner, in fact, French wine connoisseurs would have to import most, if not all, of their wine (*sacre bleu!*). In the late 1800s, a root disease known as phylloxera infected vineyards across the French countryside. France's leading experts turned to a Texas winemaker named Thomas Volney Munson of Dennison, Texas. Munson bred a strong variety of grape that resisted the disease, and helped save the French wine industry from ruin. He was awarded the Legion of Honor (and maybe even a kiss on each cheek) from the French government.

TEXAS VINES OF THE TIMES

Prohibition all but killed the state's wine industry in 1919, except for a single winery: the Val Verde Winery in Del Rio, Texas. Established in 1883 by an Italian immigrant, it survived prohibition by selling table grapes. The American wine renaissance hit Texas in the late 1960s and early 1970s. Today, over fifty wineries make Texas the fifth-largest wine-producing state in the country. The Val Verde winery is not only still going strong, but also is still operated by the original family, which has become famous for wines like its Don Luis Texas Tawny Port. Try some when you're smoking your big old cee-gar after a savory steak dinner.

* * * * *

"Here were six or eight good species of wild grapes, several of which had not been seen by me previously. I had found my grape paradise! Surely now, thought I, 'this is the place for experimentation with grapes!'"

—Thomas Volney. Munson, 1876,
Texan rescuer of the French wine industry

Tarzan, Texas, on State Highway 176 in Martin County, is the home of the Tarzan Hot Oil Company.

AS BIG AS TEXAS

It's hard to believe, but there hasn't always been a Texas. This, of course, was very long ago, when dinosaurs ruled the plains.

Meet the Texas-sized inhabitants of the plains, fields, and forests that would one day become the Lone Star State.

TEXAS PANHANDLE

The oldest dinosaurs in Texas lived in the Texas Panhandle beginning around 220 million years ago, during the Triassic period—almost as long ago as the first Dairy Queen franchise. At the time, most of the Panhandle was tropical forest surrounded by mountains.

Technosaurus: Campus Cutie

It was found near the Texas Tech University campus, hence the name, which literally means "techno lizard." About the size of a large dog, these bipedal (two-footed) herbivores (plant-eaters) noshed on Triassic shrubbery. Classified as "ornithischian," which means that it had hips like a bird, it was a favorite food of coelophysis, who you'll be meeting next.

Coelophysis: Leader of the Pack

Its name means "hollow form"—a reference to the hollow bones that gave it the speed to chase down smaller animals, like technosaurus. Theories say the coelophysis used to hunt in packs to take down prey. Standing about six-and-a-half feet tall and almost ten feet long from nose to tail, these large theropods (meaning "beast-footed") weighed only 60 pounds. They wouldn't inspire the terror of another theropod, like the tyrannosaurus, but seeing a pack of them heading your way might make even the toughest Texan duck into the nearest cave.

Shuvosaurus: Big Bird

Imagine a 10-foot long, 250-pound featherless ostrich and you've got a shuvosaurus, a Triassic ornithomimid (bird mimic).

"Shuvosaurus" means "Shuvo's Lizard," named for the son of
Lubbock-based-paleontologist Sankar Chatterjee, who discovered
the first specimen. This herbivore (who possibly also snacked on
small animals) used its short heavy beak to crack open nuts and
seeds. Its skull, found near the tiny town of Post, Texas, is the only
evidence of its existence. Meet the rest of the family in BIG
BEND, below.

CENTRAL TEXAS
Dinosaurs appeared in Central Texas about 110 to 105 million
years ago, during the early Cretaceous period, after thriving in the
area from northeast of what is now Dallas/Fort Worth and across
the Hill Country. At the time, this strip of land ran along the
Gulf of Mexico's shoreline, so everything east of U.S. Highway 35
was underwater.

Acrocanthosaurus: Stalk of Fame
With a mouthful of almost 70 serrated teeth with steak-knife
edges, this 3-ton, 30-foot carnivore (meat-eater) probably started
the tradition of eating big in Texas. First discovered in Oklahoma
in 1950, the "top-spined lizard" (named for the foot-long dorsal
spines along its back) were the top predators of their day. Finding
one today is rare; only 4 specimens have been found anywhere,
but they left their 3-toed footprints all over Texas. You can even
see a Cretaceous chase scene at the Dinosaur Valley State Park in
Glen Rose, where fossilized footprints show an acrocanthosaurus
chasing and attacking a pleurocoelus, who you'll be meeting
shortly.

Deinonychus: Captain Hook's Crew
Its name means "terrible claw," referring to the five-inch, flesh-
tearing claws on its hind feet, and as a dromaeosaur ("swift
lizard"), it's related to the velociraptors of *Jurassic Park*. The ten-
foot-long, fast-as-a-sports-car deinonychus hunted in packs, using
their deadly claws (and their powerful, clawed front limbs) to take
down prey. They're closely related to modern birds, but if you run
across a group, don't bother with your field guide—just run!

Texas towns that are four-letter words: Alto, Acme, Best, Buda, Bula, Cash, Fink, Grit, Hext ...

Pleurocoelus: Bigger is Better

This dino has the distinction of being the State Dinosaur of Texas (as mandated by Texas Legislature Concurrent Resolution No. 57 in 1997). At 10 to 20 tons and 50 to 70 feet tall, this relative of the brontosaurus was one Texas vegetarian nobody made fun of. Pleurocoelus, which means "hollow side" because of the way its vertebrae are scooped out along the side, left its huge footprints all over central and north-central Texas, and can still be seen at Dinosaur Valley State Park near the city of Glen Rose.

BIG BEND

Almost 100 dinosaur species have been discovered at Big Bend National Park. Dinosaurs found in this Texas region lived about 75 to 65 million years ago, during the tail end of the Cretaceous period and the beginnings of the Cenozoic era. At the time, a huge inland body of water stretched from the Gulf of Mexico to Alaska, and the Big Bend area was on its western bank. You'd think that much of the landscape looked pretty much like it does today, with modern flowers and trees. (Until a dinosaur walked by, that is.)

Chasmosaurus: Fashionable Frill

Funky chasmosaurus had a groovy look going on. Like his distant cousin triceratops, chasmosaurus had a big bony frill on top of its head. But this "chasm lizard" was the more stylish, since his frill had two really big holes in it, a totally different look!

Paleontologists think that the holes helped lighten the bone mass. The frill also served both to protect chasmosaurus's neck and to attract mates. Also like a triceratops, the chasmosaurus was armored, walked on all fours, ate plants, and had a toothless beak. Almost 20 feet long and weighing more than 2 tons apiece, they were also found in Alberta, Canada, just like cowboys and oil money.

Torosaurus: Toro! Toro!

Named for the large cattlelike horns over his eyes, the "bull lizard" has the biggest skull (9 feet long) of any known land animal. El torosaurus was a gentle herbivore, and so big (24 feet long, 9 tons in weight), that he might not have even noticed if a Cretaceous cowboy tried to rope and ride him.

Not to mention Lawn, Lodi, Nada, Spur, Toca, Voca, Wink, and Zorn.

TEXAS MOVIE QUIZ

Test your cinema smarts on this little Texas trivia timewaster.

Think you can spot a Texan a mile away? How about just a movie screen away? Take our little quiz and find out.

1. This Texan singer of "Baby Don't Get Hooked on Me" played quarterback Seth Maxwell in *North Dallas Forty* (1979). Can you name him?

2. Oliver Stone's *JFK* (1991) about the assassination of President Kennedy in Dallas highlights an investigation by a district attorney in another city. Which city is it?

3. Which two Rat Packers appeared together in 1963's *Four for Texas*?

4. Who was the director of 1984's acclaimed movie *Paris, Texas*?

5. Name the bar featured in *Urban Cowboy* (1980).

6. Robert DeNiro plays a bounty hunter who catches Charles Grodin and drags him across Texas in this 1988 film.

7. John Sayles's *Lone Star* (1996) starred this native Texan and Chris Cooper as father and son. Can you name him?

8. This 1985 feature film of Kevin Costner followed a road trip of five University of Texas students beginning in Austin. Name the film.

9. What *Rio Lobo* actor played Davy Crockett in 1960's *The Alamo*?

10. Can you name the Texan who starred in the original *Walking Tall* (1973)?

Answers on page 303.

The motto of Gun Barrel City, Texas, is "We Shoot Straight With You."

THE CONFEDERACY'S LAST STAND

The problem with fighting a war before the age of instant communication is that some folks don't get the news that the war is over.

The Civil War officially ended on April 9, 1865, when General Robert E. Lee surrendered to General Ulysses S. Grant at Appomattox Court House in Virginia. But the last battle of the Civil War took place in Texas more than a month later: The Battle of Palmito Ranch (a.k.a. Palmetto Ranch), at the southernmost tip of Texas in Cameron County. And it was the *Confederates* who won that battle.

JOHNNY YANK STARTED IT

Historians are generally puzzled as to why Union commander Colonel Theodore Barrett ordered his men to attack an encampment of Confederate troops near Brownsville, since, among other things, the Union and Confederate forces in Texas at the time had been operating under an unofficial agreement to keep out of each others' hair—and rifle sights. Ordering an attack wasn't in keeping with the spirit of the standing "gentleman's agreement." It could have been that, since Barrett knew about the Appomattox Court House surrender, he was simply moving to occupy Brownsville, but there's also speculation that Barrett had political aspirations, and a battle victory would look nice on his resume.

WHO KNEW?

Whatever the reason, on May 11, 1865, Union troops advanced on the Confederate forces, led by Colonel John "Rip" Ford. Ford and his men were in the dark about the status of the war—they didn't know enough to know they'd already been beat. So when the Union troops showed up at Palmito Ranch, the rebels weren't in the surrendering frame of mind. The Union troops got the jump on the Confederates and beat them back from the ranch, but in the afternoon, the Rebs counterattacked and drove back the Yankee invaders.

Fossils of 17 different kinds of dinosaurs have been found in Texas.

AND JOHNNY REB FINISHES IT

The next day the Union forces got the upper hand, but once again, the Confederate troops reorganized and this time, with the help of a two-pronged attack and six cannons, routed the enemy. The Union forces took heavy casualties and retreated. Ford and his men had earned a victory for the South. It was only after the battle that the Confederates found out that the Civil War was officially over. And ironically enough, they heard it from the Union troops they had captured.

All told, the Union troops had suffered 115 casualties, including at least 30 dead. The Confederate forces also suffered dozens injured but none fatally wounded. The last man killed at Palmito Ranch was Private John J. Williams of the 34th Indiana Volunteer Infantry, which likely makes him the last man to die in the Civil War.

THE LEGACY OF PALMITO RANCH

If Colonel Barrett had political inclinations, the Battle of Palmito Ranch didn't do him much good—after this last battle he pretty much faded from American history. Confederate Colonel John Ford, on the other hand, fared better. He never officially surrendered to the Union—two weeks after the battle, he disbanded his unit rather than surrender it. After the war, he became an editor at the Brownsville *Sentinel* newspaper and later a charter member of the Texas State Historical Association and a frequent contributor to its journal. He died in 1897 in San Antonio, the last victorious commander of the Civil War.

* * * * *

In Shamrock, Texas, you can kiss the Blarney Stone—literally. The town has a fragment of the original stone from Blarney Castle, County Cork, Ireland.

In Lubbock's Mackenzie Park, you can get up close and personal with frisky little prairie dogs that live in their own "Prairie Dog Town."

Sugar Babies, starring Houstonian Ann Miller, ran on Broadway for 1,208 performances.

LET'S HEAR IT FOR THE 'BOYS

*A quintet of games every Dallas Cowboy fan remembers—
for better or worse.*

A Cowboys fan will tell you that every game is important. Even so, some games are more important than others—and some games turn out to be flat-out legendary.

THE ICE BOWL
The Date: December 31, 1967
The Opponent: The Green Bay Packers
The first thing you need to know is that it was *damn* cold. The wind chill factor was 40 degrees below zero that New Year's Eve at Lambeau Field—the coldest New Year's in Green Bay history at the time. The Cowboys and the Packers were slugging it out for the right to advance to Super Bowl II. The field was heated, but the heating system malfunctioned, so the field was coated with ice. It was so cold the officials' whistles had frozen and wouldn't blow. With less than five minutes to go in the fourth quarter, the Cowboys were ahead 17–14 and the Packers had the ball on their own 32-yard line. Twelve plays and 68 yards later, with 16 seconds to go and no time outs left, Packer quarterback Bart Starr slipped into the end zone to crush the Cowboy's Super Bowl hopes like snowflakes under his spikes. "The Ice Bowl" is one of the greatest games in NFL history, although of course Cowboys fans wish it had ended a little differently.

90 SECONDS OF GLORY
The Date: December 23, 1972
The Opponent: The San Francisco 49ers
The Cowboys had made the playoffs for a record-setting seven seasons in a row. But things weren't looking good for America's Team toward the end of the first-round playoff game against the 49ers. Going into the fourth quarter, the Cowboys were down by twelve points. Sent to the field in the third quarter to replace

---

Fargo, Texas, is where 6,000,000 cattle crossed on their way to Dodge City, Kansas.

Craig Morton, young quarterback Roger Staubach used this game as a springboard for his legendary career. With just 90 seconds left on the clock, Staubach marched the Cowboys down the field not once, but twice, scoring two touchdowns to bring the Cowboys to a 30-28 victory.

LONGLEY'S MOMENT
The Date: November 28, 1974
The Opponent: The Washington Redskins
The 1974 season is not considered a truly great year by Cowboys standards (they went 8-6 for the year), but the Thanksgiving match-up against the Redskins remains a standout game. In the third quarter, things were looking pretty grim for the Cowboys. Washington was up 16-3 and Cowboys star quarterback, Roger Staubach had just been knocked out of the game by 'Skins linebacker Dave Robinson. Enter Clint Longley, 22-year-old backup QB, who'd spent the entire season riding the pine. Igniting the offense, Longley had the game of his life. With 35 seconds to spare, he threw a 50-yard bomb to receiver Drew Pearson for the winning touchdown and a final score of 24–23. Longley would be out of the league in a few years, but he's still fondly remembered as the Cowboys' "Mad Bomber."

HAIL MARY
The Date: December 28, 1975
The Opponent: The Minnesota Vikings
Oh, yeah, you can *bet* Viking fans remember this one. They were within two minutes of burying the Cowboys on their way to a third Super Bowl when Staubach took over the offense at the Cowboys' 15-yard line. Nine plays later, the Cowboys were at midfield with 30 seconds left. The 'Boys lined up in shotgun formation, Staubach pump-faked left, then turned right, and chucked the ball downfield . . . right into the hands of Drew Pearson, who bobbled it before tucking it in and scoring the winning touchdown. Staubach later said, "I never had a more eerie sensation on a football field than during the aftermath of our touchdown. The crowd was so shocked there wasn't a sound from the stands." He called it "a Hail Mary pass" and the name stuck.

Lolita, Texas, was named after the granddaughter of Texas Revolution veteran Charles Keller Reese.

THE CATCH

The Date: January 10, 1982
The Opponent: The San Francisco 49ers

The Cowboys had pulled out a lot of last-second victories with amazing game-winning passes, so maybe it's only fair that one of the most breath-taking plays in football happened *against* them. In 1982, longtime rivals Dallas and San Francisco squared off for the NFC championship. With less than 90 seconds to play, the Cowboys were up 27-21, but rookie quarterback Joe Montana and receiver Dwight Clark performed a miracle for the 49ers. After the ball was hiked, Montana held onto it until the last possible instant and then tossed it off his back foot. It looked like a bad pass until Dwight Clark reached up from behind the defensive player and made "The Catch." Clark brought the ball down inbounds for the touchdown. The game ended 28-27, and signaled the rise of Montana's 49ers. Guess you can't win 'em all, even if you're the Dallas Cowboys.

* * * * *

SUPER SUPER BOWLS

The Dallas Cowboys have won the Super Bowl five times!

SUPER BOWL VI
Jan. 16, 1972
Dallas Cowboys 24
Miami Dolphins 3

SUPER BOWL XXVIII
Jan. 30, 1994
Dallas Cowboys 30
Buffalo Bills 13

SUPER BOWL XII
Jan. 15, 1978
Dallas Cowboys 27
Denver Broncos 10

SUPER BOWL XXX
Jan. 28, 1996
Dallas Cowboys 27
Pittsburgh Steelers 17

SUPER BOWL XXVII
Jan. 21, 1993
Dallas Cowboys 52
Buffalo Bills 17

HIDDEN BARBECUE HOT-SPOTS

The sweet and lowdown on Texas's secret little barbecue havens.
Can't you smell 'em from here?

Oh, sure—you could settle for middle-of-the-road, corporate franchise barbecue—but why should you, when Uncle John, bless his little heart, has compiled the ultimate list of juicy, lip-smacking joints you'd be hard-pressed to find on your own.

HAROLD'S PIT BAR-B-Q
Abilene, Texas
To be renowned for barbecue in a ranching town like Abilene is no small feat. Other restaurants around the Big Country get more hype, but Harold's is where those in the know go. Menu items include chopped barbecue sandwiches, sausage, chicken, cornbread, even pints of sauce "to go." Harold Christian's pappy opened this restaurant when little Harold was just 10 years old. Now Harold's all grown up and not only runs the place, but occasionally walks onto the floor and sings gospels songs for his patrons.

JOE'S BARBEQUE COMPANY
Alvin, Texas
Between Houston and Galveston on Highway 6, Joe's Barbeque Company is far enough removed from the big city to give you that small-town Texas feel. But everything about it is big—and good. Beautiful beef, chicken, sausage, ham, ribs done up in ol'-fashioned Texas style, and even fried shrimp (the coast being only minutes away). Joe's even has a banquet hall for weddings and parties, as well as a catering service offering not just barbecue but party trays, appetizers, and ice carvings. And outsiders who pass by the little town of Alvin on their way to sample some of Houston's haute cuisine or Galveston's seafood without a clue as to what they're missing.

Marfa, Texas, took its name from a character in Dostoyevsky's *The Brothers Karamazov*.

BAR-B-Q MAN RESTAURANT
Corpus Christi, Texas
Fenced in like valuable livestock, the Bar-B-Q Man off I-37 in Corpus Christi doesn't exactly beckon visitors with its outside décor. What it beckons with is the smell of its brisket! Spare ribs, beef, and other mesquite-smoked delicacies blow away the franchise competition. But it's not all business with a patio cantina, pool tables, and a dance floor. Here's an idea: on weekdays, the refineries should just cut out the middleman and pay employees in Bar-B-Q Man brisket.

WILLIAMS' SMOKEHOUSE
Houston, Texas
On Houston's far North Side, Williams' is neither conveniently located nor interested in marketing itself to strangers—it's just a small family joint in a fading residential neighborhood. But Houstonians who know good barbecue would walk over hot coals covered in lighter fluid to get a taste of Williams' soul-food specialties. Houston restaurants spend hundreds of millions of dollars making and marketing barbecue, but Williams' Southern country barbecue pork ribs, brisket, and sliced-beef sandwiches have them all trumped.

CASSTEVENS CASH & CARRY
Lillian, Texas
Eighty-year-old Harold "Cass" Casstevens's place is a triple threat: it's a store, it's the Diamond Shamrock gas station, and it's an outstanding barbecue joint that's so exclusive that there's only one table. No cow statues. No celebrity photos. No fancy menus. But people come from all over North Texas, passing dozens of table-clothed competitors along the way, for a taste of Cass's thick brisket, pork ribs, hot links, and ham. He gets up every day while the city people are snoozing, and smokes his meats for at least a dozen hours before they pass muster. It's a great place to fill 'er up with some sweet smoky vittles and a few gallons of barbecue sauce.

The town was used as a locale for the movie *Giant* and other films, including *Fandango*.

WHISTLIN' DIXIE BBQ AND GRILL
Lubbock, Texas

To the untrained eye, it looks like just another West Texas barbecue place. But this Old South-style barbecue restaurant stands out among the dusty mesquite-smoking enthusiasts of West Texas. There's the standard barbecue fare: baby back ribs, beef, and pulled pork—plus something called "burnt ends," which are just the crispy little parts of the end of a brisket. Whistlin' Dixie gives you a choice of sauce options: Tennessee Honey, Cajun, and plain old traditional Texas sauce. Include this place in the mix when you're in Lubbock and you could taste major barbecue varieties without getting up from your seat.

NO TEETH BARBECUE
Rockdale, Texas

You don't need teeth to eat here—this barbecue is so gosh-durn good, it melts in your mouth! Proprietor Wallace Brandyburg has turned No Teeth into a real treat for interstate travelers on the road between Dallas and Houston. The brisket is so tasty it even makes grown-ups ask: "Are we there yet?" Plus his habanero-jalapeño-cayenne hot sauce can turn even the toughest Texan into a crybaby with a runny nose.

For more on Texas barbecue, see "Barbecue Basics" on page 217 and "Food Feud" on page 232.

* * * * *

"A Texas Governor has only two happy days: the day he is inaugurated and the day he retires."
                              —Joseph D. Sayers, *governor 1898–1902*

"The Texas Legislature consists of 181 people who meet for 140 days once every two years. This catastrophe has now occurred sixty-three times."
                              —Molly Ivins, *Texas columnist and author*

Texas has one natural lake—Caddo Lake. But it has 190 man-made lakes and reservoirs.

RODEO LINGO

*If you wanna be a rodeo cowboy, you'd better
learn how to talk like one.*

Just a quick list of terms, so's you know what you're talking
about next time you go ringside in Texas.

Arm jerker
A bull so strong it feels like it could yank the rider's arm out of its
socket.

Bad wreck
(Seriously, is there ever a good wreck?) This is when a rider is
bucked off hard and either horned or stomped on by the bull.

Bareback bronc
A horse without a saddle whose rider hangs onto a strap around
the horse's ribcage.

Barrel man
Nope, it's not a daredevil who pitches himself off Niagara Falls,
but he performs a stunt just as risky. You may know him better as a
"rodeo clown." The barrel man hides in a barrel during the bull-
riding event. If the rider is thrown, the barrel man springs into
action to distract the bull from trampling the rider. The barrel
protects the clown so he can protect the rider.

Bull rope
A flat braided rope that goes around the middle of a bull that riders hang on to during the bull-riding event.

Chaps
So much more than a men's cologne by Ralph Lauren, chaps are
the leather coverings that go over riding jeans.

And 80,000 miles of rivers and streams.

Cowboy up
Psyching yourself up, getting in the zone, or preparing mentally. Whatever your cliché, it's getting ready to climb up and give it everything you've got.

Crow hopper
A bull that jumps stiff-legged, straight into the air instead of bucking.

Dogie
As in, "Git along little dogie." A "dogie" is an orphaned calf.

Free hand
Just what it sounds like. The one hand that must be free at all times during riding events in a rodeo.

Freight trained
If a bull sprints over you and tramples you down, then you've been officially freight trained. Unless you're a contestant or a barrel man, you probably needn't worry.

Good bucker
A bronco or steer that gives a particularly feisty performance.

Hooker
(Watch it now.) This is a bull that throws the rider and attempts to hook him with his horns.

Houlihan
A head-over-hooves somersault that a steer can make during the steer-wrestling event.

P.R.C.A.
The Professional Rodeo Cowboy's Association.

Spinner
A bull that spins in circles while trying to shake off his rider. It kind of looks like a puppy chasing his tail.

Sucks back
When referring to a rodeo, it's when a bull bucks in one direction and then quickly switches to another. When referring to beer, it means to drink quickly.

ROADSIDE ROYALTY

The story of Texas's Dairy Queens, as told through numbers.

L ots of Texas towns don't have a mall. Or a Starbucks. Or
even a police station. But it's more than likely that they
have a Dairy Queen. In fact, the highway patrol will give
you a ticket for driving more than 20 miles without eating at a
"DQ." (That's a joke, son.)

But why all the fuss over this hamburger and ice-cream joint?
Check out the numbers.

500,000
The minimum number of dollars of net worth needed to qualify as
a candidate for getting a Dairy Queen franchise. Buying into a
Dairy Queen ranges from around $650,000 to almost $2,000,000,
which includes a $35,000 franchise fee, up to $500,000 for construction, and up to $250,000 for equipment. No wonder they're
stingy with their napkins.

1,478
The number of the official bill, filed by the 78th Texas Legislature
in 2003, recognizing two Jacksonville men for their entrepreneur-
ial efforts at a local Dairy Queen. As the bill notes, "unfavorable
market forces" brought out the creative side in the two men who
came up with the "Dude" and "Country Basket" menu items
(chicken-fried steak sandwich and steak fingers, respectively).
According to HR 1478, " . . . the House of Representatives of the
78th Texas Legislature hereby pay tribute to J. N. Grimes and the
late Ray Morrow for the clever creations that helped to earn Dairy
Queen recognition as the 'Texas stop sign.'"

1,000
The number of customers who showed up at the Dairy Queen at
Coppell, Texas in 2002 when Mark Cuban, billionaire owner of
the Dallas Mavericks basketball team, spent a few hours working
its counter. DQ bigwigs offered Cuban the gig after he was fined
$500,000 by the NBA by sarcastically saying in public that he
wouldn't hire Ed Rush, the NBA's head of officiating, "to manage
a Dairy Queen."

Texas is one of two states that have been called "the blizzard state." The other is South Dakota.

836

The mass, in grams, of one serving of a DQ large chocolate malt. In case you're wondering, that's about 1.8 pounds; the equivalent of eating around half of a copy of James Michener's 918-page *Texas: A Novel*—in hardback.

600

The number of Dairy Queen restaurants in Texas. That means Texas not only has the largest number of Dairy Queens of any state, but also that it has twice as many Dairy Queens as it does county courthouses, which total a measly 254.

169

The number of times per week the first Dairy Queen radio advertisement was transmitted in 1965.

44

The number of millions of dollars that Dairy Queen has raised in those little change jars for its favorite charity, the Children's Miracle Network, an international non-profit organization dedicated to generating funds and awareness programs to benefit kids treated at children's hospitals. Don't let your warm fuzzies melt the ice cream.

20

The number of foreign countries with Dairy Queens of their own. The list includes Bahrain, Cambodia, China, Oman, Qatar, South Korea, and the United Arab Emirates, among others.

10

Monetary value, in cents, of the enterprise's first sale of their signature soft, frozen delicious dairy treat.

2.5

The number of total fat grams in a Dairy Queen side salad (sans dressing). Despite traditional Texas-size offerings like the aforementioned chocolate malt, DQ is jumping on the light-fare bandwagon with lots of greens and plenty of roughage.

0

The cost, in dollars, of wireless Internet access at the Dairy Queen on Highway 249 in Houston.

STATE FLOWER: BLUEBONNET

Senate Concurrent Resolution No. 10, 27th Legislature, Regular Session (1901)

House Concurrent Resolution No. 44, 62nd Legislature, Regular Session (1971)

Did'ja know that Texas has five state flowers while most states just have one? What gives?

THE GREAT STATE FLOWER DEBATE
Back in 1901, the Texas legislature decided that it needed a state flower—and the battle was on. In one corner was John Nance Garner, the future vice president of the United States, who earned the nickname "Cactus Jack" as an advocate for that thorny plant. Someone else nominated the cotton boll. But the National Society of Colonial Dames of America in Texas championed the bluebonnet, *Lupinus subcarnosus*, and prevailed.

That should have been that. But *Lupinus subcarnosus* isn't the only bluebonnet on the block. The Dames-nominated variety grows along the sandy Texas coast and blooms royal blue in early spring. Another flower-frenzied faction preferred a different variety, the *Lupinus texensis*, a brighter, showier bloomer from central Texas, and rallied for seventy years to have its favorite officially adopted.

So in 1971, the Texas legislature relented and added the second species, plus "any other variety of bluebonnet not heretofore recorded" in order to avoid offending any other subspecies advocates. Since then, three more varieties have been discovered and are now included:

- *Lupinus havardii*, also known as the Big Bend or Chisos Bluebonnet, found on the flats of the Big Bend country.
- *Lupinus concinnus*, whose flowers come in white, rosy magenta, and lavender, from the Trans-Pecos region.
- *Lupinus plattensis*, the only perennial in the bunch, grows in the Texas Panhandle's sandy dunes.

Texas High: Fort Davis in Jeff Davis County is the highest town of any size in Texas, at 5,050 feet.

They've all become the symbol of Texas, much as the shamrock signifies Ireland. In fact, Texas is so bluebonnet batty that one of its state songs is . . . wait for it . . . "Bluebonnets."

LOCAL LEGENDS

Legend has it that when an Aztec maiden offered her life up as a sacrifice for her tribe's sins, her headdress dropped to the ground and the Great Spirit turned it into thousands of bluebonnets in her honor.

The bluebonnet (*Lupinus*) comes in all shades of blue and covers the fields and roadsides of Texas for a few weeks every spring. It is also a bean, which probably makes it the unofficial state bean, but that doesn't concern us here. What does concern us is the Texas love for the innocent little plant that's been nicknamed wolf flower, buffalo clover, and *el conejo* ("the rabbit" in Spanish).

PLEASE DON'T PICK THE BLUEBONNETS

Texans have been known to dress their kids up in their Sunday best and pose them for family photographs in front of the pretty blue flowers.

Smooshing the blues for photos' sake is deemed acceptable, but picking the state flower is a no-no if done in excess. You can legally get away with plucking one or two, but burgling a bunch of beautiful bluebonnets is considered defacing the roadside and against Texas law.

* * * * *

DALLAS'S DREAMBOATS

Aside from their sideline duties, the Dallas Cowboy Cheerleaders are stars unto themselves. In addition to their two made-for-television movies, they have appeared on episodes of *The Love Boat*, battled the Dallas Cowboys on *Family Feud*, and made appearances on *The Tonight Show*! They also had a featured role in Robert Altman's *Dr. T and the Women*, also starring Richard Gere.

The Texas citrus industry has trademarked names for Texas red grapefruit: Rio Star and Ruby Sweet.

WAYLON JENNINGS: THE FIVE-SONG BIOGRAPHY

Just a good ol' boy with a leather-covered guitar, fightin' the Nashville system with his Texas outlaw ways. A sketch in five songs.

Waylon Jennings: Inspired by Buddy Holly and an inspiration to musicians as diverse as Travis Tritt and Metallica, this Texas music master did things the hard way, but also did them his way. In the process, he helped launch the "outlaw" music genre with fellow Texan Willie Nelson, and helped country music make a declaration of independence from the comfortable rut it had settled into by the late 1960s. For this, country music made him a star—proof that being Texas tough can pay off.

THE BUDDY YEARS: "JOLE BLON"

Any biography of Waylon Jennings that omits Buddy Holly—even a five-song biography—would be woefully incomplete. Jennings, born in 1937 in Littlefield, Texas, met up with Holly in 1955 in Lubbock, where the young Jennings was working at radio station KLLL. Holly took a shine to Jennings and helped him with his career, working on songs with his friend and producing his first single, the Cajun-tinged "Jole Blon," in 1958. Jennings also served as a backup Cricket for Holly, playing bass for him during Holly's final tour. In a well-known bit of trivia, Jennings was supposed to be on the plane trip that claimed Holly's life on February 3, 1959, but gave up his seat to fellow Texan, "The Big Bopper" J. P. Richardson, who had a bad head cold and wanted to get some extra rest. The crash also claimed the life of "La Bamba" singer Ritchie Valens.

Jennings was devastated by the death of Holly and spent the better part of two years mourning his friend. "Buddy was the first guy who had confidence in me," he later told a reporter. "Hell, I had as much star quality as an old shoe. But he really liked me and believed in me."

In 1921 a hurricane deposited 23 inches of rain on Texas in one day.

EARLY HITS: "ONLY DADDY'LL WALK THE LINE"

In 1960 Jennings hit the road. After stops in Phoenix and Los Angeles, Jennings landed in Nashville in 1965 with an RCA contract. Luck gave him Johnny Cash as a roommate; the two developed a life-long friendship. Jennings's first Nashville hit was "That's the Chance I'll Have to Take" in 1965; from there, his popularity grew, culminating in 1968 with a string of top ten hits including the top five hit "Only Daddy'll Walk The Line," in which Jennings griped about being wrapped around this gal's little finger. But despite his popularity, Jennings wasn't satisfied with the work and began to chafe under what he saw as musical restrictions of Nashville, where producers tried to tame his honky-tonk sound to make it safe for "decent" people's ears.

THE OUTLAW YEARS: "HONKY TONK HEROES"

Jennings started on the outlaw path in 1970, when he took a chance on a young songwriter named Kris Kristofferson and used his songs to make the albums *Singer of Sad Songs* and *Ladies Love Outlaws*, which laid the foundation for the tougher, rawer "outlaw country" sound. Then in 1972, Jennings got RCA to agree to let him produce his own work and choose his musicians; with that new freedom he released his first masterpiece, 1973's *Honky Tonk Heroes*, which featured the songs written by Billy Joe Shaver and wrenched a number of emotional performances out of Jennings, from the elegiac "We Had it All," and the wanderlust classic "Willy the Wandering Gypsy and Me," to the wry opening honky-tonk salvo of the title track.

Jennings was doing it his way, and it paid off: in 1974, he charted his first number one with "This Time." The Country Music Association voted him Male Vocalist of the Year in 1975. And in 1976, pop stardom hit when *Wanted! The Outlaws*, a compilation album featuring Jennings, his wife Jessi Colton, and Willie Nelson, hit number one on the national charts.

THE SUPERSTAR YEARS: "GOOD OL' BOYS"

The late 1970s and early 1980s were very good for Jennings. He notched a string of ten number-one hits, including three with his old friend Willie Nelson, with whom he recorded the classic *Waylon & Willie* album in 1978, which featured the ironic hit "Mammas Don't Let Your Babies Grow Up to Be Cowboys." He

---

Texas was an independent nation from 1836 to 1845.

also achieved international fame by singing "Good Ol' Boys," the theme song he wrote, and becoming "The Balladeer," the off-screen narrator for the hit TV show *The Dukes of Hazzard*, in which he would describe the zany goings-on of Hazzard County in that wry, folksy voice of his.

The series' theme song was one of his ten number-one hits. Jennings topped off this period of his career in 1985 by joining forces with old friends Nelson, Cash, and Kristofferson to form The Highwaymen, outlaw country's first and only "supergroup," whose album *Highwayman* featured a number-one song about reincarnation. Really.

THE LATER YEARS: "MOST SENSIBLE THING"
Things slowed for Jennings after the mid-1980s, as the musician switched labels from RCA to MCA, then to Epic, and later to smaller labels like Justice, for whom he recorded 1996's *Right For the Time*, which featured the retrospective ballad "Most Sensible Thing," in which he looked back at some of the excesses of his earlier days. He also became a spokesman for education: the high school dropout earned his GED in 1989 and after that became a proponent of the program. He also released a children's album, called *Cowboys, Sisters, Rascals & Dirt*, in 1998, which provided the toddler set a little taste of outlaw country with songs like "All My Sisters are Girls," and "Dirt," a salute to, well, getting dirty.

In his final years, Jennings struggled with his failing heath brought on in part by diabetes. In 2001, his foot was amputated due to complications brought on by the disease, which would later contribute to his death in February 2002.

A LASTING LEGACY
As a gauge of Jennings's influence on music, one need look only as far as the contributors to I've *Always Been Crazy* and *Lonesome, On'ry & Mean*, the two tribute discs released in 2003. There you'll find not only country stars Kris Kristofferson, Travis Tritt, and Kenny Chesney, but also a few surprises like Henry Rollins, Metallica's James Hetfield, and jazz chanteuse Norah Jones, whose smoky take of "Wurlitzer Prize (I Don't Want to Get Over You)" makes a good argument for music lovers not getting over Jennings anytime soon.

STATE REPTILE: TEXAS HORNED LIZARD

House Concurrent Resolution No. 141, 73rd Legislature,
Regular Session (1993)

*Better known as the "horny toad," the Texas Horned Lizard isn't
a toad at all. It's one of the Lone Star State's smaller critters and
averages about four inches in length. Why, then, was it chosen to
represent a state that's known for its hugeness?*

HERE'S BLOOD IN YOUR EYE

For one thing, horny toads have a unique bag of tricks. When threatened by predators, they lay flat on the ground, their brown and gray coloring acting as camouflage. If that doesn't work, they can puff themselves up to twice their normal size. (Now, that sounds more Texan.) And with two rows of spiny scales running up and down their bodies, their natural enemies think twice about snacking on them. If all else fails, the horny toads have one last surefire tactic—and it isn't pretty. They squirt blood from their eyes.

Horny toads like to hibernate during the fall and winter months; when they emerge in the spring, they laze around in the sun, mate during late May and early June, then the female lays up to 45 eggs, buries them in a makeshift nest, and walks away. And never looks back. When the babies hatch several weeks later, they're completely on their own.

HORNY AND HUNGRY

They dine mostly on red harvester ants, but they'll sometimes scarf down a beetle or two for variety. Here's a problem, though: pesticides have depleted their food supply. With fewer red ants to go around, the horny toad's population has significantly decreased. (Of course, the fact that they like to sunbathe in the middle of the road doesn't help either.) Because of their declining numbers, Texas has identified them as a threatened species and banned the collection of horny toads as pets. In 1993, Texas adopted this odd little creature as their official state reptile—bloody tears and all.

Texas boasts the nation's largest herd of whitetail deer.

PICK-UP TRUCK
POP QUIZ

*In most states, pick-up trucks are the ride of the working man and
woman: farm hands, construction workers, factory folks. But in Texas,
almost everybody loves the personality and practicality of a pickup—
from white-collar workers to housewives. How much do you know
about Texas's favorite form of transportation?*

1. What was the most stolen vehicle in Texas in 2003?
   A. 1994 Chevrolet C1500 4x2
   B. 2001 Ford F150 4x2
   C. 1989 Honda Accord
   D. 1998 Dodge Ram Pick-Up

2. Who developed one of the earliest four-wheel drives, a
   battery-powered vehicle with one motor per wheel, in 1900?
   A. Henry Ford
   B. Ransom Eli Olds
   C. Charles F. Kettering
   D. Ferdinand Porsche

3. In 2004, a straight-off-the-assembly-line Dodge Ram SRT-10
   earned the *Guinness Book* record for the fastest production
   truck in the world. What does SRT stand for?
   A. Street-Legal Race Team
   B. Special Response Transmission
   C. Street and Racing Technology
   D. Specialty Road and Track

4. Which major pick-up manufacturer has a factory between
   Dallas and Forth Worth where it's made 7.5 million vehicles
   over the last five decades?
   A. Ford Motor Company
   B. General Motors Corporation
   C. Toyota Motor Sales, U.S.A.
   D. Land Rover North America, Inc

One of every five Texans is employed in an agriculture-related industry.

5. "Shift on the Fly" lets you do what?
    A. Alternate between automatic to manual transmission
    B. Shift without using the clutch
    C. Tow especially heavy loads at high speeds
    D. Go between two- and four-wheel drive while moving

6. Which hardcore 4x4 last rolled off the line in October 1980, less than two decades after it had been introduced?
    A. The Ford Bronco II
    B. The Chevy Blazer
    C. The Subaru Brat II
    D. The International Harvester Scout

7. According to statute 545.414 of the Texas Department of Public Safety, what's the only thing that would make it legal to drive a pick-up truck with a person under 18 in the bed?
    A. It's their birthday
    B. You're at the beach
    C. The youngster is related to you
    D. You're driving slower than 5 mph

8. Which Texas country music legend composed and wrote the "Pick-up Truck Texas"?
    A. Waylon Jennings
    B. Gary P. Nunn
    C. Lightnin' Hopkins
    D. Rick Cardwell

Answers on page 301.

The first event in the Houston Astrodome was on April 9, 1965.

NEIMAN MARCUS PUTS "GAUD" BACK IN CHRISTMAS

Known to his employees as Mr. Stanley, he took the company that his father, aunt, and uncle founded in Dallas and added a spark that brought it worldwide fame as the ultimate source of Texas excess. All it took was a touch of moxie, a few diamond-encrusted stuffed tigers, personal submarines, and His and Hers camels.

Texas's signature department store almost never happened. Herbert Marcus, his sister Carrie, and her husband, Al Neiman, were operating a sales promotion company in Atlanta, Georgia, when they received two buyout offers: one for $25,000 cash, the other a franchise for an up-and-coming soft drink called Coca-Cola. They took the cash and moved to Texas where they would make department-store history.

GRAND OPENINGS
They ran a full-page ad on September 8, 1907, in the *Dallas Morning News* announcing the opening of a "New and Exclusive Shopping Place for Fashionable Women." In 1913, disaster struck when the original store burned to the ground along with its entire inventory. The plucky Neiman-Marcuses set up a temporary store and reopened seventeen days after the fire. In a year, the store would reopen *again* at a new, larger location in "uptown" Dallas. This flagship store publicly proclaimed that it had "25 specialty shops in one building."

STYLISH EYE FOR THE TEXAS GUY
Soaking it all in was an impatient-to-grow-up Stanley Marcus, the oldest of Herbert's four boys. Stanley didn't have time for sports, but at his mother's insistence took elocution lessons so he could learn to speak on his feet. Luckily, he could think on his feet, too. After

seeing a Neiman Marcus ad that read, "We are dreaming of expansion," Stanley quickly left the Harvard Graduate School of Business and hightailed it back to Texas to begin his career at the store.

TEXAS CHUTZPAH
Mr. Stanley, as he was called, was an idea man with an eye for fashion. In 1927, he started the first weekly retail fashion show and even provided the commentary for it. He had the audacity to advertise in fashion magazines alongside the New York big shots; Neimans was the first retail establishment outside of New York to do so. A professional name-dropper and charming character, Stanley also knew how to make a lasting impression, which he did when he donned a sequined cowboy shirt to give Coco Chanel a tour of the store.

STANLEY, OSCAR, AND GRACE
Stanley solidified Neiman Marcus's reputation as a fashion leader when he created what would become known as the "Oscar" of the fashion industry. The Neiman Marcus Award for Distinguished Service in the Field of Fashion has been given out yearly since 1938 to such distinguished fashion plates as Christian Dior and Princess Grace of Monaco.

MR. STANLEY STEPS UP TO THE COUNTER
On his father's death in 1950, "Mr." Stanley became president and CEO of the family dynasty. He stressed the importance of customer service and quality merchandise, once ordering a buyer to get rid of $40,000 of popular but ugly wooden purses. He said it was up to the store to decide whether an item should be sold, not if it would sell.

BLAME IT ON WALTER CRONKITE
As the new boss, Stanley was under pressure to expand the store into other cities, an idea he was afraid might water down his emphasis on customer service. But Walter Cronkite gave him another idea.

The native-Texan television newsman would routinely call the week before Christmas wondering what unique items the rich

---

The first oil gusher in Texas came in 1901, near Beaumont in East Texas. It was called Spindletop.

oil folks were buying. Sensing that Cronkite didn't want a plain answer—and true to his own Texas nature, Stanley would exaggerate a little and tell Cronkite about a man who bought over-the-top, ultra-extravagant gifts, like mink coats for all of his daughters.

IT'S BEGINNING TO LOOK A LOT LIKE CHRITMA
It didn't take long for the light bulb to go off. The store had been publishing its *Neiman Marcus Christmas Book* since 1939, a 16-page special catalog that was sent only to select customers and contained a treasure trove of gifts: fur coats, perfumes, toys, you name it. Stanley could use the catalogue to sell outlandish items, and the store would rake in endless media attention. Whether anyone bought them or not—the publicity would be priceless. The idea quickly developed into one of the store's most popular gift offerings—"His-and-Hers" gifts on a very grand scale.

No idea was too outrageous: His and Hers bathtubs, airplanes, blimps, mummy cases, two-person submarines, gold-encrusted wigs, and even camels. During a bad recession, Stanley thought up matching gifts for pessimists and optimists. The negative-minded could buy a made-to-order ark á la Noah, and the optimists could get oak seedlings. The rumor is that he sold 1,500 oaks and nary an ark. (Does that mean that only optimists shop at Neimans?)

DEATH OF A RETAILER
Stanley retired in 1975 and handed over the reins to his son Richard. His death in 2002 was mourned, but his retailing legacy still lives. The store now has 32 locations, and its annual quirky *Christmas Book*, is now available to you for only $15 a pop. The 2003 His and Hers gifts? Life-size robots.

* * * * *

RETAIL REASONING
"There is never a good *sale* for Neiman-Marcus unless it's a good *buy* for the customer."
—Herbert Marcus

The tidewater coastline of Texas contains more than 600 historic shipwrecks.

THE CUT-THROAT WORLD OF TEXAS CHEERLEADING

Cheerleading is serious business in Texas. Deadly serious.

Have you heard the one about the mom who put a hit out on another mom, all because of a cheerleading competition? Then pull up a chair and get the facts behind this Texas-sized scandal.

WHO WAS "THE TEXAS CHEERLEADER MOM"?
She was (and is, because she's still alive as of this writing) Wanda Holloway, who in 1991 lived in the small blue-collar Houston suburb of Channelview, worked as a secretary, and played piano for her church.

WHAT DID SHE DO?
She tried to hire a hitman to kill the mother of a rival cheerleader at her daughter's middle school.

WHY ON EARTH WOULD SHE WANT TO DO THAT?
Wanda really, really, *really* wanted her daughter, Shanna Harper, to be a cheerleader. Young Shanna had tried and failed to make the cheerleading squad at her junior high school because of "improper campaigning." Her mother had given away pencils and rulers with Shanna's name on them to promote her (apparently a big no-no), so Shanna was disqualified.

So Wanda decided to give her daughter an extra edge the following year, when Shanna would be competing for the freshman cheerleading squad at Channelview High School. By helping her with a routine? Well, no, actually. Wanda decided to murder their neighbor, Verna Heath, whose daughter Amber would also be trying to make the cheer squad. Wanda thought that Amber would be so distraught at the death of her mother that she wouldn't be able to find it in herself to cheer—thus opening the door for her own little Shanna to make the team.

Scott Joplin, known as the King of Ragtime Music, is from Bowie County in Texas.

WHY VERNA HEATH?

Apparently, in addition to their competing daughters, the two women just didn't get along, though Holloway and Heath had been by all accounts reasonably friendly before their daughters began to compete. And while Amber Heath showed a facility for cheerleading, Shanna wasn't as much of a standout.

In the seventh grade, Amber and Shanna went head-to-head trying to make the cheerleading squad. Amber made the cut, but Shanna didn't. Then came Shanna's eighth-grade disqualification, which her mother attributed to malice on the part of Verna Heath; witnesses at the trial said Wanda believed that Heath plotted to have Shanna disqualified. Another witness said that Wanda even believed that someone was spying on Shanna and turning the information over to Verna Heath. In reality, Shanna had been disqualified because her mother had tried to bribe the judges.

DID VERNA HEATH GET BUMPED OFF?

No. Before the deed could be done, the police arrested Wanda.

HOW DID THAT HAPPEN?

Because (thankfully for Verna Heath) Wanda Holloway chose her conspirators poorly. The twice-married Holloway approached her former brother-in-law Terry Harper about finding someone to do the deed; Harper decided this was all way too wacky for him and informed the authorities about Holloway's ambitions. He then wore a wire for the police when he went to talk to her about the contract.

Holloway toyed with the idea of killing both Verna and Amber Heath but balked at Harper's $7,500 asking price. She chose instead the more economical route of bumping off only the mom, a bargain at a mere $2,500. Holloway said, and this is a direct quote from the tape: "Maybe I should go with the mother. Ah, the kid, she can just be screwed with the murder. Maybe it would mess with her mind." Later Holloway met with her undercover "hitman" and handed over a pair of diamond earrings in payment. Which is solicitation for capital murder. And a crime.

SO WHAT HAPPENED TO "THE TEXAS CHEER-LEADER MOM"?

Well, she was put on trial in 1991 and was convicted to 15 years in the slammer. But wait! A mistrial was declared when it was

---

Many Texas towns and cities are named for women, but only one county—Angelina.

discovered that one of the jurors was improperly impaneled. Turned out he was on probation for cocaine possession, which apparently is enough to fling a fella out of the jury pool in Texas.

In 1996, Wanda pleaded no contest to solicitation of capital murder and was sentenced to ten years in prison. However, after just six months (most of which Holloway spent on "hoe detail," cleaning up Houston-area interstates), she was released on strict probation, which included 1,000 hours of community service, psychiatric examinations, and (this is probably key) a requirement to stay away from both Verna and Amber Heath.

HEY, DIDN'T THEY MAKE A MOVIE ABOUT "THE TEXAS CHEERLEADER" MOM?

Actually, two movies were made about this story of cheerleading rivalry gone wrong. The first was a made-for-TV version, 1992's *Willing to Kill: The Texas Cheerleader Story.* Lesley Ann Warren starred as Holloway, but the film's quality wasn't up to snuff. ABC ended up paying Holloway an undisclosed amount so that she wouldn't sue them.

The second and much superior film was released in 1993 on HBO; *The Positively True Adventures of the Alleged Texas Cheerleader-Murdering Mom* starred Holly Hunter as Wanda and Beau Bridges as Harper. The film itself was a critical smash in 1993, and both Hunter and Bridges won Emmys for their performances.

AND WHAT HAPPENED TO THE HEATHS?

Well, the whole ordeal was quite traumatic, as you might imagine. The Heath family did receive a $150,000 settlement from Holloway's insurers as well as a sum from the HBO movie made of the story. But the money didn't make it all better. "It's almost a dirty feeling," Verna Heath told the *Houston Chronicle* in 1994. "It's like my kids' school years, the innocence, the happiness, the fun, were taken away."

DID SHANNA MAKE THE CHEERLEADING TEAM THAT YEAR?

No. But Amber Heath was on the cheerleading squad throughout high school.

TEXAS VITTLES

Texans know good eatin' and drinkin', so it's no surprise that these treats all have Texas roots.

Foodies (and drinkies) have a lot to thank Texas for. Here are the stories behind some of the Lone Star States greatest hits.

THE CORN DOG

Take a hot dog, impale it on a stick, cover that sucker with cornmeal, and what have you got? The beginning of a battle, that's what. On one side is the Texas State Fair, which says the corny dog (corn dog to some) was invented by a couple of vaudevillians, Neil and Carl Fletcher of Dallas, who sold them from a fair booth in 1942. The other contender is Springfield, Illinois, which tries to convince the world it's the site of the first dog of a corny nature. Thing is, even they credit Texas. Here's how it went.

Ed Waldmire, Jr., claims he saw a strange sandwich in Oklahoma consisting of a wiener baked in cornbread. When his friend came up with a mix that would stick to a wiener so it could be deep-fried, Ed stuck a stick in it and called it Crusty Cur. At his wife's urging, he changed the name to Cozy Dog and eventually sold it—and many more—in a Springfield restaurant of the same name. Thing is, the actual inventing took place while Ed was stationed at an Air Force base in Amarillo. So either way, the corn dog was invented in Texas.

DEEP-FRIED ONION RINGS

The Pig Stand's original Dallas location was the first on a number of fronts. It was the first drive-in restaurant in the world to offer curb service when it opened in 1921. It went on to bigger and (ahem) batter things when, as legend has it, a cook accidentally dropped a ring of onion into batter and deep-fried it up. *Voila!* The modern onion ring was born. In its prime the Pig Stand was a famed franchise across the Midwest, but today only seven remain, all in Texas.

CHICAGO-STYLE PIZZA

University of Texas football player Ike Sewell went into the liquor business after Prohibition was repealed and ended up in Chicago. But he pined for the Tex-Mex food of his home state and decided to open Chicago's first Mexican restaurant. He hit up bar owner Ric Riccardo with the idea, but Riccardo found Sewell's vittles inedible and refused to invest.

Fortunately, Sewell had a backup plan. Pizza. And like a true Texan, he wanted his pizza to be bigger than life. More dough, more sauce, more meat and tomatoes. Pizzeria Uno was born and the world rejoiced at Chicago-style pizza. These days it's a popular chain with more than 150 restaurants. Sewell finally got his Mexican food in the 1960s when he opened Su Casa, next door to the original Uno's.

THE FROZEN MARGARITA

Nobody is sure who invented the Margarita, but one theory claims that a party-loving Margarita Sames of San Antonio concocted them for her Acapulco Christmas bash in 1948. Others give the credit to Juarez bartender Pancho Morales who supposedly created it in 1942 when he got confused about a patron's weird drink request. Then there are the Californians who swear that a Palm Springs drink jockey created it to resemble a shot of tequila followed by a slurp of lime and salt.

But none can deny a Texan first took a batch of the tequila (which is Aztec for "volcano") and lime mixture, froze it to perfection, and made it available to the masses.

Mariano Martinez, Jr., learned about Margaritas at his father's Dallas Mexican restaurant where the old man would concoct them from a secret recipe. When Junior opened his own place, dad handed over the recipe. But bartenders couldn't get it right.

Frustrated, Mariano found a solution in 1971 while in line at 7-Eleven watching kids crowd the Slurpee machine. He and a partner developed an automated frozen Margarita machine and the frozen Margarita became a major hit with customers. Since Martinez never bothered to patent it, the frozen Margarita machine spread like a Texas wildfire.

Still doubt the Margarita's Texas roots? Just ask Jimmy Buffett, the singer who praised the frozen concoction in his ditty "Margaritaville." Buffett tasted his first frozen Margarita at Cocina del Sur restaurant in Austin in 1976. Afterward, he sat on the deck of a friend's house and penned the legendary song.

Eight-five percent of the public libraries in Texas were founded by women's clubs.

THE FRITZ RITZ

Texas puts up some lucky German prisoners of war, which is right hospitable of 'em, doncha think?

Since the days of the Texas Republic, Germans have flocked to Texas seeking prosperity, adventure, and community. In fact, they were and continue to be one of Texas's largest ethnic populations, ranking behind Hispanics as the largest ethnic group (17.5 percent) But during World War II, a heck of a lot of Germans came not as immigrants, but as prisoners of war.

TEXAS AND GERMANY

With such a strong German heritage, Texans swallowed a bitter pill when war was declared on Germany. And it didn't help matters that the daring German U-boat commanders in the Gulf of Mexico were having a good year. Though the press kept it quiet, many a Texas oil tanker lost inventory, ships, and lives at the hands of German submariners. Almost everyone in Houston, Galveston, or Corpus Christi had a story to tell about a friend or relative's terrifying encounter with a U-boat.

Texas had twice as many prisoner-of-war (POW) camps as any other U.S. state. The Geneva Convention of 1929 requires that POWs be sent to a climate similar to that from which they were captured. And many thought Texas's climate similar to North Africa, where General Erwin Rommel's Afrika Korps surrendered in 1943 (which makes sense, but only in a bizarre sort of way). Pair that with plenty of wide open spaces, and Uncle Sam made Texas its favorite destination for detainees. By 1943, over 30 POW camps in Texas housed almost 80,000 prisoners.

DAY IN THE LIFE

Many Germans recall their stay in Texas as the adventure of a lifetime. For the most part, they lived like other soldiers in Texas. In fact, the camps were designed just like any other military base: military barracks covered in sheet iron or tarpaper, filled with cots, footlockers, and even a pot-bellied stove. The only differences

---

Texan Lyndon Johnson was the first president to host a barbecue on the White House lawn.

were the watchtowers, barbed wire, and occasional dog patrols—
and the lack of freedom to come and go as you please. Germans
being German, they pretty much organized and disciplined themselves. The guards, often the second-round draft picks of the U.S.
military, even ate and mostly lived with the prisoners.

PART OZ, PART JUNIOR COLLEGE

The German POWs kept busy. The ones who worked were reimbursed with canteen coupons—good for things like food or beer at
the commissary. With Texas's most fit young men off to war, there
was a huge dearth of available local labor, especially for farming.
So the War Department allowed prisoners to pick cotton, gather
pecans, or work in the rice fields. They didn't *have* to work, but
those who did worked hard, and the Texas farmers liked them;
many kept in touch after the war. And since they couldn't begin
to spend the money they earned, the prisoners would pool earnings and make donations to local charities. Texas ladies liked
them, too, attracted by their good looks, dark tans, and muscles
that bulged from all that hard work. One Galveston lady passing
the nearby camp of Fort Crockett remarked: "They were just beautiful!"

They played soccer, read German books, or took university-level
classes in everything from Engineering to English (designed to such a
caliber that the credits they earned would be accepted by German
universities when they returned). There were theater groups, orches-
tra groups, and even a camp-wide newspaper. Pretty plush.

HEINREICH'S HEROES?

Some of them itched for freedom, or maybe just a change in routine, so quite a few tried to escape. But not a single German prisoner ever escaped for more than a short while. For one thing,
Texas is big—at a lot of camps a man could walk for days through
scrub or slush before reaching a city of any significance. In addition, Northerners still stood out in a crowd during 1940s Texas—
much less young men who spoke with heavy German accents and
clicked their heels. Anyone who escaped was easy to find. One
escapee from the camp even called for help after being chased up
a tree by a bull.

Athens, Texas, lays claim to having created that all-American meal, the hamburger.

GOODBYE TO THE COUNTRY CLUB LIFE

At the close of the war, most German POWs were sent to France or Britain to aid in rebuilding those countries before finally being reunited with their nation and families. Texas POW camps were dismantled and the buildings put up for sale. Fort Crockett became a recreational facility for military personnel. Parts of Camp Fannin, near Tyler, became Tyler Junior College. The Huntsville camp would eventually become Sam Houston State University.

One German POW left the following message on a typewriter at Camp Swift, near Austin: "Goodby [sic], big country, rich country, after 1,000 days I'm leaving you forever. Goodby you level farmland, you cotton raising state, you proudest soil under the sun: 'My Texas' . . . Goodby levelly [lovely] stenographers, with silk stockings, powdered faces and rouged lips. I was amazed seeing you sitting leisurely at hard work with 'Cokes' at hand. Goodby America: I'm going to England now as a young slave . . . Goodbye—You swell life."

* * * * *

GREAT REASONS TO VISIT TEXAS

1. Beautiful scenery (267,000 square miles of it! Including 17 national wildlife refuges, 4 national forests, and 5 national grasslands)

2. Attractive beaches

3. State parks (Over a hundred!)

4. Lakes and boating (1 natural lake, Caddo Lake, and 190 man-made lakes and reservoirs)

5. Freshwater and saltwater fishing (80,000 miles of rivers and streams)

6. Good campgrounds

7. Lots of hiking trails

8. Dude ranches

Fletcher Davis, who owned a downtown cafe, said he invented the hamburger in the 1880s.

UNIQUE TEXAS MUSEUMS

The Smithsonian. The Louvre. The British Museum.
Ha! They've got nothing on Texas.

I f you like museums of the nonstuffy kind, you'll love these offbeat Texas museums.

DUTCH WINDMILL MUSEUM
Nederland, Texas
The town of Nederland—seven miles southeast of Beaumont—
was founded by Dutch settlers in 1896, and much of the region
was developed by financing from the Netherlands. The Dutch
Windmill Museum, an exact replica of a 49-foot Dutch windmill,
houses a strange combination of memorabilia from Holland—and
the personal effects of early cowboy star "Tex" Ritter (father of
actor John Ritter), who was born in Nederland.

BULLFIGHT MUSEUM
El Paso, Texas
Most museums forbid food and drink near the exhibits, but the
Bullfight Museum is actually housed within the walls of the Del
Camino restaurant on El Paso's Alameda Street (U.S. 80 East).
Let the smell of sopapillas and salsa be your guide as you browse
the artifacts, capes, costumes, and all sorts of memorabilia relating
to both the Spanish and Mexican art of bullfighting. And there's
no admission price—just the cost of a couple of tacos, and maybe
a margarita or two.

BUCKHORN HALL OF HORNS
San Antonio, Texas
Housed in the Lone Star Brewery (the "National Beer of Texas"),
The Buckhorn Hall of Horns is a giant-sized collection of every
imaginable type of animal horn and antler. The collection started
at the Buckhorn Saloon in downtown San Antonio, which

The Dallas/Ft. Worth Airport is larger than New York City's Manhattan Island.

opened its doors in 1881. Its proprietor, Albert Friedrich, started the collection and over the years, his customers—hunters, trappers, and the like—would come in and swap him an antler for a lager. The Lone Star Beer Company eventually acquired and expanded the collection—adding such elaborations as a "Hall of Fins" and "Hall of Feathers." Years later, when Lone Star Brewery moved to Longview, Texas, Albert Friedrich's granddaughter, Mary Friedrich Rogers, fought to keep the collection in San Antonio. She and her husband acquired the collection and moved the Buckhorn Saloon & Museum to its present location, just a few blocks from the original 1881 site.

HERTZBERG CIRCUS MUSEUM
San Antonio, Texas
Local lawyer Larry Hertzberg donated this huge collection of circus memorabilia—one of the largest on the planet—to the San Antonio library in 1940. Its curiosities range from posters and handbills to memorabilia from Buffalo Bill's Wild West Show. There's even a full-scale 1920s circus tent. The museum is home to noncircus curiosities, too, including a top-drawer rare book collection of nearly 15,000 volumes, including a first edition of Sir Walter Raleigh's *History of the World* published in 1614.

U.S. ARMY MEDICAL DEPARTMENT MUSEUM
Fort Sam, Houston, Texas
This weird museum offers room after room of nothing but army medical equipment, including uniforms, implements, photographs, and even medical supplies captured from enemies on the battlefield. It's not for the faint of heart; one look at some of the saws and scalpels and you're sure to stop bad-mouthing modern medicine forever. Don't forget to hit the gift shop, where you can pick up a copy of *Cadet Nurse Stories*, an Army Nurse Corps leather bookmark, or even a stained glass angel wearing a stethoscope.

TEXAS TORNADO MUSEUM
Amarillo, Texas
To explore exactly how much Texas weather can suck and blow, visit the Texas Tornado Museum, located in the parking lot of the legendary Big Texan Steak Ranch (see "Steak Yourself to a Free

Meal" on page 45) The museum is a little place, but it's big
enough to house a whirlwind of tornado history and trivia, including interactive displays and lots of educational information. You'll
recognize it by the authentic tornado debris strewn around it.

NATIONAL MUSEUM OF FUNERAL HISTORY
Houston, Texas
Coffins. Hearses. Pictures of dead people. The National Museum
of Funeral History is probably not a good choice for a first date.
Despite the macabre first impression, this museum reverentially
and objectively explores "one of our most important cultural
rituals." The intricate 1860 German "Glaswagen" coach and gold-
plated hearse are especially impressive, as is the original JFK
Eternal Flame that still burns in honor of our fallen 35th president. On your way out, be sure to stop by the gift shop to pick up
our favorite souvenir, a coffee mug that reminds us: "Any day
above ground is a good one."

MUSEUM OF PRINTING HISTORY
Houston, Texas
Tucked into a back street near downtown Houston, this terrific
surprise has everything from ancient papyrus to rare handwritten,
pre-Gutenberg era books. Antique lithographs, presses, and plates
are not only on display—but are also available for artists who like
to work in these traditional mediums. It even has typewriters to
demonstrate, for younger Texans, just what "carriage return"
means.

ART CAR MUSEUM
Houston, Texas
The "garage-mahal" opened in 1998 as a private institution dedicated to contemporary art from around the world. The museum's
showroom takes the corporate conformity of America's status-
burdened, car-crazy culture and turns it on its ear with four-
wheeled, drivable likenesses of a giant cockroach, a red stiletto
high-heeled shoe, and a white killer rabbit. From low riders to
"conventional" exhibitions, the Art Car Museum has much higher
creative octane than your typical roadside attraction.

BEHIND THE
SCENES AT BIG OIL

When people think big oil, they tend to think of seegar-chompin' fat cats who'll stop at nothing to bring in the big bucks and bring down their rivals. Well, this isn't about them. It's about the hard-working Texans who do the real work finding energy, making sure it gets delivered, and consumers like us who use it, sometimes with abandon.

EXPLORATION AND PRODUCTION: FINDING OIL AND GETTING IT OUT
For hundreds of millions of years, organic materials such as plants have been transferring sunlight into energy through photosynthesis, thus creating the fossil fuels we burn today as one of our sources of energy.

Meet some of the behind-the-scenes people who help find these fuels and get them out of the ground:

Geologists
There are more than 16,000 working geologists in Texas who spend most of their time identifying places where oil and gas is likely to be found. This includes studying samples of rock, maps, working oil wells, and seismic data.

Engineers
The processes of finding oil and gas and getting them out of the ground without going broke—or blowing something up—takes a lot of engineers, from specialized petroleum engineers to computer experts who write custom software. The Society of Petroleum Engineers, based in Houston, has more than 55,000 members (and that's a lot of mechanical pencils).

Drillers
Tough and sleep-deprived men and women who supervise drilling crews at the well site, they've mostly worked their way up through the crew ranks, learning each of the well's systems, parts, pumps, gauges, and controls. Like train conductors, drillers have a long-

---

Corn has been cultivated in Texas for at least 2,000 years, says the Texas Historical Commission.

levered brake that stops the well immediately if anything goes wrong. Between 1982 and 2000 there were 274,866 wells drilled in Texas.

Landmen and Accountants

Landmen are lawyers who nail down land leases and clear up any legal obstacles to drilling; the accountants make sure that everyone who has a stake in the well gets paid. It's hard to roll a bowling ball in Dallas, Houston, or Odessa without hitting a landman (or woman).

Royalty Owners

These are the "Beverly Hillbillies" of the world. They get a check from the oil company for anywhere from $5 to hundreds of thousands of dollars every month—often without doing anything. ExxonMobil alone shells out royalty payments to 39,000 folks from its Texas-based operations and pays the state of Texas upwards of $1 billion in royalty, severance, franchise, sales, property, and payroll taxes annually.

REFINING AND MARKETING: TURNING OIL INTO SOMETHING USEFUL

Underground deposits of oil and gas aren't like swimming pools—pockets of liquid or gas. Rather they're soaked into the rock, like water in a sponge, and brought to the surface together, where they're separated and sent to refineries and processing plants that turn them into saleable products like gas for your car, heating oil, and chemicals used to make things like plastics and bathroom disinfectants.

These are some of the folks who help:

Refinery Workers

Like John Travolta in *Urban Cowboy*, these guys and gals climb up towers, turn wrenches, and generally do really dangerous things so the rest of us can have StainMaster carpets and drive Hummers to pick the kids up after soccer. There are hundreds of roles involved in running a refinery—from safety personnel and construction contractors to chemists and electricians.

In Texas it's against the law to shoot a buffalo from the second story of a hotel.

More Engineers

Petroleum consists almost entirely of hydrocarbons—molecules composed of carbon and hydrogen atoms. An army of chemical, mechanical, electrical, and petroleum engineers sit in the cubicles of each refinery trying to perfect materials ranging from jet fuel to fiberglass surfboards. Design engineers in Houston get the squeaky-clean downtown lifestyle, but lots of maintenance, safety, electrical, computer, mechanical, and construction engineers spend their days onsite, wearing fireproof suits in 100-degree heat.

Firefighters

Refineries are a firefighter's Mount Everest. Almost everything in a refinery is not only flammable, but also potentially explosive, toxic, or volatile. Hundreds or thousands of on- and off-site fire-folks stand ready to keep refineries from blowing sky-high on a daily basis. And let's not forget the bottom line: just a few refinery fires could affect the price of oil nationwide.

Salespeople

Their job isn't particularly dangerous, but without them, the business of business would grind to a halt. They sell plastics to Ford for car parts, natural gas to local power plants, or plain old gasoline to area retail stations. The Houston-based Shell Oil Company, for instance, has over 9,000 gas stations in the United States—most with very little bathroom reading, no doubt—but hopefully clean.

ENERGY CONSUMPTION: GEEZ, AT LEAST CARPOOL, WILL YA?

For better or worse, U.S. consumers ultimately run the oil and gas business. Drilling and production activity is fueled by the American consumer's energy-intensive lifestyle. Driving cars, flying in planes, and even just plain living all require energy and lots of it.

Home Owners

Natural gas plants generate an increasing amount of home electricity. American homes consume over 7,000 trillion BTUs (British Thermal Units) of energy a day. A single BTU equals the energy of burning a wooden match; it takes plenty of them to do

The first black explorer in Texas was Esteban, a Moor who traveled with Cabeza de Vaca.

big jobs like heating and cooling homes and small jobs like keeping your microwave's digital clock running (which never turns off if you've noticed). In 2000, Texas consumed 11.6 quadrillion BTUs, putting it first in the nation's energy consumption.

Planes, Trucks, and Automobiles
The average American spends five times more time in cars than on vacation. In 2000, there were 128 million cars on the road traveling 2.3 trillion miles, sucking up 8.2 million barrels of fuel daily. Texas alone has over 13,300,000 motor vehicles; its population is just under 21,000,000. Travelers by air stoke the U.S. demand for jet fuel, which in 2003 averaged 1.60 million barrels per day.

So it looks like all those folks behind the scenes of the oil industry will be in business for a while, at least as long as the demand for energy and the supply of oil and gas keeps up.

* * * * *

THAT'S ONE BIG FISH

Located in Athens, Texas, is the Texas Freshwater Fisheries Center. Lately visitation seems to have picked up. The cause? A new record-setting blue catfish named Splash has made the Center her home. Formerly of Lake Texoma, Splash weighs in at 121.5 pounds and is 58 inches long. Visitors have been flocking to see her swim in the dive tank at the Center.

Cody Mullennix of Howe, Texas, caught her back in January 2004. It took him over 30 minutes to reel her in! Seeing the big catch, Cody decided to let her live and contacted the Park Service to see if they were interested in Splash. He currently holds the state rod and reel record for blue catfish.

The first Texas ranches were the 18th-century Spanish mission ranches along the San Antonio River.

TASTING TEXAS BREW

There's a law in Texas that forbids microbreweries to sell their beer where they brew it—unless they're also a brewpub, in which case they can sell their beer only on the premises. Which means that if you want to sample the wares of the following brewpubs, you gotta go there. If that's not an excuse to travel all over the heart of Texas, we don't know what is.

AUSTIN: THE BITTER END

This brewpub is widely praised for its pale ale, but offers a number of other brew selections edging toward the eclectic (mead, anyone?). The Bitter End also offers an unusual food menu with items like South Texas Fried Antelope and Wood Fired Beef Tenderloin with Yukon Gold Mashed Potatoes and a Cassis Peppercorn demiglace. If that's a bit much for you, you can scare up some regular pub food or sashay over to the more relaxed B-Side Lounge and Tap Room.

DALLAS: TWO ROWS RESTAURANT AND BREWERY

Beer lovers rave about Two Rows' IPA (that's India Pale Ale), so if it's in stock when you're visiting, you need to give it a try. Other popular choices are the highly regarded Imperial Stout and, for the more adventurous, a serving or two of Barleywine. The menu includes a blackened chicken Alfredo pizza, fish tacos, and arrabiata seafood pasta. Two Rows has expanded to Houston and two other locations, but the Dallas brewpub is the original.

EL PASO:
JAXON'S RESTAURANT & BREWING COMPANY

There's some debate among Texas beer cognoscenti as to whether the quality of Jaxon's brews have declined since brewer John Pilhofer left in 2002 to start up Sunset Brewery, also in El Paso (the way to judge for yourself—try both!). Be that as it may, the IPA is well praised, but with a 6 percent alcohol content, it's not for beginners, who may be better off with the pilsner-like Silver Star.

Cattle baron Richard King first earned his riches as a Rio Grande steamboat captain.

LUBBOCK: HUB CITY BREWERY

More than one local wit has noted that Hub City Brewery should get credit for trying to brew anything using the local water supply, a comment that makes us glad we've switched over to the bottled kind. All the same, the Red Raider Ale (named after Texas Tech's sports teams) gets praise from all comers, as does the Christmas brew. And the brewery's American Brown Ale won a gold medal at the 2001 Great American Beer Festival, so say what you will about the water, we'll have another.

SAN ANTONIO: BLUE STAR BREWING COMPANY

People can't seem to say enough about the cask-conditioned pale ale here (it seems like pale ales are something of a Texas brew specialty), but the raves also extend to the chocolate stout, which is the dessert to have when someone else is driving you home. If you need something to wash it down, make it the pork green chili. If pork or beef aren't your thing, there's a surprisingly wide selection of vegetarian dishes. Blue Star also offers live entertainment with jazz most Tuesday nights.

And don't forget to drink your beer responsibly. Your local Texas law enforcement official and you hang-over-free body will both thank you for it.

* * * * *

DID YOU LOCK YOUR HORSE?

A cowboy went into a bar for a beer. When he came out, his horse was gone. He rushed back into the bar and loudly demanded to know what happened to his horse or "I'm gonna do what I did in El Paso!" Everyone looks around nervously and stays quiet. Again, the cowboy says, "Tell me what happened to my horse or I'm gonna do what I did in El Paso!" One brave voice pipes up, "What did you do in El Paso?" And the cowboy says, "I walked home."

J. R. EWING, PHILOSOPHER

The nighttime soap opera, Dallas, ran for a whopping 13 seasons, and its central character, J. R. Ewing, was the glue that held the series together. Here are some of his more outrageous sayings.

ON PRIVACY
"I am not having you followed, and you want to know why? I do not care who you're with, or what you do, or where you go. I just don't give a damn!"

ON FAMILY
"What's a family for if it can't take care of its losers?"

"Momma should have had her tubes tied after I was born!"

ON REVENGE
"Revenge is never stupid, darling—it's the single most satisfying feeling in the world."

ON CONVERSATION
"Saying terrible things is part of my charm, I suppose."

"Talking's the second best thing I do."

ON RISK-TAKING
"Higher you fly, further you fall!"

"Anything worth having is worth going for—all the way."

ON WEALTH
"Do I look like a man that likes to sit on the grass with ants and chiggers?"

"Don't be so glum Lucy; rich folks are always happy!"

"There are a few things that J. R. Ewing can't afford, but patience is one of them!"

ON ETHICS
"A conscience is like a boat or a car. If you feel you need one, rent it."

"Never tell the truth when a good lie'll do!"

"Once you give up integrity the rest is a piece of cake."

ON FAITH
"There is God after all, and right now He's smiling at ole J.R.!"

For more dirt on Dallas, *see "Ten Things You Didn't Know You Didn't Know About* Dallas" *on page 37.*

THE CAPITAL CAPITAL OF THE WORLD

Today Texas—tomorrow the world!

Enhancing the Texas reputation for doing things bigger and better than anywhere else, these Texas cities have crossed state lines to go global with their specialties.

THE COWBOY CAPITAL OF THE WORLD: BANDERA
It shouldn't come as any surprise that the Cowboy Capital is in Texas. Bandera has held the title for more that a hundred years, from the days when it was a staging area for the legendary cattle drives of the late 1880s. After the Civil War, many Confederate officers became "contract drovers," who drove cattle from Texas to market in places like Kansas, Missouri, or Louisiana. Today, Bandera honors modern cowboys with a bronze monument on the courthouse lawn, commemorating the many National Rodeo Champions who call Bandera home.

THE ROSE CAPITAL OF THE WORLD: TYLER
Tyler's 22-acre municipal rose garden is a testament to its devotion—nearly 40,000 rose bushes and 100,000 annual visitors. Every fall, Tyler holds the Texas Rose Festival, where among other things, the "Rose Queen" is crowned and attendees "take tea" with her. In addition to the pageantry, commercial growers around Tyler ship hundreds of thousands of bushes to nurseries throughout the U.S. and around the world.

THE ENERGY CAPITAL OF THE WORLD: HOUSTON
It's tough to argue with this claim to fame, especially if you've heard of energy giants Halliburton, Chevron, and ConocoPhillips? They all live in Houston and, according to the Greater Houston Partnership, about 5,000 energy-related businesses, including 44 of the U.S.'s 200 largest publicly traded oil and gas exploration and production businesses live there, too. In fact, Houston is home to

The El Capote Ranch at Seguin provided horses for Theodore Roosevelt and his Rough Riders.

companies representing virtually every sector (oil and gas, electro and petrochemical) of the energy industry

THE LIVE MUSIC CAPITAL OF THE WORLD: AUSTIN

Does making your official city slogan "The Live Music Capital of the World" make it true? Austin isn't just whistling Dixie: actual serious research has shown that per capita, Austin has more live music venues than Nashville, Memphis, Los Angeles, and New York City. This "creative economy" generates upwards of $500 million per year and produces some of the most progressive, distinctly Texas music around. And Austin is home to thousands of professional musicians, over 100 recording studios, and over 100 record labels. As if that wasn't enough, the city itself works to help the music community by setting up a "Band of the Week" web site so locals can check out up-and-coming bands.

THE SPINACH CAPITAL OF THE WORLD: CRYSTAL CITY

Crystal City erected a huge statue of its patron saint, Popeye the Sailorman, across from the city hall in 1937. The city holds an annual Spinach Festival every November, complete with cook-offs and a Miss Spinach pageant. The whole megillah started in the 1930s when the town was a primary center for packing, processing, and shipping vegetables for a local Del Monte plant. The rest is history.

THE BLACK-EYED PEA CAPITAL OF THE WORLD: ATHENS

Over the years, Athens has grown a mess of black-eyed peas (which aren't peas at all, but legumes). They're also known as cowpeas because they were used strictly for the feeding of cattle in the South until those dastardly Union troops destroyed every other crop and there was nothing else to eat. So chances are when Texans of the past observed the tradition of eating "blackeyes" on New Year's Day, their peas usually came from Athens. Every October, Athens celebrates that fact with an annual Black-Eyed Pea Fall Festival. It holds a cook-off (what else?) that attracts competitive cooks from across the country (even New York City!).

Teddy Roosevelt rode an El Capote horse, "Seguin," at the Battle of San Juan Hill (1898).

Some recent winners: "Pea-nut Butter Pea," and "Darned Ole Dirty Peas."

THE PECAN CAPITAL OF THE WORLD: SAN SABA

Post-World War II harvesting of pecans was crackin' in San Saba, which is home to both the Pecan Fest (held every November) and the Miss Pecan Pageant. Of course, there's something of a dispute between San Saba and Albany, Georgia, regarding their respective claims to worldwide pecan preeminence. But Texas may have an historical edge since paleontologists have found pecan fossils in San Saba dating back 80,000,000 years. Take that, Georgia!

THE GOOSE HUNTING CAPITAL OF THE WORLD: EAGLE LAKE

Itching for some good goose hunting? Just stop by Eagle Lake, located west of Houston on Interstate 10. The burg is nestled smack-dab under what's known as the United States "Central Flyway," a migratory path for waterfowl that stretches from Canada's Northwest Territories to the tip of South Texas. Birdwatchers can view over 250 different species of migratory birds each autumn. So whether you like to watch birds or shoot 'em, Eagle Lake is the place to be.

THE KILLER BEE CAPITAL OF THE WORLD: HIDALGO

We've been hearing about "killer bees this and killer bees that," and "What are we gonna do when they get here?" since the 1950s. For gosh sake, are they on their way from South America to ravage the North American continent? Should we run for our lives? Turns out, killer bees have already made the scene, and lucky Hidalgo has garnered world capital status as a result. African killer bees were first found in the U.S. just outside Hidalgo in 1990. So the city entered the bee biz and even constructed a "World's Largest Killer Bee" statue to commemorate their arrival after all those years of waiting. Glad to hear they finally made it. We can stop waiting now.

PRIMETIME TEXAS

Because there's more to Texas TV than Dallas.

Got a hankerin' to see how Texas has played on the small screen? Well, some of these shows are true classics—and some stunk like a squashed armadillo in a hot West Texas summer. But they've all got that Lone Star something.

TALES OF THE TEXAS RANGERS
The premise of the show was simple enough: Two Texas Rangers (named Pearson and Morgan) solved crimes the Texas Ranger way, and for extra verisimilitude, the crimes were from actual Texas Rangers files. What was interesting about the show is that while the characters remained the same, the show moved backward and forward in time: Some shows took place in the 1830s while others took place in the (then) present day. The show had three incarnations: as a radio drama from 1950 through 1952 (with movie star Joel McCrea as Pearson); as an afternoon television drama from 1955 through 1958, then briefly as an evening drama in 1959.

TEXAS JOHN SLAUGHTER
A show that never stood on its own two feet, *Texas John Slaughter* was a recurring feature of *Walt Disney Presents*, one of Disney's attempts to find another show as popular as its *Davy Crockett* series had been. As such, it failed. At least 13 episodes of *Texas John Slaughter* aired over three seasons, from 1958 through 1961. The title character—played by Tom Tryon, who gave up acting in the 1960s to write a series of best-sellers, including *The Other and Crowned Heads*, both of which were made into movies—was based on a real-life Texas Ranger "Minuteman" and cattle baron of the same name. Texas John's adventure weren't confined to the Lone Star State; as with his namesake he also adventured into Arizona in the episodes "Range War at Tombstone" and "Trip to Tucson."

The park has carefully bred the animals to retain only true Longhorn characteristics.

THE TEXAS WHEELERS

This alleged comedy featured a motherless clan of Texans trying to make their way in the world. Father Zack (played by Jack Elam, known better to audiences for his malevolent gunslinger roles) was something of a ne'er do well, so it fell to young Truckle (played by Gary Busey, known better to audiences as a guy who rides motorcycles without a helmet) to lead the family. The 1974 ABC show lasted only one season, but is notable for launching the careers of Busey, who would go on to portray another Texan in *The Buddy Holly Story*, for which he received an Academy Award nomination, and Mark Hamill who played Truckle's younger brother Doobie (seriously, who thought up these names?). Hamill, of course, would literally rocket to fame as Luke Skywalker in *Star Wars*.

FLO

A 1980 spin-off of the TV show *Alice*, featuring the character of Flo Castleberry, a waitress whose signature line "Kiss my grits!" became the late 1970s mantra of saucy overworked people everywhere. Flo reopens a broken-down diner in her hometown of (get this) Cowtown, Texas, which naturally becomes the home base for all manner of zany, offbeat characters. Despite being reasonably funny, *Flo* went the way of most spin-offs, lasting just one and a half seasons before getting her grits tossed out the door by CBS in 1981. Is that any way to treat a Texas lady?

TEXAS

Dallas was so hugely successful in 1980, why not a daytime soap opera based in *Texas*? To avoid confusion, it would be called *Texas*, presumably to point out its connection to that great state in case anybody missed it. The producers of the daytime soap, *Another World*, picked up the idea and ran with it, spinning off one of that show's most popular characters, Iris Cory Corrington (Beverlee McKinsey), sending Iris to Houston to reunite with Alex, an old flame. Alas, what worked in the nighttime didn't work as well in the day: *Texas* lasted only from August 1980 through December 1982.

San Angelo's restored Fort Concho has been called the best preserved western fort in the U.S.

HOUSTON KNIGHTS

Chicago cop Joey La Fiamma (Michael Pare) messes with the Mob and is hustled off to Houston for his own safety. There he's partnered with Houston cop Levon Lundy (Michael Beck), whose ancestors were Texas Rangers (not all of them—just some). They hate each other at first, of course, and then they fight crime. What could possibly go wrong? Well, *something* did, because this 1987 show lasted exactly one season. Just prior to this series, Michael Beck had played famous Texan and Alamo defender Jim Bowie in the TV movie *Houston: The Legend of Texas*. But it didn't do him any good in this case.

WALKER, TEXAS RANGER

Eighties action star and martial arts master Chuck Norris spent nine seasons, 1993 through 2001, playing Cordell Walker, a Texas Ranger who solved crimes the old-fashioned way, if you consider beating the boots off of this week's bad guy to be the old-fashioned way. Walker was partnered with former Dallas Cowboy Jimmy Trivette (played by Clarence Gilyard, Jr.), who served as the brains of the outfit. He concentrated on forensics and computer science while Walker concentrated on putting his feet into bad guys' jaws.

KING OF THE HILL

Everybody's second favorite animated television series follows the adventures of Texas Everyman, Hank Hill, purveyor of propane and propane accessories (voiced by series creator Mike Judge) and his family and friends in Arlen, Texas. Texans might have had reason to be concerned about how Judge, the creator of the famously rude MTV show *Beavis & Butthead*, would take on their beloved state, but they needn't have worried. The show gently ribs the state of Texas, but it never insults it. Notable guest stars have included famous Texans Ann Richards and Willie Nelson. The show debuted in 1997 on the Fox network as a companion to *The Simpsons*, and of this writing is still going strong.

The 1891 Fayette County Courthouse at La Grange was the site of the movie *Michael*.

THE SECRET LIFE OF SAM HOUSTON

Uncle John exposes the rough-and-tumble real life of a true Texas hero.

By the time he passed away of natural causes in 1863, Sam Houston had the ultimate hero's resume. He fought in the War of 1812 with Andrew Jackson. He led Texas forces to a victory against the Mexican government, securing Texas's independence and eventually the West for the United States. He was the President of the Republic of Texas. Twice. And the only person ever to be governor of two states—Texas and Tennessee (though not at the same time).

But behind the key-to-the-city achievements hid an ornery six-foot two-inch lover of women, whiskey, and bar brawls.

YOU WANT A PIECE OF ME?

Early on, Houston preferred the earthy Cherokee way of life to the mundane existence of American domesticity so he ran away from home to live among them. And his love of scrapping and fighting wasn't even cooled by his three near-fatal wounds in the War of 1812. At the Battle of Horseshoe Bend, on the Tallapoosa River, after taking an arrow to the thigh, he ordered a lieutenant to pull it out (and threatened that if he didn't, Houston would skewer him with his sword). Once the arrow was out, a medic declared Houston no longer fit to fight that day, but Sam pushed his way back out to the battlefield.

After the war, his political career underway, he beat a Congressman from Ohio—not in an election, but with a cane in the streets of Washington, D.C., over a perceived insult. In another instance, through his endorsement of a political rival, Houston made an enemy of the Postmaster of Nashville who challenged Houston to a duel and hired a professional duelist to confront Houston on his behalf. When the duelist met with Houston, Houston's reply was "Try me." Rather than try Mr. Houston, the duelist took the next boat out of town. When the postmaster's friend stepped in to settle the duel, Houston shot him down. But Houston didn't settle all his affairs with violence. Sometimes

At La Grange, Texas, The Jersey Barnyard is home to Belle, the singing cow.

words did just as well. When challenged to a duel by 5'1" David Burrnett, Houston retorted "I don't fight downhill." Game over.

BIG DRUNK

Houston was a big man with big appetites, and whiskey was no exception. During his time with the Cherokee, he earned the nickname: "Big Drunk." In Tennessee he and a friend got riotously drunk on the day the local militia was conducting drills in the streets. In crisp uniforms, the militiamen tried to march in step with the most serious of expressions. Only they couldn't concentrate. Houston and his friend brought a set of drums into the streets and began beating them so loudly it disrupted the unit's rhythm. The red-faced weekend warriors stumbled—out of order, rifles swinging in all the wrong directions—until they gave up and demanded that Houston stop. He was fined $5 for: " . . . annoying the court with the noise of a drum. . ."

COURTING IS ALWAYS IN SESSION

Houston courted women like Davy Crockett shot squirrels—often and well. He won them over with his confidence, stylish clothing, and his large, masculine frame. When he was governor of Tennessee, his first marriage ended almost immediately in a cloud of secrecy—though rumors spread of infidelity on her part, not his. So he resigned his position and ran away again to live among the Cherokee (where he temporarily took an Indian wife whom he left behind when he came to Texas). He married three times, and he was never too busy for the ladies. At the Battle of San Jacinto, while a surgeon was digging a bullet out of his ankle, Houston took the opportunity to write a love letter to the daughter of a wealthy Pennsylvania colonel.

MARK TWAIN WITH A TWANG

Houston could be funny, too, in a nineteenth century sort of way. When he helped close the sale of New Mexico to the United States, he commented that it was "the best sale ever made of poor land and a disputed title." People even used to call him "a party unto himself," to which he once replied: "From that I rather derive some consolation because I know that I could not be in better company, and no differences can arise between myself and myself."

Belle stars in Blue Bell ice cream commercials.

STATE LARGE MAMMAL: THE LONGHORN

House Concurrent Resolution No. 178, 74th Legislature, Regular Session (1995)

Texas is big enough to warrant both an official small mammal, the armadillo, and a large mammal, the Texas Longhorn.

HERE'S THE BEEF

Descended from Spain's robust Andalusian cattle, Texas Longhorns are a hearty lot. It's believed they were the first cattle brought to North America; they existed on brush and cactus, going for days without water. It's no wonder that by the 1840s, there were something like 300,000 Longhorns on the loose—some with horns measuring up to eight feet across.

Texas landowners literally helped themselves to the cattle booty, rounding up wild herds and branding them. By the end of the Civil War, Texas Longhorns numbered in the millions; no wonder beef is a favorite amongst Lone Star citizens. But even Texans could only eat so much steak. To turn a profit, ranch owners had to herd their cattle beyond state lines.

THERE GOES THE BEEF

And so, since Longhorns could be rounded up and traveled well by hoof, the cattle drive was born. Over the next few decades, hardworking cowboys drove millions of longhorns to American cities as far away as Chicago. Forty years later, the overzealous ranchers realized that they'd depleted the herds and what was once the pride of Texas was threatened by extinction.

In 1927 the federal government stepped in, rounded up a small longhorn herd in South Texas, and took them to the Wichita Mountains Wildlife Refuge in Oklahoma. Texans themselves followed suit by protecting the cattle in their own state parks. Soon longhorn numbers were once again on the rise. This

---

The Sterling McCall Old Car Museum in Warrenton houses more than 80 classic and antique cars.

time, surplus animals were sold to breeders who carefully managed their herds. Today, Texas Longhorns are known for their high quality and in 1995, the State of Texas recognized this symbol of the west as their official state large mammal. It was about time, since the University of Texas had officially adopted the Longhorn as their proud symbol way back in 1904!

For more on Texas cattle drives, see "Designated Drovers" on page 147.

For more on Texas cattle drives, see "Designated Drovers" on page 147.

* * * * *

RAYBURN'S REASONING

Texas son Sam Rayburn served as the Speaker of the U.S. House of Representatives longer than any other person. It figures he has some great advice.

"Don't try to go too fast. Learn your job. Don't ever talk until you know what you're talking about . . . If you want to get along, go along."

"Any jackass can kick a barn down, but it takes a carpenter to build one."

"Don't count the crop until it's in the barn."

"You cannot be a leader, and ask other people to follow you, unless you know how to follow, too."

"You'll never get mixed up if you simply tell the truth. Then you don't have to remember what you have said, and you never forget what you have said."

"When you see a man get stuffy or arrogant because he holds a big job, it means he was not big enough for the job when he got it."

"No one has a finer command of language than the person who keeps his mouth shut."

BEACH TRINKET BINGO

*Grab your metal detector, slap on some sunscreen,
and check out these booty-filled Texas beaches!*

Since 1554, thousands of ships have sunk along the Texas coast—many of them laden with gold, silver, and precious jewelry. Add some buried treasure and you've got yourself a fortune just waiting to be found.

SOUTH PADRE ISLAND

Known simply as "Padre," this is the mecca of Texas treasure hunters and beachcombers. Because of the naval traffic nearby, and its centrality on the Gulf, Padre Island tales of beach treasure are as countless as they are true. One of the best documented is the wreck of three treasure-laden Spanish ships that had been on their way back to Spain in 1554 from what is today Veracruz, Mexico. There were four ships in this fleet, carrying the equivalent of $34,388,152 in gold in today's dollars.

As they passed Padre Island, they were slammed by a brutal Gulf storm. Three of the ships sank; the fourth managed to escape the storm. Most of the sailors on the three lost ships drowned, but a few made it back to Veracruz with the bad news. Two months later, a salvage party reclaimed some of the loot on one of the ships. The site remained untouched until almost 400 years later when, after suing an out-of-state company already beginning excavation of one of the ships, Texas worked at recovering some of the treasure from the second ship. It was filled to the gills with silver coins, and silver and gold bullion. But the third shipwreck was scattered when a channel was dredged, and its bounty is still to be discovered.

SOUTH PADRE ISLAND

John Singer, a New Yorker and younger brother of the man who developed the Singer sewing machine, had invested money in his brother's company and was rewarded handsomely. After his family's ship was wrecked off the coast of Padre Island in the

1840s, he began a life there—ranching, selling land and growing vegetables. Because of his experience with ships wrecked in the area, he was made the region's "wreckmaster," making his money by salvaging wrecked ships, a very good gig when gold was still such a common currency.

But when the Civil War rolled around, the Singers were sunk. They were Yankees, with Yankee beliefs. They were run out of town, taking with them only what they could manage, and forced to bury a fortune—at the time around $80,000 in Spanish gold coins, silver, and jewelry—until they could come back. In fact, Singer did come back after the war to reclaim his treasure, but the sandy landscape had been changed by wind and water. Neither John Singer, nor anyone else, ever found the buried fortune.

CORPUS CHRISTI'S NORTH BEACH

Long before German-style beer gardens were all the rage in Texas—in the late 1800s to be exact—a man named Jacob Ziegler owned a popular beer garden in Corpus Christi. Since Texans are a notoriously thirsty bunch, Mr. Z. did very well for himself. The gold in his study piled up high—too much, in fact, to keep on hand, so one day he hauled $50,000 of it into the grove of cedars at North Beach. He died before retrieving it or telling anyone its exact location. For all this time, treasure-seekers have been scouring the place looking for it, but so far no one has found the Ziegler stash.

GALVESTON ISLAND

Fifty miles southeast of Houston is the sand barrier island of Galveston. If Texas legend holds true, the island buckles under the tremendous weight of gold and silver wedged into its sands. Nineteenth-century pirate Jean Lafitte, known as "The Pirate of the Gulf," once used the island as his headquarters. One visitor noted that at the little town Lafitte built for himself, "Doubloons were as plentiful as biscuits." It's said there's treasure lost or discarded from his activities—or buried to keep them hidden—not just all over the island but up the Texas coast as far as the Louisiana border. Even if you don't find any buried treasure, it's such a popular place to swim and fish that maybe you can find some modern treasure without much effort. Check under the sofa cushions at your B&B.

Its guestbook has included Gen. George A. Custer, Robert E. Lee, Sam Houston and Jesse James.

TEN DAYS IN THE LIFE OF THE BATTLESHIP *TEXAS*

Believed to be the only surviving pre-World War I dreadnought (that's battleship to you, pardner), the battleship Texas has had a history worth talking about.

The battleship *Texas* was once the most powerful weapon on the planet. Today, moored near the San Jacinto Monument in Deer Park, the once-great vessel is the scene of guided tours, educational programs, a gift shop, and an on-board conference facility. More than that, the old girl serves as a reminder of engineering excellence and military might. Here are ten days in her extraordinary career.

DAY 1. I'M READY FOR MY CLOSE UP, UNCLE SAM
May 18, 1912: Newport News, Virginia
Fifteen thousand spectators watched as the young daughter of a Texas Republican National Committee member smashed a bottle of champagne across the *Texas's* bow in what's thought to have been the first U.S. Navy ship launch recorded through moving pictures. The brand-new ship housed one of the most advanced naval reciprocating engines (the precursor to turbines) of the time.

DAY 2. RUNAWAY REVOLUTIONARY
April 21, 1914: Vera Cruz, Mexico
The *Texas* got its first taste of war carrying U.S. forces to Vera Cruz, Mexico. Mexican dictator Victoriano Huerta had recently led a coup, killing off Mexican President Francisco Madero in the process. President Woodrow Wilson despised Huerta's antidemocratic ways, and when a handful of U.S. sailors were detained in Tampico, Wilson got the excuse he'd been looking for. Demanding satisfaction, he dispatched the *Texas* to Vera Cruz. Huerta resigned and fled to Spain.

DAY 3. HILFE! THE EYES OF *TEXAS* ARE UPON US!

April 24, 1918: The North Sea
With the British Sixth Battle Squadron, the *Texas* gave chase to
the German High Seas Fleet, getting a chance to open up its
28,100 horsepower engine (the equivalent of over 70 brand new
Ferraris). The Germans escaped, but failed in their attempt to
attack a nearby convoy. The *Texas* had them in its sights when the
fleet eventually surrendered.

DAY 4. TOP GUN IN ITS INFANCY

March 10, 1919: Guantanamo Bay, Cuba
On this day the *Texas* became the first American battleship to
launch an airplane from its deck. The plane, a Sopwith Camel
biplane flown by Lt. Commander Edward O. McDonnell, was
launched from a platform that was laid across the ship's long
gun turrets.

DAY 5. NAVIGATING THE ELECTRIC CURRENT

January 4, 1939: Norfolk, Virginia
Government technologists tried out an experimental system
known as the CXZ, designed to locate objects using reflected radio
waves. The commanding officer of the *Texas* encouraged further
development into what he thought was a revolutionary concept.
Electronics giant RCA pursued the project, which would come to
be known as radar.

DAY 6. ANCHOR AWAY!

November 13, 1942: Port Lyautey, Morocco
Off the Moroccan coast, while supporting American troops in
Algeria (and also hunting U-boats), the *Texas* landed war correspondent Walter Cronkite at Port Lyautey. Cronkite returned
home with the ship, and as they neared Norfolk, Virginia,
Cronkite boarded a plane on the *Texas* to go tell America the
"way it was" at war.

DAY 7. BEACH BOMBING AT NORMANDY

June 6, 1944: Normandy, France
On D-Day, the *Texas* bombarded Omaha Beach in preparation for

landing troops. Ernest Hemingway wrote of the soldiers landing at the beach, "watching the *Texas* with looks of surprise and happiness. Under their steel helmets they looked like pikemen of the Middle Ages, to whose aid in battle had suddenly come some strange and unbelievable monster."

DAY 8. SHOWDOWN AT IWO JIMA
February 16, 1945: The Pacific Ocean
Texas and the rest of what was known as Task Force 54 pounded the beach at Iwo Jima in preparation for a U.S. Marine landing, coordinating its efforts with air forces. The Japanese were entrenched like gophers, but the *Texas* continued to pound enemy strongholds until all of Iwo Jima's hard-won soil had fallen to the Allies.

DAY 9. DESTINIES ON DISPLAY
April 21, 1948: Deer Park, Texas
On the anniversary of Texas Independence and 34 years into its service, *Texas* was decommissioned and named the U.S.'s first memorial battleship. As an official national historic landmark, the ship was permanently moored next to the San Jacinto battlefield and monument. Admiral Chester Nimitz, a native Texan, was largely responsible for seeing the ship to Texas waters.

DAY 10. DON'T GIVE UP THE SHIP!
September 8, 1990: Deer Park, Texas
By the late 1980s, the *Texas* was in trouble—rusting and near ruin. Despite its powerful engine (which is itself a national engineering landmark), it couldn't outrun old age. Texans across the state rallied to the cause, including school kids who gave up their pennies to save the ship. In 1988 the *Texas* was towed to a shipyard in Galveston for a major makeover. Parts of the hull were replaced, a new wood deck installed, cabins restored, and 9,000 gallons of paint covered the ravages of years of neglect. She was returned to the park in 1990; her restoration will continue with another phase planned for 2005.

JANIS JOPLIN: TRUE OR FALSE

Think you know a little about Port Arthur's favorite daughter? We'll just see about that.

Janis Joplin represents a lot of things to a lot of people. Music historians and fans think of her as one of the great blues and rock singers. Feminists have claimed her as an icon of free thinking independence. To most, she was a template for the free-spirited hippie chick. But what do you know about this exceptional Texas native? Or more to the point, what do you *think* you know? Test your JQ—"Janis Quotient"—by figuring out what's true and what's false.

True or False: Janis Joplin felt comfortable in her hometown of Port Arthur, Texas.
False. By all accounts Joplin was a cheerful, happy kid, but by the time she was a teenager, she'd begun to recognize that she wasn't much like the other kids, who seemed pretty conservative to her. On one hand she liked being different, but on the other hand being different undermined her self-confidence, a problem she'd wrestle with for her whole life. Friends remember her looking forward to returning to Port Arthur for her tenth high school reunion in 1970—but leaving it feeling even further distanced from her old classmates and her town. Joplin died in Los Angeles a few months later; her will specified that her ashes were to be scattered over the ocean.

Whether she was happy in Port Arthur or not, the city sponsors an annual "Janis Joplin Birthday Bash." A bust of Joplin also sits in the local library (now that she can't make any noise anymore).

True or False: Janis Joplin's California friends once passed the hat to raise money to ship her back to Texas.
True. But it's not as mean as it sounds. Joplin came to California after disastrous college stints at Lamar State College of

Technology and the University of Texas at Austin, where she was memorably (and for her, painfully) nominated as "Ugliest Man on Campus" by some jerks. California's blooming counterculture appealed to Janis in a way that Texas never did. From 1963 through 1965 she took to the streets of San Francisco.

The good news was that her singing was getting her noticed in coffee shops and clubs all over the city; the bad news was that she was getting so strung out on drugs that her weight dipped dangerously south of the 90-pound mark. That's when her friends put her on a bus back to Port Arthur and back to her parents to recuperate. But Joplin would be back in California in 1966, when she got a chance to join the psychedelic rock band, Big Brother and the Holding Company.

True or False: Joplin made all her records with Big Brother and the Holding Company.
False. In fact, Joplin made only two albums with the band: *Big Brother & The Holding Company* in 1967 and *Cheap Thrills* in 1968, the latter of which went to number one on the strength of the hit "Piece of My Heart." But after that success, Joplin was interested in working on her own and ditched Big Brother—except for guitarist Sam Andrew who joined her new Kozmic Blues Band, with whom she released *I Got Dem Kozmic Blues Again Mama!* in 1969. Her final album, *Pearl*, was cut with yet another band, the Full Tilt Boogie Band. The jury's still out on which band best backed Joplin's distinctive, expressive voice, but over time Big Brother is getting the nod; they could be sloppy, but they had heart, and exactly the same thing could be said of Janis.

True or False: Joplin lived long enough—just barely—to see "Me and Bobby McGee" become a number-one hit single.
False. Joplin was recording *Pearl* when she met up with one of her old drug dealers in the lobby of the Landmark Hotel in Hollywood. She bought some heroin and overdosed; her body was found on October 4, 1970. *Pearl* was released in 1971, and "Bobby McGee," written by former lover Kris Kristofferson, hit number one in February of that year, and became one of the songs most identified with Joplin (one more, the a cappella "Mercedes Benz," is also on *Pearl*).

True or False: Joplin's life has been the subject of a Hollywood film.
True, sort of. First, a 1974 documentary Janis, then 1979's *The Rose*, a thinly fictionalized version of Joplin's life, with Bette Midler, in her first starring role. The movie was a hit, as was the film's title song; Midler was nominated for an Academy Award and won a Grammy for "The Rose." Since then a number of Joplin biopic ideas have been tossed around; actress Lili Taylor was reportedly attached to one such project, and musician Melissa Etheridge, who gave Joplin's induction speech for the Rock and Roll Hall of Fame, was attached to another. As of this writing, Oscar-winning actress—and Texas native—Renee Zellweger is slated to take on the Joplin role in another biopic scheduled for 2005.

* * * * *

THE OTHER JOPLIN FROM TEXAS

You may not know Scott Joplin's name, but you know his music. Anyone who's sat through the Paul Newman-Robert Redford film *The Sting* is sure to recognize the strains of Scott Joplin's ragtime music. Joplin was born in northeast Texas around 1867. When he was seven years old, the Joplin family moved to Texarkana, where Scott would grow up.

His musical talent was obvious early on in his life. Jules Wiess, a local German-born music teacher, took Scott under his wing and instructed him in music with an emphasis on European art forms, including opera.

Joplin got his professional start playing piano in saloons and other venues. He traveled up to St. Louis, Missouri, around 1890 and really dug into ragtime and its bouncy, upbeat style, influenced by European and African musical traditions. His two most famous compositions *Maple Leaf Rag* and *The Entertainer* were just a small part of his impressive repertoire, which included the opera *Treemonisha*. He would continue to compose until his death in 1917.

Seventy percent of the population of Texas lives within 200 miles of Austin.

THE TEXAS MAP
<u>GOES DUCKY</u>

*Before we plunged on in, we wanted to make sure that we knew
the lay of the land that makes up the great Lone Star State. So our
little ducky left his marks all over the map so's you can orient
yourself while you're readin'.*

NORTH
Morning sure does become Electra (9), especially when the Miss
Goat BBQ contest rolls around. Read all about it in "Isn't She
Lovely?" on page 23.

EAST
Due South of Tyler (23) lies Houston (7), home to some fine-tastin'
barbecue at Williams' Smokehouse. Texas is jam-packed with
"Hidden Barbecue Hot-Spots!" (find more on page 88.)

SOUTH
Beautiful South Padre Island (21) boasts of hidden treasure like
other Texas towns. Read more about them in "Beach Trinket
Bingo" on page 134.

WEST
If you fancy chili, then Terlingua (22) might be the place for you.
For more on Texas chili and where to eat it, check out "Hotter 'n
a Burnin' Stump" on page 17.

CENTRAL
Wanna know more about on Austin (3), the state capital of Texas
and the World Capital of Live Music? Then check out "The Age
of Austin-ius" on page 187.

*These are just a few of the many excellent places in Texas. We only wish
we could cover them all. Such are the burdens of being a kickass state.*

The least populous Texas county: Loving, with 67 residents. Most populous: Harris, with 3.4 million.

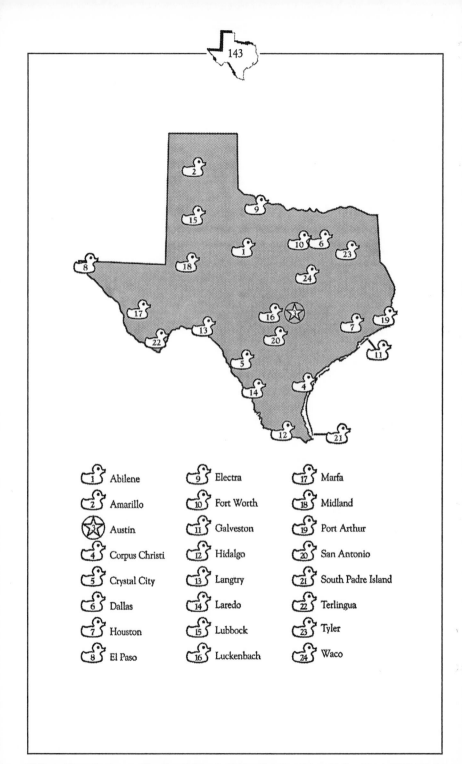

El Paso, Texas, is closer to Needles, California (516 miles) than it is to Dallas, Texas (571 miles).

ALAMOLOGY 101: A PRIMER

Remember the Alamo? Here's a question-and-answer guide to remind you if you don't.

WHAT IS THE ALAMO, ANYWAY?

The famous Alamo church, the only surviving part of the original structure, has come to be the most popular image of this famous Texas landmark. Actually, the Alamo was much more than one building. It was more formally known as Mission San Antonio de Valero (named after Saint Anthony of Padua and the Duke of Valero, who was the Viceroy of New Spain). The Franciscan mission was founded in 1718 to convert and educate the local Native Americans.

Spanish officials secularized San Antonio's missions in 1793, so the site was no longer used for religious purposes. In the 1800s, the Spanish stationed a cavalry unit there and the former mission would house the military until the Texas Revolution. Just before the battle, the building was being used as a barracks for the Mexican Army. The compound had made a great mission, with enough buildings and land to support a community, but it wasn't the most impregnable fort.

HOW DO YOU GET "THE ALAMO" FROM "MISSION SAN ANTONIO DE VALERO"?

You don't. There are two explanations as to why the building is known as the Alamo. One is that the Mexican soldiers stationed there were from the town of Alamo de Parras, Mexico; the other is that there was a grove of cottonwoods on the mission grounds (the Spanish word for "cottonwood" is "Alamo"). The place had long been known as "El Alamo" long before the Texans got to it.

IF IT WAS A MEXICAN ARMY BARRACKS, WHAT WERE THE TEXANS DOING IN IT?

At the time, Texas was part of Mexico, and the Texan citizens were agitating for independence. In December 1835, Texans led by Ben Miliam and Frank Johnson attacked the forces of Mexican General Martín Perfecto de Cos, that were stationed at what is now San Antonio. The resulting Siege of Béxar forced General Cos and his men to hightail it out of there. The Texans occupied the Alamo as a result and stayed in it—against the sage advice of Texan leader Sam Houston, who was concerned that it would be tough to hold with a small number of Texan troops. But you know Texans. They're just stubborn.

Turns out that Sam Houston was right. Angry at losing his fort, Mexican General Antonio Lopez de Santa Anna wanted it back. On February 23, 1836, Santa Anna showed up with thousands of men to lay siege to the Alamo. With reinforcements, the Texans (comprised of Texas Army regulars and Texan volunteers) numbered no more than 189. So the odds were pretty steep odds, even for Texans.

A LITTLE ABOUT THE TEXANS

If you know anything about the Alamo, then you've probably heard of the "big names" who fought there, including Davy Crockett and Jim Bowie, the latter of whom commanded the Texas volunteers. The other Texans involved came from all over: from 19 American states and territories (not counting Texas, which was neither at the time) as well as England, Ireland, Scotland, Wales, Germany, and Denmark. One defender, known only as "John," was a black freedman. In other words, it was a real melting pot.

SO, HOW DID IT END?

Badly. Santa Anna ordered a blood-red flag flown from his headquarters at the Cathedral of San Fernando, within view of the defenders of the Alamo, which meant that he wasn't planning to take any prisoners. Even if the Texans surrendered, they would be killed. The reason for this was pure and simple. In Santa Anna's eyes, these uppity Texans needed to be taught a lesson about the futility of fighting against the mighty Mexican army—a lesson that other rebellious Texans could take to heart.

On the morning of March 6, after laying siege to the Alamo for nearly two weeks, Santa Anna's forces attacked and overwhelmed the defending Texans. The Texas fighters were killed to a man—in that respect, Santa Anna was as good as his bloody word.

DID ANYONE SURVIVE?

Yes. The figures aren't exact, but it's believed that about 15 people survived the seige of the Alamo: women, children, slaves and servants of the defenders. A notable survivor was Susanna

Dickinson, the wife of Texas Army captain Almeron Dickinson, who gave a number of accounts of the fall of the Alamo and attested to seeing the bodies of some of its more notable defenders, including Crockett. She also noted that Jim Bowie, dreadfully sick in his bed, nevertheless managed to kill two Mexican soldiers before he himself was killed.

Santa Anna allowed these survivors to live because he wanted them to spread the word of the defeat at the Alamo, the presumption being that the stories of the loss would dishearten the Texan rebels and put an end to their revolution. As anyone who remembers the cry "Remember the Alamo!" knows, it pretty much had the opposite effect: the fact that just over 180 Texans held back the Mexican Army for as long as they did reinforced the idea that Texans were just too tough to be kicked around.

WHAT HAPPENED TO THE BODIES OF THE TEXAN DEFENDERS?
Their bodies were burned by the Mexicans and, as legend has it, were buried under the sanctuary railing of the old church. In fact, in 1936 some charred remains were discovered in that very spot. (But it's not entirely clear if the remains really belong to the defenders of the Alamo.)

WHAT HAPPENED NEXT?
Texas had declared its independence on March 2, 1836—four days before the Battle of the Alamo, but they needed to defeat Mexico to hold on to it. Things took a turn for the better after the eighteen-minute Battle of San Jacinto on April 21, 1836, when Sam Houston routed Santa Anna's forces. Texas had successfully defended its independence and would go on to become its own country.

The Republic of Texas existed independently for almost a decade before joining the United States in 1845 by way of a treaty rather than by annexation—the only American state to do so. After Texas joined the Union, the Alamo was used to quarter troops and store supplies. In the 1880s Texas took control of the building, and today it's an historical site and one of Texas's main tourist attractions. It still serves as a reminder that you don't mess with Texas—and you don't mess with the 'Mo.

For more on Santa Anna, see "Without a Leg to Stand On" on page 208.

DESIGNATED DROVERS

What's the best way to get a bunch of ornery cattle from the middle of Texas to the plates of hungry Easterners?
Walk.

HOME ON THE RANGE

After the Civil War, Texas was packed with longhorn cattle, living half-wild out in the scrub and prairies. You could even call them free-range cows: they were rarely branded and therefore could be rounded up by the first man with a horse and a rope.

The men coming back from the war saw these ornery longhorns as money on the hoof, particularly when it became clear that there were a lot of non-Texans out there who were starving for a nice, juicy steak.

At the time, the railroad was just beginning to reach across Kansas from the East. This meant that if Texas cattlemen could move their herds up to Kansas, the railroad could take them to Chicago where they became Porterhouses, filet mignons, prime ribs, and New York strips for the rest of the U.S., particularly the East.

ROUND 'EM UP, BOYS

The great era of the Long Trail Drive began in the late 1860s and lasted barely 20 years. By the mid-1880s, rail lines had spread out into Texas and most cowboys could reach one by driving cattle only a couple hundred miles at most rather than all the way to Kansas. In the heyday of the cattle drive, Texas drovers pushed hundreds of thousands of cattle thousands of miles up the trail from the vast grasslands of central Texas to wild and wooly cow towns of Kansas, like Wichita and Dodge City. It was hard, dirty, and sometimes dangerous work.

A drive started in Texas with the spring roundup: cowboys picked out mature cattle that were fat enough to go to market. Big ranches would have enough head to make a drive on their own, but smaller ranches usually banded together to create a trail herd. Sometimes these herds numbered in the thousands.

Pete is on U.S. 290 at Main Street. He's 11 feet tall and 20 feet long.

DRIVING A TAURUS TO WORK

Usually there was one cowboy for every 250 to 300 head of cattle. The trail boss rode out front and senior cowboys rode "point," ahead of the herd and the kicked-up cattle dust. They were followed by the boys on both sides of the herd riding "swing" and a bit farther back on "flank." Then came the poor pokes riding "drag," trailing thousands of cows, breathing through sweaty kerchiefs for every hot, stinking, dusty mile. The herd moved across the prairie in one big line that could stretch a mile or two wide. To overcome the big distances, the cowboys learned to communicate with hand signals adapted from Plains Indian sign language or by making different gestures with their hats. Generally, the cows and the cowboys covered about 15 miles per day and usually completed the trip to Kansas in one to three months.

The outfit provided the horses for the cowboys; a cowboy rarely owned his own horse (and didn't usually sing to it, either). The extra horses traveled up the trail in a group called a "remuda," along with the wranglers who handled them.

THEY'RE GOOD FOR YOUR HEART

Besides cows, cowboys, and horses, a trail drive included the all-important chuck wagon, which was invented by ranching pioneer Charlie Goodnight. Every day, the chuck wagon drove ahead and set up where the herd was going to bed down for the night so "Cookie" could prepare some grub for the boys to eat when they dragged in, covered in dirt and sweat, and ready to collapse for a few hours sleep before they had to get up and ride night rounds. Actually, a good cook was a valuable commodity on the trail and earned much more than a cowboy, which admittedly wasn't a hard thing to do.

What did they eat? Well, *Blazing Saddles* wasn't too far off the mark. Beans were popular, as were bacon, eggs, and the occasional bowl of Texas chili. Sounds like being downwind from a cowboy could be just as much fun as being downwind from a cow. Oooo-ee!

TRAIL'S END

Cowboys earned a dollar per day; food (also known then as "found") was included. If a cowboy were lucky—after three

---

"Tex" Avery, the animator who created Droopy Dog and Porky Pig, was born in Taylor, Texas.

months in the saddle under the blistering Texas sun dealing with cantankerous cows that might stampede if a twig broke at the wrong time, not to mention biting bugs, poisonous snakes, swollen rivers, violent thunderstorms, cattle rustlers, and all sorts of general annoyances—a cowboy might earn $100 when he reached the end of the trail in early autumn. Still, this was a good chunk of change for these fellows, and being responsible citizens, some would then promptly blow it on whiskey, women, and cards, all readily available in Kansas. After which they'd saddle up and head back to Texas, praying they could get the same low-paying, filthy, dangerous job next year.

STAY AT HOME, LITTLE DOGIE?
The cattle drives boomed for about 20 years; cattle prices kept going up and up and up, so it seemed safe to the barons to assume that trend would just keep on keepin' on. Not so. In 1871, a record-setting 700,000 cattle made their way to Kansas, but a slack economy and fewer buyers meant that half of them went unsold. The leftovers had to winter in Kansas at a great cost to their owners. The following years weren't much better and by 1873 some cattlemen were forced into bankruptcy. When the railroad came to Northern Texas and the refrigerated car along with it, it marked the end of the cattle drive's Golden Age.

For more on cattle drives, check out "Goodnight, Mr. Goodnight Wherever You Are," on page 214.

* * * * *

"It is remarkable that during my ten years on the trail I rarely ever had a man who would shirk his duty; had he been so inclined, he would have been ridiculed out of it."—Charlie Goodnight

"Boys, the secret of trailing cattle is never to let your herd know that they are under restraint . . . In this manner, you can loaf away the day, and cover fifteen to twenty miles, and the herd in the mean time will enjoy all the freedom of the open range."
—Jim Flood, trail boss as quoted in *The Log of a Cowboy* by Andy Adams

---

In 2002, Texas's peach crop weighed 11,400,000 pounds!

TEXANS IN
TERRIBLE TROUBLE

Television is fraught with lurid tales of true crime, and Texas has sure had its share. Can you match the Texan on the left with his or her crime?

_____ 1.   Joe Ball

_____ 2.   T. Cullen Davis

_____ 3.   Robert Durst

_____ 4.   John Wesley Hardin

_____ 5.   Clara Harris

_____ 6.   Genene Jones

_____ 7.   Ronald Clark O'Bryan

_____ 8.   Walker Railey

_____ 9.   Charles Reynolds

_____ 10.   Darlie Routier

_____ 11.   Jeff Skilling

_____ 12.   Karla Faye Tucker

_____ 13.   David Waters

_____ 14   Charles "Tex" Watson

_____ 15.   Andrea Yates

A. Acquitted cross-dresser who shot his neighbor, cut up the body, and dumped it in the Galveston Bay. 2004

B. Convicted murderer. First person executed via electric chair in Texas. 1923

C. Tavern owner who allegedly fed his waitresses to his pet alligators. 1938

D. Pediatric nurse convicted of killing children by injection. 1984

E. Acquitted of murder in the shooting of two people in his Fort Worth mansion. 1976

F. Executed for murder. Became a born-again Christian while on death row, but was denied request for clemency. 1998

G. Former minister charged with the attempted murder of his wife. 1992

H. Convicted of murdering her two sons, but maintains innocence and claims an intruder attacked the family. 1997

I. Manson family member who fled to Texas after his participation in the Tate and LaBianca murders. Extradited and convicted. 1970

J. Convicted of murdering her philandering husband by running him over with her Mercedes. 2002

K. Enron CEO charged with insider trading, fraud, and conspiracy. 2004

L. Murderer of atheist Madalyn Murray O'Hair, her son, and her adopted daughter. 2001

M. "The Man who Killed Halloween" by lacing his son's Halloween candy with cyanide in order to claim insurance money. 1974

N. Convicted of drowning her five children in the bathtub. 2001

O. Outlaw who allegedly gunned down more than 40 victims. Pardoned by Governor Hogg. 1894

Answers on page 305.

Hog Island, in the Ship Channel, was at one time a Lover's Lane for Baytownians.

IT JUST AIN'T WRIGHT

Believe them or not, a few stories of the Texans who took to the skies before that famous day at Kitty Hawk in 1903.

BOING!
The first powered flight in the United States was undertaken by Joseph Brodbeck, a school supervisor in Fredericksburg, Texas. Brodbeck constructed a crude airplane in 1865 (or maybe 1863) that was powered by giant springs (which did not "boing!" him into the air, but powered the propeller). His plane actually worked—it was said to have risen twelve feet off the ground and traveled about 100 feet before the springs unwound completely and the plane crashed into a chicken coop. Brodbeck's investors considered this a setback and bowed out of the project. Brodbeck was unable to raise more money and had to flush the whole project. None of his drawings or blueprints survived.

TRIP TO NOWHERE
Then there's the possibly apocryphal story of an unnamed railroad agent in McClellan County who, in 1897, built a plane that made a five-mile round trip. The story goes that even though it was successful—and remarkably so, given the technology of the day— nothing more came of it.

TRIP TO HEAVEN
Of all the stories, the Reverend Burrell Cannon's takes the cake. A Baptist preacher, lumber mill owner, and confessed tinkerer from Pine, Texas, the reverend ran across a Bible passage that he found especially inspiring. From the Old Testament book of Ezekiel, he read: "The appearance of the wheels and their work was like unto the color of beryl and . . . when the living creatures were lifted up from the earth, the wheels were lifted up . . ." The passage seemed to suggest a flying machine to Reverend Cannon; he read it again and again, and thought about nothing else.

He moved to Pittsburgh, Texas, looking for investors. He spent years sketching, calculating, and revising, and finally fin-

---

Four kinds of Texas pecans: Pawnees, Choctaws, Cheyennes, Kiowas.

ished his design (wheel-shaped wings, an eighty horsepower engine, and lots and lots of wheels) in 1901. *The Dallas Morning News* reported that: "The unique features of this machine, is [*sic*] its motive power and propelling apparatus, and the most astonishing feature of it is that the whole machine and all of its intricate parts is fully set forth in the Holy Bible."

But when one of Cannon's workers got the machine airborne in 1902, it started vibrating uncontrollably and crashed into a fence. The plane had gone 167 feet. The backers disappeared, and the reverend moved back to Pine. But he didn't give up on his aeroplane.

TODAY PINE, TOMORROW THE WORLD'S FAIR
The 1904 World's Fair in St. Louis, Missouri, seemed the perfect place to wow the public and sniff around for more investors. The aeroplane was loaded onto a flatbed train car for transport to the North. But it would never leave Texas soil; the very instant it reached the Texas-Arkansas border, the black finger of a Texas twister smashed into the train and its winged cargo. Maybe Ezekiel was trying to tell him something.

WHAT THEY CALL GROUNDED IN FAITH
More than Cannon's plane was crushed by the tragic accident. He declared: "God never willed that this airship should fly; I want no more to do with it." But he didn't really mean it; he had to try one more time. So he built another plane, and in 1911—the Wright Brothers having stolen his thunder eight years earlier—tried again. This time the test pilot crashed the plane into a telephone pole— itself a relatively new invention.

And the preacher who thought he could get to heaven by taking the shortcut gave up for good.

In 2001, the total Texas pecan crop weighed 75,000,000 pounds!

MORE GHOSTLY GALS OF TEXAS

Three more lady ghosts—one of them definitely not a Texan—who do their haunting on Texas college campuses.

Who: Sarah Morgan
Where: Texas Tech University, Lubbock, Texas
What: Haunts the halls of the Texas Tech University biology building; her bloodstain will not dry.
When: Starting in 1968
Why: Texas Tech University is the only campus in the state that's home to a major university, law school, and medical school. So keeping its campus clean is a tough job. In 1967, Sarah Morgan was one of the hundreds of people who stayed after hours to help pick up.

One morning, Morgan was found hunched over an aquarium in Room 331 of the biology building. She had been murdered—practically decapitated with a razor-sharp scalpel and her key to the building had been stolen. At the same time, a physiology professor noted that one of his premed students suddenly began "earning" great grades, where prior to the murder he was in peril of flunking out. A police investigation revealed that this student had broken into the building to steal an upcoming test. When surprised by Morgan, he panicked and killed her. He was arrested, convicted, and sent to prison in Huntsville.

Today the ghost of Sarah Morgan is seen walking the third-floor halls of Tech's Chemistry/Geosciences Building, sometimes peeking into the classrooms and shaking her head in disappointment. Room 331 is now an administrative room, with carpet covering the linoleum bloodstain from decades ago. But on the anniversary of the murder and during exams, legend says that the stain on the floor grows as wet and dark as the day it was spilled.

Who: Elizabeth Barrett Browning
Where: Baylor University, Waco, Texas
What: Walks the library in a white nightgown, holding a candle
When: Starting in the 1950s
Why: We bet you're wondering why on earth Elizabeth Barrett Browning—an English poet who died in Florence, Italy, in 1861—would be haunting a university in Texas. So were we. Here's the seeming explanation.

In 1912, Dr. Andrew Joseph Armstrong became the Chairman of the English Department at Baylor. A big fan of Robert Browning (Elizabeth's poet-husband), he often peppered his lectures with Browning quotes, like "A minute's success pays the failure of years." Armstrong made over 29 pilgrimages to Europe, where he amassed a Texas-sized collection of the famous couple's manuscripts, first editions, personal effects, and mementos. That's how it came to be that the largest Browning collection resides, not in London or Florence, but in Texas—at Baylor's Armstrong Browning Library.

And so, Elizabeth Barrett Browning—or some ghost-impersonator who looks a lot like her—has been seen floating along in the library wearing a white gown, shielding a candle, and watching the live people work. She's also been seen staring out of the top floor window. Even her statue, in front of the library building, has been said to move its arms every once in a while.

Who: "Georgia" (real name unknown)
Where: Texas Wesleyan University, Fort Worth, Texas
What: Mysterious middle-aged lady seen sitting in the Fine Arts Building Theater, watching closed rehearsals in Victorian dress.
When: Starting in the early 1980s.
Why: Texas Wesleyan University is a private liberal arts university with fewer than 4,000 students. "Georgia," as the students named her, seems to appear in the theater at random—always keeping to herself and staring straight ahead, face expressionless—even when students rehearse for upbeat musicals and comedies.

The students started calling her "Georgia." Theater director Mason Johnson and his students saw her often, and on occasion had to pause rehearsals while she moved about or made noise. It was frightening and disruptive at the time, but every time she appeared, the production they were rehearsing became a big hit. The actors and staff, normally superstitious anyway before opening night, came to accept her as a good-luck omen.

Texas ghost specialist and author Docia Schultz Williams speculates that the ghostly guest could be the spirit of Sarah Dobkins, the resident of a cemetery on which the university was built. Dobkins's brother was the college's first physician; she was buried in 1896, a year that would be consistent with the descriptions of her clothing.

According to an interview Williams conducted with Mason Johnson before he died, one night (around 10:45 p.m.) during a closed rehearsal of *Brigadoon*, he saw someone he didn't recognize sitting in the audience. He waited for a pause in the action and started down the aisle toward the lady, who ignored him. As he drew nearer, she disappeared.

* * * * *

SOMETHING ABOUT TEXAS

"The sun has risen, and the sun has set, and I ain't out of Texas yet."—*Old Texas Saying*

"Texas is a state of mind. Texas is an obsession. Above all, Texas is a nation in every sense of the word."—John Steinbeck

"There is a growing feeling that perhaps Texas *is* really another country, a place where the skies, the disasters, the diamonds, the politicians, the women, the fortunes, the football players and the murders are all bigger than anywhere else."—Pete Hamill

"Texans ignore 'better,' long ago forgot the useless word 'good.' Everything in Texas is 'best.'"—Edward Smith

W. Lee "Pappy" O'Daniel was a flour salesman and host of a country-music show . . .

COWBOY TALK

*We went waaaaay back into the Uncle John's archives for this little
beauty from Uncle John's Fifth Bathroom Reader. Well, maybe you
can't be a cowboy, but you can still talk like one. Here are a few
phrases to practice. And smile when you say them, son.*

**"He's crooked enough to sleep
on a corkscrew."**
He's dishonest.

**"Raised on prunes and
proverbs"**
A religious person.

"Fat as a well-fed needle"
Poor.

"Deceitful beans"
*Beans that give you gas. (They
talk behind your back.)*

**"Got a pill in his stomach that
he can't digest"**
Shot dead.

**"She's like a turkey gobbler in
a hen pen."**
She's proud.

**"He's like a breedin' jackass
in a tin barn."**
He's noisy.

"Fryin' size but plumb salty"
A senior citizen.

**"Quicker 'n you can spit 'n
holler 'Howdy!'"**
Very fast.

"Studying to be a half-wit"
Stupid or crazy.

"Built like a snake on stilts"
Tall.

**"Shy on melody, but strong on
noise"**
A bad singer.

"Weasel smart"
Very crafty.

**"Scarce as bird dung in a
cuckoo clock"**
Hard to find.

**"Dry as the dust in a
mummy's pocket"**
Very dry.

**"In the lead when tongues
was handed out"**
Talks too much.

**"If he closed one eye he'd
look like a needle"**
Very skinny.

"He died of throat trouble"
He was hung.

"Coffin varnish"
Whiskey.

FROM UNIQUE TO EUNUCH

It's probably a safe bet that Lajitas, Texas, is the only town that has a goat for a mayor. But it's an even safer bet that Lajitas is the only town with a beer-drinking, castrated goat for a mayor!

The good citizens of Lajitas were all in agreement. It was Clay Henry who put the sleepy Rio Grande town (population 100) on the map. Visitors flocked to watch Clay perform his unusual stunt—imbibing prodigious numbers of beers. And so, in 1986, the townspeople of Lajitas elected Clay Henry their mayor. Which may not seem particularly noteworthy, except for the fact that Clay Henry is a goat.

The current mayor of Lajitas is Clay Henry III, the grandson of that original beer-guzzling political animal. Like his father and grandfather before him, Clay III can knock them back with the best of them. But his rise to power has not been an easy one.

A POLITICAL DYNASTY
In 1992, "Hizzoner," the first Clay Henry, was in his pen, blotto as usual. His son, Clay Henry, Jr., following in his dad's footsteps, was also drunk in the same pen. Tragically, it happened to be rutting season. Clay Henry, Jr., killed his own father in a horny drunken brawl over a she-goat. Clay Henry, Sr., has since been stuffed and now stands watch over The Trading Post—the very place where people buy beer to feed to the mayoral goats.

With the demise of Clay Senior, the good people of Lajitas had no choice but to elect Junior as their mayor. Clay Henry Jr. did the town proud, drinking as he did some 35 to 40 beers a day. He appeared on television, including a segment of *The Sally Jesse Raphael Show*, and a bit part in *The Streets of Laredo* series.

THE HEIR APPARENT
Following the family tradition after the death of his father (from natural causes, it's presumed), Clay Henry III was elected mayor of Lajitas in 2000; the town's 300 citizens enthusiastically picked him

over his opponents: a cigar store wooden Indian and a dog. Like his predecessors, Clay III was happy just to hang around his pen slurping up liquid refreshment as payoffs from loyal subjects like Steve Smith, Austin millionaire-turned-owner of the Lajitas Resort. Smith has fully embraced the Clay Henry phenomenon: the resort's bar, "The Thirsty Goat," serves a drink special called the "Clay Henry Margarita." But Clay Henry himself still prefers beer.

AIN'T THAT JUST LIKE A JIM BOB?

Everything seemed to be going fine for Clay Henry III. Not only was he a local celebrity, he had all the free beer he could drink. But in August 2002, disaster struck.

On that fateful Sunday, Jim Bob Hargrove jealously watched Mayor Henry III swill his beer. Hargrove would have liked to join the mayor, but local blue laws prevented him from buying any beer for himself. In a jealous rage, Hargrove castrated the hapless goat. Clay Henry III lost a lot of blood and darn near died, but he pulled through.

Jim Bob Hargrove was charged with felony animal cruelty. Luckily for him, his first trial ended with a hung jury.

Clay Henry III made a full (if, perhaps, not complete) recovery. The Lajitas Resort's marketing director probably summed it up best when he told the *Houston Chronicle:* "It doesn't seem to have traumatized him . . . He drinks as much as he ever did. Or, maybe, he drinks a little more."

And thus sadly, ends a promising political dynasty.

* * * * *

TERRIBLE TUESDAY

One of the worst single tornadoes in recorded Texas history hit Wichita Falls on April 10, 1979. Forty-two people were killed, 1,740 injured, and an estimated 20,000 left homeless. Dubbed "Terrible Tuesday," the storm system caused an estimated $400,000,000 (in 1979 dollars) worth of damage, one of the costliest storms in American history.

SQUISHING YOUR SUPPER

More than the folks in any other state, Texans seem to have a preoccupation with roadkill. Maybe it's just 'cause there's so much of it.

With its long straight roads, dusty flatlands, and remote landscapes, Texas highways are just plain built for speed. The temptation to go too fast can be hard to resist, much to the misfortune of the local wildlife, or as it's postmortemly called, "roadkill." Whether they shoot it or smoosh it, some Texans think roadside critters are good eats.

IT'S FRESH AND ORGANIC

Unlike West Virginia and Tennessee, in Texas it's illegal to take your roadkill home and set it on the supper table—a state of affairs that isn't to the liking of every Texan. In 2002, local members of People for the Ethical Treatment of Animals (PETA) petitioned State Representative Fred Brown, requesting he introduce a bill in the Texas House of Representatives repealing the prohibition.

PETA argued that animals killed on the road were healthier eats than critters raised on factory farms, where they're shot with hormones and antibiotics and run through automated slaughterhouses. Roadkill, in essence, is the ultimate free-range food. Taking it to a higher plane, PETA went so far as to suggest that the law stood as a violation of a person's freedom of choice.

Representative Brown weighed their arguments but respectfully declined to pursue the matter. So Texas roadkill connoisseurs will have to live outside the law.

EAT, DRINK, AND CELEBRATE ROADKILL

As the "Roadkill Bill" was dying in the cavernous halls of the legislature, the roadkill phenomenon reincarnated elsewhere. Texans took to the notion of eating roadkill and incorporated the idea into their eateries and their entertainment. Over in Leakey, for example, is Toad's Roadkill Café. In Bellaire, just outside of

Houston, is the Roadster Grill, featuring Roadkill Burgers on its menu. (Of course, everyone knows it's really a chicken burger.)

Then there's a creative bartender who concocted the Texas Roadkill Shooter, which we suspect may be named after the half-ounce of Wild Turkey in it.

If you're knocking back a Shooter in some San Antonio bar you may be able to catch the rhythms of cowboy honky-tonk brought to you by Gary Wright and the Roadkill Band. Down the road, Fort Worth also has some drop-dead good rhythms—Texapeno music played by Mink Dean Averitt and *his* Roadkill Band.

THE SINCEREST FORM OF FLATTENING

Other states are catching on to the roadkill trend. In Oregon a petition is circulating to legalize the consumption of roadkill. Recipe books have hit the ground running, including Buck Peterson's best-selling *Totaled Roadkill Cookbook*. The book was published in California and features such recipes as Queasydillo, Ricocheted Rabbit, Pepe Le Stew, and Tar Tartare.

For more adventures in roadkill, try "Eat It or Wear It?" on page 277.

* * * * *

GOOD GOLLY, MISS MOLLY (IVINS)

Texas pundit Molly Ivins has a way with words and she sure doesn't mince them.

"I dearly love the state of Texas, but I consider that a harmless perversion on my part, and discuss it only with consenting adults."

"The first real Texan I ever saw on TV was *King of the Hill's* Boomhauer, the guy who's always drinking beer and you can't understand a word he says."

"But what still makes Texas Texas is that it's ignorant, cantankerous and ridiculously friendly . . . It is the place least likely to become a replica of everyplace else. It's authentically awful, comic and weirdly charming, all at the same time."

THE OTHER
MAN IN BLACK

*Destined to become one of the most easily recognized voices—
and faces—in rock, Roy Orbison had his humble beginnings in the
oil fields of West Texas.*

He was born in 1936 in Vernon, Texas, but early on his family moved to Wink. That's in Texas, too. At 13, Roy Orbison, future shade-wearing man in black, started his first band, the Wink Westerners, with a bunch of kids from school. Roy sang lead vocals and played guitar. The kids booked gigs at school functions, local theaters, clubs, and dance halls all throughout West Texas, and even had their own radio show. This early brush with success whetted Roy's appetite; in his high school yearbook he was quoted, "To lead a western band is my after school wish, and of course to marry a beautiful dish."

SCHOOL OF ROCKS
Young Roy enrolled in North Texas State University (Pat Boone was enrolled there at the same time) where he majored in rocks—geology, that is—figuring he could fall back on his degree just in case his musical career didn't pan out. He met some other musicians at the university with similar musical aspirations, and it was all over. Roy dropped out of school and, with a couple of old band mates from the Wink Westerners, joined his new friends to form the Teen Kings.

The new band didn't play country western; this was the 1950s, after all, and if rock wasn't yet king, it was prince and heir apparent of American popular music. The Teen Kings covered some popular rock and roll songs and then came out with their own rockabilly classic "Ooby Dooby" in 1956. A friend played the recording over the phone to Sun Records owner Sam Phillips (the man who "discovered" Elvis). Sam loved "Ooby, Dooby," and asked the Teen Kings to record it again for Sun. Roy and the gang started touring the South, playing alongside stars as huge as Johnny Cash, whose influence, it's said, was the reason that Roy started wearing black.

TOP OF THE CHARTS

In 1958, Orbison quit Sun Records, citing personal differences, and left most of his band mates behind when he returned to West Texas. In Odessa, he met and married his wife, Claudette Frady, for whom he wrote the song "Claudette," which turned out to be a so-so hit for the Everly Brothers. A record deal with Monument Records in Nashville led to 15 "Top 40" hits between 1960 and 1965, including, "Only the Lonely," "Crying," "In Dreams," and "Oh, Pretty Woman." His melodies were addictive and tailor-made for his clear-but-quavery three-octave range. Elvis once called him "the greatest singer in the world."

THE TEXAS INVASION

Orbison toured Britain regularly during the early 1960s; he even came to call it his "second home." The trademark dark sunglasses he started wearing while he was there weren't to screen out the sunshine, heaven knows, but to cover up his astigmatism. On his earlier tours there, he shared the stage with the Beatles, before they made it big in the States. Legend has it that their first number one hit in Britain, "Please Please Me," was a tribute to Orbison.

A GOOD REVIEW FROM THE BOSS

Roy flew under the pop music radar during the late 1960s and the 1970s—while stars like Van Halen and Linda Ronstadt covered his songs (how many times have you heard Linda sing "Blue Bayou" on the radio?).

The stage was set for a triumphant return in the 1980s: first a Grammy win for his duet with Emmylou Harris on "That Loving You Feeling Again," followed by "In Dreams" being featured on the soundtrack of David Lynch's *Blue Velvet*, which introduced the Orbison sound to a whole new generation. When Roy was inducted into the Rock and Roll Hall of Fame in 1987, Bruce Springsteen said of him, "In '75, when I went to the studio to make 'Born To Run,' I wanted to make a record with the words like Bob Dylan, that sounded like Phil Spector, but most of all, I wanted to sing like Roy Orbison." The other man in black was back.

TRAVELIN' ON

Within a year, Roy joined Bob Dylan, George Harrison, Tom Petty, and Jeff Lynne, a.k.a. The Traveling Wilburys. Their debut album was a major success, but less than a month after its release, on December 6, 1988, Orbison suffered a fatal heart attack at his mother's house in Hendersonville, Tennessee. He was 52.

But that wasn't the last word from the man from Wink. The album *Mystery Girl*, released posthumously in 1989, was Roy's most successful album ever: "You Got It" and "She's A Mystery To Me" topped the charts.

His legacy endures. Any barroom jukebox worth its salt will stock "Oh, Pretty Woman." And the town of Wink honors Roy Orbison with a festival every year in June.

* * * * *

WILD AND WOODEN

Texas is home to some of the finest wooden roller coasters in the United States. Just take a gander at these classic coasters:

TEXAS CYCLONE
Location: Six Flags Astroworld, Houston
Introduced in June 1976, this big wooden coaster was inspired by the 1927 Coney Island Cyclone, only the Texas version is both taller and faster. With a height of 93 feet, the Texas Cyclone reaches a top speed of 65 mph.

TEXAS GIANT
Location: Six Flags Over Texas, Arlington
One of the top wooden roller coasters in the world, this huge ride is 143 feet tall and reaches speeds of 62 mph. The first drop is the scariest; you plummet down 137 feet at a 53-degree angle.

JUDGE ROY SCREAM
Location: Six Flags Over Texas, Arlington
While not as tall as its Texas cousins (Roy is only 71 feet tall), this classic coaster packs the thrills in too. After a 65-foot drop, the coaster gets up to 53 mph on its trip round the 8-acre site.

WHY ALL THE WILDFLOWERS?

A First Lady's living legacy carpets the Lone Star State each spring.

For Texans, who endure long and scorching summers and shorter but freezing winters, spring's brief appearance signals cool and sensory delights—including the colorful fields of native flowers that appear as if by magic: bluebonnets, Indian paintbrush, teacup sage, and black-eyed Susans, to name just a few of the more than 1,000 species. While Mother Nature certainly put them in place, another woman is responsible for propagating them: Mrs. Lyndon Baines Johnson, the First Lady from Texas.

PETAL PUSHER

Lady Bird Johnson was a First Lady with more on her mind than inaugural ballgowns and White House redecoration. She turned her aesthetic eye to country's landscape. "Ugliness is so grim," she once said. "A little beauty, something that is lovely, I think, can help create harmony which will lessen tensions." Mrs. Johnson used her sense of beauty with her political know-how to transform the Texas practice of sowing wildflower seeds (a tradition since the 1920s) into a firm national tradition.

Born Claudia Alta Taylor in the town of Karnack, Texas on December 22, 1912, the future First Lady was declared "purty as a lady bird" by her baby nurse, and the name stuck (despite Claudia's dislike of it). She graduated from the University of Texas at Austin in 1934 and shortly thereafter married a forceful young congressional aide, Lyndon Johnson.

Although Lady Bird had told her husband "I would hate for you to go into politics," he proceeded to do so at a breakneck pace which she followed, with her characteristic grace. While he served in World War II, she became an entrepreneur, buying an Austin radio station (WLBJ is still in place). After the tragic assassination of President John F. Kennedy made her husband the nation's chief executive, Lady Bird Johnson became increasingly concerned with the revitalization of America's roadsides, and in 1965 the first

---

The kangaroo rat is built so that it never needs to drink water.

major legislative campaign ever launched by a First Lady, the
Highway Beautification Act ("Lady Bird's Bill"), was passed.

A PLACE TO SMELL THE FLOWERS

But although Mrs. Johnson loved beautification, she also loved
conservation. "Getting on the subject of beautification is like
picking up a tangled skein of wool," she wrote in a 1965 diary.
"All the threads are interwoven—recreation and pollution and
mental health, and the crime rate, and rapid transit, and highway
beautification, and the war on poverty, and parks—national, state,
and local. It is hard to hitch the conversation into one straight
line, because everything leads to something else."

When the Johnsons returned to their "Texas White House,"
Lady Bird Johnson became more and more interested in local
flora, and the project of a research center for indigenous Texas
plants came to mind. In 1982, the National Wildflower Research
Center was founded by Mrs. Johnson with help from her friend,
the actress Helen Hayes. The Center moved to its current southwest Austin location in 1995, which allowed it to be expanded.
Renamed in 1998 for its founder, the Lady Bird Johnson
Wildflower Research Center has structures that Mrs. Johnson said
should "look as if God himself did it."

From the sandstone blocks in Spanish mission style to the
limestone blocks reminiscent of German immigrants to Texas, all
materials and building styles harmonize with each other and the
landscape. A 6,000-gallon cistern is part of a rainwater-harvesting
system that produces up to 300,000 gallons per annum. Trails, a
library, a café, and gift shop—the center offers many ways for visitors to enjoy the beauty of native plants.

However, Mrs. Johnson was adamant that visitors understand
beauty is only half of the Center's mission. These bright flowers
are more than just pretty faces—they're also ecologically wise
choices for the local landscape.

HUMPING ACROSS TEXAS

That shore is a funny-lookin' horse you got there.

Mules were nineteenth-century man's equivalent of an SUV: they could to carry a lot of baggage but they didn't get great mileage. The hardships of 1800s travel in the American West—food shortages, dehydration, and fatigue—often proved too much for them. They'd just plain give out when crossing the desert, shipping supplies cross-country, or defending the frontier. Texas's answer? The camel.

THE GREAT UNKNOWN

In the 1800s, much of North America was still uncharted. Most of it hadn't been surveyed or explored in great detail. This was especially true of the American West, which many considered to be nearly uninhabitable. One of the biggest problems with the West, including West Texas, was simply getting around. The land just spreads way out, offering little chance to feed or water livestock. Pair this with heavy loads that need carrying and indigenous peoples who were understandably hostile, and you could be stuck with an extremely sore ass, or even an exhausted one.

THIS SOUNDS LIKE A JOB FOR A CAMEL

On March 3, 1855, the Secretary of War, Jefferson Davis, asked Congress to appropriate $30,000 to conduct an experiment to determine the usefulness of other pack animals in helping to solve the problems posed by the West Texas landscape. The idea of using camels was suggested to Davis by George Perkins Marsh, who some call the father of American environmentalism. Perkins, who worked for the Smithsonian, had traveled to Egypt and had come back a big fan of the camel's desert practicality. He even gave a lecture on the topic at the Smithsonian. Soon after his lecture, the funds were awarded: "under the direction of the War Department in the purchase of camels and the importation of dromedaries, to be employed for military purposes."

It was time to go camel shopping.

BUYING A PACK OF CAMELS
In May 1855, Major H. C. Wayne traveled to North Africa and then back to Indianola, Texas, with 33 camels and a handful of Middle Eastern camel experts. On July 8, 1855, sixty miles west of San Antonio, the government established a headquarters for its promising camel study. Davis planned to use this western camel depot, called Camp Verde, for secure and dependable long-distance overland communication via camelback. Soon after, a second batch of forty hump-backed beasts arrived.

WESTWARD HO!
Camels flew in and out of Camp Verde like teenagers through a fast-food drive-thru. In the spring of 1857, a contingent of camels were used to survey a wagon road from Fort Defiance, New Mexico to Fort Tejon, California—almost 700 miles! This was followed by a camel-only expedition of the previously unexplored Big Bend, the mountainous badlands of Texas south of the Davis Mountains. And countless other camel caravans carried Uncle Sam's supplies from town to far-flung town across the young West. It seemed that the camel was destined for domestic greatness. Lieutenant Edward Beale, who led the Fort Defiance expedition, wrote in his journal that: "They pack water for others for days under a hot sun and never get a drop. They pack heavy burdens of corn and oats for months and never get a grain. They eat worthless shrubs and not only subsist, but keep fat."

GOOD IDEA . . .
It looked as though the concept couldn't fail. Not only could these magnificent mammals walk around carrying 600 pounds like a cowboy carries a Stetson hat on his head, they could plod on forever without water and would eat almost anything green. Plus, they really took to their Southwestern surroundings. So why didn't they take the mule's job?

. . . BAD SMELL
The ugly truth is that people just didn't like them. Their strong smell was not only unpleasant for people, but also downright frightening to Texas horses, dogs, cattle and other regional

During the Depression, armadillos were a popular food supplement.

mammals. One whiff of a camel and they went crazy with fear. And a lot of handlers found them too difficult to work with. Even West Texas Comanche Indians—proven warriors and horsemen—called them "The Devil's Goats."

GIVING UP CAMELS

Plus, the timing was bad. The Civil War, which lasted from 1861 to 1865, not only changed the ownership of Camp Verde, but also scattered camels to the four winds: they were auctioned, slaughtered, sold, or shipped away.

After the war, some Texas civilians tried importing camels for profit, but with no demand to meet supply, the camels were eventually let loose to roam the streets and countryside. Today, the ruins of Camp Verde have been reconstructed as a ranch house along with an historical marker from the Texas Centennial Commission. Some say the unappreciated specters of hump-backed ghosts can still be seen in the West Texas desert. There's no word if their smell lingers on, but our guess is that it would be hard to miss if it did.

* * * * *

SMART LADY BIRD

Brief bits of wisdom from Lady Bird Johnson.

"The First Lady is an unpaid public servant elected by one person—her husband."

"Every politician should have been born an orphan and remain a bachelor."

"Any committee is only as good as the most knowledgeable, determined and vigorous person on it. There must be somebody who provides the flame."

"No news at 4:30 a.m. is good."

THE FOLKIES
ON THE HILL

Despite threats of bankruptcy and the ever-looming rainstorm, the Kerrville Folk Festival is the place to be for folk music fans.

Every year since 1974, folk music fans from around the world have gathered in the Texas Hill Country between Austin and San Antonio to enjoy the world's longest continuously operating music festival.

SEND IN THE MARINE!

It took a stubborn ex-Marine to pull it off: Rod Kennedy, a hustling former broadcaster, was running promotions for an Austin radio station when he got the idea for the festival. The folk-protest scene of Joan Baez and Bob Dylan was winding down, but a grassroots revival—an almost-underground movement—was emerging from the ashes. Kennedy wasn't about to give up on folk music; he was just getting started. The first festival was a smallish event held indoors at the Kerrville Municipal auditorium in 1972. The tickets went for a whopping $2.50.

FAN OUT, FOLK FANS!

In 1974, Kennedy moved the event outdoors to the 63-acre Quiet Valley Ranch, a green oasis just outside of Kerrville, where a corny-but-cute sign greets visitors with a "Welcome Home." Funky folk music fans show up early with their own tents and scope out the best camping spots. Most campers actually stay for the whole 18-day festival and return year after year. Festival true believers are dubbed Kerrverts; newcomers are Kerrvirgins. Their campsites go by such "official" monikers as Camp Stupid, Camp Dysfunctional, and Camplicated.

It's an around-the-clock lyrical love fest. Fresh from the stage, performers gather around the campfire with banjos and guitars for a never-ending jam session with their often less-talented fans.

It's estimated that Texas has more than 3,000,000 deer.

THE NOT-SO-GREAT OUTDOORS

Moving the festival outdoors into the sun seemed to be a natural for folks who like natural. You won't find disposable cups at the Kerrville Folk Festival. But you can gobble vegetarian goodies and attend your choice of folksy mass or Shabbat services on week-ends—tie-dyed shirt optional.

It's certain that Mother Nature appreciates the fest's natural approach, but she's always got a few tricks up her puffy sleeves. Like rain, dude. Lots and lots of rain. The year 1985 was Rod Kennedy's personal hell. A few hearty Kerrverts braved the shows, huddled under shower curtains, but the bills were mounting and the telephone service was cut. Kennedy was ready to quit. Looking back on it, the head folkie credits his Marine training for helping him to stick it out through the rough years. It's all about "integrity of position," he says. That means hanging on until you absolutely have to retreat. And he never did.

EXPLETIVES DELETED

From a swiveling captain's chair backstage, the head folkie surveyed the stage for 31 years. And he didn't forget his days as a Marine, as the new recruits found out when they crossed the line. Singer-songwriter Eliza Gilkyson blurted out a naughty word backstage and was banned from the event for a while. But unable to hold a grudge, Kennedy let his big heart win out in the end and invited her back to perform. He even pretended not to hear when she accidentally said the same word again!

Kennedy retired in 2002 at age 72, but the Kerrville Folk Festival continues, rain or shine.

* * * * *

TAKES ON TEXAS WEATHER

"If you don't like the weather now, then just wait five minutes."
—*Old Texas Expression*

"One Texas claim is that it does not have a climate, just weather."
—J. Frank Dobie

Texas harbors nearly 600 species of birds, more than any other state.

DO THE MATH

In a place as big as Texas, there are a lot of towns. (The counties are in parentheses.) Put 'em all together and what have you got?

FOR THE KIDDIES

	Dog Ridge	(Bell)
	Cat Claw	(Callahan)
+	Bird Town	(Blanco)

Classic Rivalries

	Ernies Acres	(Brazoria)
	Burt	(Comal)
	Elmo	(Kaufman)
	Kermit	(Winkler)
	Oscar	(Bell)
+	Grover	(Guadalupe)

Are we on Sesame Street or in Texas?

| | Linus | (Panola) |
| + | Lucy | (Atascosa) |

Peanuts Sibling Rivalry

EMBARRASSMENT

| | Thompson Chapel | (Fort Bend) |
| + | Groom | (Carson) |

Left at the Altar?

DRAMA!

| | Thelma | (Bexar) |
| + | Louise | (Wharton) |

Female Buddy Movie

| | Sweeney | (Brazoria) |
| + | Todd | (Grayson) |

The Demon Barber

	Paris	(Lamar)
	Helena	(Karnes)
+	Troy	(Bell)

Homeric Soap Opera

RECREATION

	Ace	(Polk)
	King	(Coryell)
	Queen City	(Cass)
	Black Jack	(Cherokee)
+	Ten Mile	(Dallas)

A Texas Straight

DELECTABLE DISHES

| | Sweeten | (Brazoria) |
| + | Teacup | (Kimble) |

A Perfect Cup of Tea?

Charlie's Angels star Jaclyn Smith was born on Oct. 26, 1947 in Houston, Texas.

Butter Krust   (Travis)
Sugar Hill   (Panola)
Chocolate   (Calhoun)
+   Pecan   (Delta)

Tasty Dessert

Bacontown   (Jackson)
Cereal   (Floyd)
Pancake   (Coryell)
+   Coffee City(Henderson)

*The Hearty Way to Start
the Day*

Holder's Gin (Bastrop)
+   Olive   (Hardin)

Happy Hour

JUST TWO GOOD OL' BOYS . . .

Boss   (Tarrant)
Hogg   (Burleson)
Roscoe   (Nolan)
Duke   (Fort Bend)
+   Daisy   (Hopkins)

*Campy Car Chase
Classic*

VANITY

Bald Knob   (Wise)
+   Whig   (Carson)

Covered Pate

HOLIDAYS

Darling   (Maverick)
Hart   (Castro)
FlowerMound (Denton)
+   Valentine   (Jeff Davis)

Be Mine 4 Ever?

Ghost Hill   (Ellis)
Witcher   (Milam)
Spider Mountain (Burnet)
Black Cat   (Hunt)
+   Dark Corners   (Bee)

Trick or Treat!

Mayflower   (Newton)
Pilgrim   (Gonzales)
Plymouth (Collingsworth)
+   Turkey   (Hall)

Let's All Give Thanks

Fellow *Angel* Farrah Fawcett is also a Texan. She was born Feb. 2, 1947, in Corpus Christi, Texas.

KIDNAPPED!

Like something out of a tale by Robert Louis Stevenson, Cynthia Ann Parker was kidnapped as a child and raised by the Comanche. When it came time to rescue her, she wasn't too thrilled about it.

Cynthia Ann Parker's life was like an adventure novel. She was born in Illinois in 1825 and when she was 10 years old her family moved to Texas. They settled out in the middle of nowhere on the Navasota River at a place they called Fort Parker, which was actually a real fort with walls to protect them from Comanche and Kiowa.

But living in a fort didn't help all that much because, in 1836, a Comanche party raided it and captured some of the Parkers, including young Cynthia Ann. This sort of thing was pretty common on the wild Texas frontier; some tribes would take settlers captive and then ransom them back to their families. In this case, four of the five captives returned home within a few years. But not Cynthia Ann.

NEW FAMILY TIES

A Comanche family adopted Cynthia Ann and loved her like their own daughter. In 1840, a trader named Len Williams encountered her in her village and offered to ransom her, but her Comanche father wouldn't give his adopted daughter up. Apparently Cynthia Ann herself learned to love her new family and the lifestyle on the open plains. When Williams spoke to her, she refused to go with him.

CYNTHIA ANN MARRIES UP

Cynthia's name was now Naudah, meaning "Someone Found." About five years later, another attempt was made to get her back, but by then she was married to Peta Nocona, a young Comanche up-and-comer and soon-to-be chief. The couple had several children. Some stories say that her brother John Parker, who had been captured too and lived with the Comanche for some years before being ransomed, begged her to come back. But Naudah refused. She wanted to stay right where she was.

CYNTHIA ANN FOUND

In 1860, a contingent of Texas Rangers staged a raid on Comanche territory. The group included Lawrence Sullivan Ross, later governor of Texas, and Charlie Goodnight, later the state's greatest cattle baron. Goodnight took a female prisoner named Naudah and her baby girl. Oddly enough, the woman had blue eyes. She spoke no English and seemed completely Comanche, but a member of the Parker family later identified her as the long lost Cynthia Ann.

Naudah and her daughter, Prairie Flower, were taken far from the Comanche to live with Cynthia Ann's relatives. The "rescue" thrilled all of Texas; the legislature voted her some money and land as a token of respect for her ordeal.

NAUDAH WANTS TO GO HOME

But Cynthia Ann wasn't Cynthia Ann anymore; she was Naudah, and all she wanted was to go back to her old Comanche home. She once begged another former Comanche captive named Coho Smith to take her back to her husband and sons. She promised that her tribe would lavish him with horses, wives, and guns. Of course, Smith knew that if he returned poor Cynthia Ann to the Comanche, he could never show his face in Texas again. Naudah made several attempts to run away on her own, but never succeeded. The Parkers promised her that she could visit her Comanche family when the Civil War ended, but that didn't happen. Some accounts say she died in 1864, but others say she lived into the 1870s. No matter when she died, Naudah never saw her husband or sons again.

MOM WOULD BE SO PROUD

Cynthia Ann's son Quanah grew up to become the last great chief of the Comanche and led their last war against the whites in 1873–1874. He later became a spokesman for Indian affairs and a national celebrity with many famous friends, including Charlie Goodnight, the man who "rescued" Cynthia Ann Parker from her happy life with the Comanche. Quanah had his mother's body moved from where the Parkers laid her to rest and buried her in her Comanche homeland.

A GUY NAMED DORIS

Aside from the factual errors in the movie Pearl Harbor *(like it's 1941 and nobody is smoking), the genuine hero was given short shrift on the big screen.*

Doris Miller was born in Waco, Texas, in 1919. A fullback on his high-school football team, Miller was a large man who stood 5'9" and weighed in at about 200 pounds. (No wonder he earned the nickname "Raging Bull" from his teammates.) Doris worked on his father's farm before enlisting in the U.S. Navy in the late 1930s. He wanted to see the world and earn some money for his family. Luckily, the name "Doris" didn't stick. Most everybody called him Dorie.

THE COLOR BARRIER
At the time of Dorie Miller's enlistment, the U.S. Armed Forces restricted African-Americans to steward service: our hero started out as a Mess Attendant, Third Class; advanced to Mess Attendant, Second Class; then First Class, and subsequently was promoted to Ship's Cook, Third Class. Most of the fighting Miller got to do was in boxing matches; he excelled at boxing and was the USS *West Virginia*'s heavyweight boxing champ. Things would change on that fateful day in December at Pearl Harbor.

THE DAY THAT WILL LIVE IN INFAMY
Ships' cooks had assigned combat tasks—just in case—so on the morning of December 7, 1941, when the call to battle stations went out, Miller dropped the laundry he was carrying (not the elegant tray of coffee service Cuba Gooding, Jr., was toting in the film). He rushed to his assigned station: an antiaircraft-battery magazine. When he saw that it had been damaged by torpedo fire, he went above decks to help carry the wounded to safety.

DON'T GIVE UP THE SHIP!
Word came that the captain and the executive officer were injured, so Miller went to the bridge and carried the captain down

to the first-aid station. After which he returned to the deck and manned an antiaircraft machine gun. He hadn't been formally trained on its use, but in his own words:

> "It wasn't hard. I just pulled the trigger and she worked fine. I had watched the others with these guns. I guess I fired her for about 15 minutes. I think I got one (of the planes). They were diving pretty close to us."

But meanwhile, the battleship *West Virginia* was sinking out from under him—a result of massive damage done by two armored bombs that had fallen on deck and five aircraft torpedoes that impacted on the port side. The crew abandoned ship, and the *West Virginia* sunk to the bottom of Pearl Harbor. Of the 1,541 men on board, 130 were killed and 52 were wounded.

LIFE AFTER PEARL
A few days later, Miller was transferred to the USS *Indianapolis*. In May 1942 he became the first African-American to be awarded the Navy Cross, for courage under fire during the Pearl Harbor attack, presented to him directly by then Admiral Chester W. Nimitz, Commander in Chief, Pacific Fleet. The following spring he was assigned to a newly constructed escort carrier, the *Liscome Bay*. That November, while cruising near Butaritari Island in the South Pacific, the *Liscome* was hit by a single torpedo from a Japanese submarine and sank within minutes. Only 272 of the *Liscome*'s 918 sailors survived. Dorie Miller wasn't among them. He was listed as missing and officially presumed dead on November 25, 1944, a year and a day after the *Liscome* sank.

BACK IN WEST VIRGINIA
The ship that Miller had so valiantly defended lived to fight another day. The *West Virginia* had been dredged up from the bottom of Pearl Harbor, repaired, and modernized. It served in the Pacific theater through the end of the war in August 1945. But both the ship and its cook-hero went down in history: Miller's bravery at Pearl Harbor afforded him a reputation far above his rank. In 1973 the U.S. Navy commissioned a new frigate—the USS *Miller*—in honor of this brave Texan hero.

They kill, cook, milk, and eat hundreds of rattlers, but there are always plenty more the next year.

STATE FRUIT: TEXAS RED GRAPEFRUIT

House Concurrent Resolution No. 75, 73rd Legislature, Regular Session (1993)

Jimmy Buffett had it right. A little morning grapefruit can do wonders for the soul and the heart and body. Bright red and rich in potassium, Vitamin C, and a whole other host of good things, a little ol' grapefruit or even a big ol' grapefruit can be a great way to keep on the sunny side of life.

THE FORBIDDEN FRUIT

Grapefruit didn't originate in Texas, but once it got there no one grew it bigger, better, or redder. Cultivation had its beginnings in Barbados in the mid-1700s. In those days it was known as "the forbidden fruit" because it was thought—for a while at least—to be the tree of good and evil from the Garden of Eden. A natural hybrid of the pummelo (*Citrus grandis*) and the sweet orange (*Citrus sinensis*), it was christened "grapefruit" by a Jamaican farmer because it grew in grapelike clusters. Grapefruit seeds probably traveled to Florida by way of French or Spanish settlers. From there, Spanish missionaries most likely carried the fruit to southern Texas.

It wasn't until 1893 that an actual grapefruit grove was planted on Lone Star soil. John H. Shary, the "Father of the Citrus Industry," bought 16,000 acres of southern Texas brush land where he planted white, then pink, grapefruit from seeds.

YOU'VE HEARD OF SHOCKING PINK?

Then, something weird but providential happened. In 1929, a *red* grapefruit was discovered growing on a pink grapefruit tree in McAllen, Texas! Over the next several years, more red mutations appeared—each one named after the individual grower who found it. By the late 1940s, Texas was growing more grapefruit than any other state. Over the years, Texas growers began to concentrate more on the showy reds. The grapefruit industry registered two trademarked red categories, Ruby-Sweet and Rio Star.

How many rattlers have been turned in at Sweetwater since 1958? 120 tons' worth.

The State of Texas will be forever grateful to nature's misstep and proved it by declaring the red grapefruit its official state fruit in 1993.

IT ISN'T JUST FOR BREAKFAST ANYMORE
And Texas makes very good use of its state fruit. You make think of grapefruit as a breakfast treat—either in its pulpy, sliced-up state or as a tall glass of juice. But did you know that there's so much more to this versatile star player? Resourceful recipe writers have come up with grapefruit salsa, grapefruit coleslaw, grapefruit gazpacho, grapefruit and avocado salad, and Rio Star grapefruit pie. So many grapefruits, so little time.

* * * * *

ISN'T IT ROMANTIC?
Quite a few other books set in Texas are strong sellers according to *USA Today*. The strongest seem to be very romantic, which may just be proof that Texans are both lovers and fighters. So find a comfy chair, plenty of hankies, and settle in for the warm fuzzies Texas can bring.

FERN MICHAELS
Texas Rich
Texas Heat
Texas Fury
Texas Sunrise

DEBBIE MACOMBER
Texas Two-Step
Dr. Texas
Promise, Texas
Return to Promise

JODI THOMAS
When a Texan Gambles
The Texan's Wager
The Texan's Dream
To Kiss a Texan
To Wed in Texas
Twilight in Texas

Texas proverb: "Don't make love by the garden gate, because even if love is blind the neighbors ain't."

SPINDLETOP: A LIFE-CHANGING EVENT

On January 10, 1901, on a hill south of Beaumont, an ocean of oil started to spew 100 feet into the air. Spindletop spawned a wave of prosperity that made the California Gold Rush look like a garage sale. It also changed a lot of lives—for the better and the worse.

MARCELLUS E. FOSTER

Before Spindletop: In 1901, Foster was a reporter at the *Houston Post*, the city's flagship newspaper. A frustrated, overworked journalist, he was dispatched to report on the unusual goings-on at nearby Spindletop Hill. When he got there, he started to sweat. People were flooding into the city from New York, Pittsburgh, and Chicago. The hotels, restaurants, and streets were filling to overflowing. This was big time! Realizing the historic gravity of what he saw taking place, and not content to be a mere bystander, he gambled a week's pay on a single well option.

After Spindletop: Foster's gamble paid off. That single option brought him the equivalent of well over $100,000 in today's dollars. Loving his work but hating his job, he returned to Houston to start his own newspaper: the *Houston Chronicle*. Now his old bosses were his top competitors. Working from a ratty three-story hovel on Texas Avenue, Foster grew his paper—which originally sold for two cents a copy—into one of the nation's top 10 newspapers. Today, the *Chronicle* is owned by the Hearst Corporation and has a Sunday readership approaching two million. The *Houston Post* went out of business in 1995.

ROBERT ALONZO WELCH

Before Spindletop: Welch boarded a train from his native South Carolina with $10 in his pocket. He arrived in Houston and landed a few odd jobs as a bookkeeper and salesman at a paint store. Oil was big news in those parts and Welch took such great interest in the petroleum industry, that his friends nicknamed him

"Pete." His excitement soon got the better of him, and he bought an acre in the middle of the Spindletop oilfield in 1901.

After Spindletop: Welch sold his single acre for a $15,000 profit—a fact which he was very proud of. That is, until the person he sold it to resold it for over $1,000,000 a few weeks later! Still, a profit was a profit and he sunk all of his earnings into new and more exciting Texas oil ventures. He chose a lot of winners. At the time of his death in 1952, "Pete" Welch was worth over $52 million (over $340,000,000 in today's dollars). And even as his fortune grew, he held on to his job at the paint store.

GEORGE WASHINGTON CARROLL

Before Spindletop: Carroll was president of his father's lumber company, and after it was sold to Texas lumber baron John Henry Kirby in 1900, found himself in quite the comfortable situation. A religious family man, he was content to quietly enjoy a life of fortune, good health, and God-fearing philanthropy in Beaumont. But one day a friend of his from the First Baptist Church offered him an excellent investment opportunity in oil: a chance to invest in a well on Spindletop Hill. Carroll put up some cash, hoping to increase his family fortune just a little bit more.

After Spindletop: When Spindletop struck oil, Carroll became the wealthiest man in a town full of millionaires. He now had a lumber fortune *and* an oil fortune—a seemingly bottomless wellspring of capital. But modest little Beaumont had changed. With oil came the usual vices: drinking, gambling, and prostitutes so busy they needed administrative assistants. Carroll couldn't bear it; he wouldn't let the heathens have his town. He waged an all-out war on this new, fast lifestyle—he lectured and donated extravagant sums to Baylor University, the Young Men's Christian Association, and the First Baptist Church of Beaumont. He ended up giving everything away, and died frustrated and penniless in a room at the YMCA, a building that his once-vast fortune had financed.

Texas sass: "Ugly? She'd make a freight train take a dirt road."

ALWAYS AN AGGIE?
LIFETIME LONGHORN?

Set. Down. Hike. Inside Texas's college football feud.

If college football is your game, then you surely know about the long-standing rivalry between two of Texas's institutions of higher learning. In Texas, you'd better know whose side you're on. So if you not an alumnus, how do pick your team?

GO WHITE! GO BLUE!
Every year, the University of Texas Longhorns face off against Texas A & M Aggies in a heated gridiron battle traditionally fought on Thanksgiving weekend.

The stereotypical view of each school may help you pick a team. Traditionally, UT has been seen as the elite state university and A&M the hard-working agricultural school (the "A&M" stands for agricultural and mechanical, which refers to the first programs offered by the university when it opened in 1876.) Blue collar versus white collar, it's an age-old tale.

Or maybe some statistics will help. The two teams have played each other since 1894; their annual match-ups began in 1915. In their century-old rivalry, the Longhorns have the edge with 70 wins to the Aggies' 34; they share 5 ties between them. So if you like the underdog, then Aggies all the way. If you prefer odds-on favorites, the Longhorns should be your team.

FIGHT, TEAM, FIGHT!
Nothing says football like a good college fight song. Both A&M and UT are noted for the ditties that charge up their fans and energize their teams. The "Aggie War Hymn" is filled with great, nonsensical words sung several times throughout the fight song, written by alumnus J. V. "Pinky" Wilson.

> Hullabaloo, Caneck, Caneck
> Hullabaloo, Caneck, Caneck
> All hail to dear old Texas A & M
> Rally around Maroon and White

Texas-born choreographer Tommy Tune: "I think Texans have more fun than the rest of the world."

The hymn continues on to poke fun at UT's school song, "The Eyes of Texas":

> The eyes of Texas are upon you.
> That is the song they sing so well,
> So, good-bye to Texas University,
> We're goin' to beat you all to—
> Chi-gar-roo-gar-rem!

The song concludes with a lot of yelling about sawing off the horns of TU's mascot, the longhorn.

The University of Texas mentions A&M in their fight song as well. "The Eyes of Texas" may be the school's official song, but its fight song is properly called, "Texas Fight." The melody closely resembles a sped-up version of "Taps," the song played at military funerals. "Blondie" Pharr, the Longhorns' band director from 1917 to 1937, penned the lyrics:

> Texas Fight, Texas Fight,
> And it's goodbye to A&M.
> Texas Fight, Texas Fight,
> And we'll put over one more win.
> Texas Fight, Texas Fight,
> For it's Texas that we love best.

Now that you know the songs—which one will you be singing next football season?

WHO STARTED IT?

The ongoing squabble as to where rodeo competitions officially started.

During the 1600s Spanish settlers traveled north across the Rio Grande into modern-day Texas, bringing their live stock in tow as well as their method of mooooo-ving them along in big herds. In fact, the word "rodeo" comes from the Spanish word *rodear*, which means, "to go around" or "round up," as in cattle. To these settlers, rounding up their livestock was all in a day's work.

ROUNDING UP THE EVIDENCE
By the mid-1800s, the modern roundup began to change from hard labor into a hard sport. Every day on the plains, cowboys rode horses, corralled sheep and cows, and tied up livestock. A cowboy would boast that he could break a bronc faster than the next cowpoke. Then he might brag that he could rope that bronc even faster. Before anybody knew it, the spirit of competition between ranch hands grew into what we now call the rodeo.

THE QUESTION IS . . .
Texas in 1883 or Colorado in 1869? Pecos, Texas, and Deer Trail, Colorado, both claim to have held the first rodeo in the United States. Colorado's contest was held on July 4, 1869 and was officially called a "bronco busting competition." First prize was a pair of jeans from a Denver dry goods store. Pecos's cowboy competition took place on July 4, 1883, and more closely resembled the modern rodeo. Cowboys from the Pecos area came to rope, ride, and test their skills in all sorts of events. The "West of the Pecos Rodeo" became an annual event in 1929, and today even reenacts the events from the 1883 spectacle.

PUTTING ON A RODEO FOR FUN AND PROFIT
Buffalo Bill Cody is a contender, too, in a way. He was the first to use the term "rodeo" to describe an exhibition of cowboy skills. As the American frontier continued to expand west, so did America's

obsession with the Wild West culture. So in 1882, a year before the first Texas competition, Buffalo Bill Cody capitalized on this fascination and created his first Wild West show featuring real live cowboys and cowgirls who showed off their skills and competed for prizes in bronco riding, roping, and other events that would become part of the modern rodeo.

MORE BANG FOR THE BUCK

As the show evolved, cowboys began to look less like real cowhands and more like performers, sporting colorful neckties, fancy chaps, and studded boots. Female performers also got into the act by wearing skirts with open sides while they were breakin' broncs. The grand finale always included bull riding to see which rider could stay on the back of an irate bull for the longest amount of time.

LEANING TOWARD COLORADO

But if you're looking for the resting place of the man who *popularized* the rodeo, you won't find him in Texas. Buffalo Bill is buried on Lookout Mountain in Colorado.

Uncle John doesn't take sides, so Colorado and Texas will have to continue to fight it out. But as they say back East, "rodeo, shmodeo," it's still a lot of fun. Bring on the buckin' broncs.

* * * * *

HE NAMED HER WHAT?

Governor James "Jim" Hogg has been the victim of an ugly urban legend. Supposedly he had three daughters named: Ima, Ura, and Wera. What kind of father would he be to saddle his three girls with names like that? Well, the truth is he only had one daughter to saddle with a name and he chose "Ima" for her; Miss Ima Hogg became a well-known philanthropist in spite of her father's creative name choice.

Bevo, a Texas Longhorn, has been a longtime fixture at UT games.

TEXAS TRUISMS

Trust these little slices of wisdom from the sages of Texas.

"Never trust a man whose eyes are too close to his nose."
—Lyndon Baines Johnson

"Never go out on the golf course and beat the president."
—Lyndon Baines Johnson

"Never ask a man if he's from Texas. If he is, he'll tell you. If he ain't, no need to embarrass him."—Anonymous

"The here and now is all we have, and if we play it right it's all we'll need."—Ann Richards

"The perils of duck hunting are great—especially for the duck."
—Walter Cronkite

"There is no such thing as a little freedom. Either you are all free, or you are not free."—Walter Cronkite

"Love is a fire. But whether it is going to warm your hearth or burn down your house, you can never tell."—Joan Crawford

"Americans will put up with anything provided it doesn't block traffic."—Dan Rather

"The only way to know how much is enough, is to do too much, and then back up."—Jerry Jeff Walker

"If you're paranoid long enough, sooner or later you're going to be right."—Kinky Friedman

"Don't compromise yourself. You are all you've got."—Janis Joplin

"If you think you can, you can. If you think you can't, you're right."—Mary Kay Ash

"Today, you have 100% of your life left."—Tom Landry

Tejas, which became Texas, is the Spanish spelling of a Caddo word taysha.

THE AGE
OF AUSTIN-IUS

Austin has a long, proud hippie past

Nothing in Austin is quite the same as it is anywhere else in Texas. Clouds of bats fly from under the Congress Avenue bridge, music streams out of every other window, and the food is as likely grown in a restaurant garden as shipped in from somewhere else. Given this eclectic state of affairs, it's no wonder that the state capital is predominantly Democratic, even though it's surrounded by a state that's predominantly Republican. But free-spirited Austinites don't let that get them down. They've stayed true to nonconformity—call it hippie, call it alternative, call it earthy, crunchy, or granola. Whatever you choose, denizens of Austin have already found their way there.

THREADBARE AT THREADGILL'S
Modern Austin history officially begins in 1872, the year that the city won its rights as the state capital over larger burgs Houston and Waco. Locals lost no time in founding the area now known as Sixth Street, where all the music happens (once known as "Guy Town"), and by 1908 the funky Driskill Hotel was in place, providing an excellent spot for speakeasy-bound groups to congregate (and really, any group—the Driskill was where LBJ gathered his cronies during the 1964 presidential elections to count votes).

But it was another funky little corner of town that fueled the live music revolution in Austin. In 1933, Kenneth Threadgill bought a beer license (you can still see "Travis County Beer License 01" on the wall) and turned a North Lamar filling station into the landmark now known as Threadgill's. Back then, it was a bar with a houseband that was "straight hillbilly," according to *Texas Monthly*. Threadgill knew good music when he heard it, so in the early sixties when a girl with an autoharp strolled in to one of his Wednesday night "Hootenannies," he let her play, too. Janis Joplin never forgot the man who gave her a start, and she told her friend Kris Kristofferson about him. Threadgill's may have been more well-known for its musical offerings, but the food is pretty good too. From their chicken-fried steak to their yummy spinach casserole, the menu tempts you to chow down while you're getting down.

DOIN' WHAT COMES NATURALLY
The next step in Austin's hippie formation was when the Armadillo World Headquarters, the live-music venue opened in 1970—the hallowed ground of Willie Nelson, Kinky Friedman, Asleep at the Wheel, and Waylon Jennings, in addition to rockers like The Clash, Bruce Springsteen, Frank Zappa, Van Morrison, and more. With its trashy beer garden, funky murals, and easygoing decorum, the "Armadillo" quickly became the center of Austin's musical renaissance, its influence brought to a wider public through the popular PBS show, *Austin City Limits* that showcased so many of its headliners.

All of this alternative music seems to have fueled a taste for other forms of alternative entertainment, including the peaceful stretch of beach along Lake Travis known as "Hippie Hollow." There, 350,000 visitors per year enjoy this "nudist oasis," but beware of visiting without being prepared. First-timers are nearly always immediately identified and then christened as "cottontails," for their lily-white posteriors.

But while plenty of folks enjoy going au naturel at Hippie Hollow, the local government has recently been taking a hard line (snicker) about letting them do what comes naturally. Travis County park officials have cleared out underbrush and tree limbs to discourage people from uh, well, enjoying themselves, by themselves, too often.

FÊTE FOR A DEPRESSED DONKEY
Freewheeling, free-living Austin has its most typical and most charitable annual event each April at Pease Park: Eeyore's Birthday Party. Depending on whom you ask, either in the early 1960s University of Texas professor James Ayres or in the early 1970s student Lloyd Birdwell, Jr., founded this celebration of Winnie-the-Pooh's gray donkey friend Eeyore, because Eeyore was always sad that no one ever threw him a birthday party. It's morphed into a huge, daylong party (11 a.m. until dark; children's

area closes at 6:00 p.m.) on varying Saturdays each year that benefits numerous local organizations. Local Austinites and visitors of all ages and stages come to enjoy an outdoor fest that combines a street fair with a rave with a pagan springtime celebration. While these days the thirty-odd year party has incorporated a lot of mainstream elements, there's still a Hippie Queen pageant, drum circles, and a whole lotta tie dye going on.

SOUTH BY SOUTHWEST
Another unique Austin festival has put it on the globe. South By Southwest, the annual live-music festival in Austin, The Live Music Capital of the World. (Acts come from as far away as New Zealand!) "SXSW," as it's colloquially known, has become one of the music industry's premier events for scouting out new acts, while remaining the music lover's premier event for hearing lots of great music of all kinds.

A possible new slogan: SXSW—It's Not Just For Music Anymore. Nope, the street fest that evolved from Austin's live-music scene has evolved from a low-key, overgrown jam session to a much hyped, overgrown event with a capital "E." Now there's a separate Film Festival and an equally separate Interactive Festival, both of which draw crowds.

2004's SXSW Music Festival featured 1,100 musical acts on 58 different stages and venues. Annually, the event also brings about 10,000 visitors to the Texas state capital, including about 6,500 media and industry folk out to schmooze their way through SWSX days filled with festival-sponsored parties. Panels are hosted by musical heavies, from indie-rocker Ani DeFranco to country outlaw Willie Nelson. But attendance isn't cheap—the going price for an all-admittance pass is in the $775 range.

SXSW is something you've got to see to believe—and like most of the best things in Austin, something you've got to participate in to enjoy. Whether you're chilling at the lake, jamming at a live-music gig, or digging into a platter at Threadgill's, you're part of the action—which is what keeps Austin the hip, human, and way cool city it is.

As of 2002 Texas had 14,639,132 licensed drivers.

THE DARING
<u>RED ADAIR</u>

Meet the man who never met a fire he couldn't put out.

Even as a kid in Houston, Red Adair lived on the edge: he broke horses and ran moonshine for after-school money. But risk-taking wasn't just a hobby.

OIL FIRES 101

By the time Paul "Red" Adair was born in 1915, east Texas was a pin-cushion of oil rigs. The black gold came with a heavy price. Almost anything could cause an eruption (a "blowout" in oil biz slang): leak-ing gas, uneven pressure in a well, sparks from a metal tool, you name it. And once ignited, oil well fires are hell to put out—fed as they are by intense heat and an almost limitless supply of fuel.

Underground oil and gas often share the same space, sealed under immense pressure from the ground above. To capture them runs the risk of fires, to say nothing of leaking toxic gas. Fires can't be left to burn themselves out or spew into the atmosphere; besides destroying billions of dollars of reserves, the effect on the environment would be catastrophic.

To extinguish an oil well fire long enough to recap it usually requires an explosion (just as with grease fires, water doesn't cut off the oxygen to put the fire out). So, to put out an oil fire, a fire-fighter has to walk into an inferno and place the explosive charges with perfect precision. In the early days of oil firefighting, most who did it, didn't do it for long. If they didn't crack from the stress, they died from a mistake—it only took one to end a career.

RED'S TRUE CALLING

A man would have to be crazy to get into the oil firefighting busi-ness. Red Adair was just the opposite: cool, calculating, resource-ful, and a whiz at improvisation. During World War II, he served with a bomb disposal unit—the first hint of his life to come. After the war, Adair went to work for Myron Kinley, the original pio-neer of oil well fire and blowout control. Adair made a name for himself there when he successfully snuffed an offshore oilrig fire

---

W.W. "Foots" Clements started as a delivery-truck driver in 1935 and became CEO of Dr Pepper Co.

off the coast of Louisiana. Eighteen wells had caught fire, and Red was the first man to conquer the offshore monster. After fourteen years, Red left to form the Red Adair Company, Inc.

BEELZEBUB'S BIC

In 1962 Adair got a call to put out a well fire that had been burning 550 million cubic feet daily for six months. Other experts had written it off, suggesting the field should simply be allowed to burn itself out. Red figured differently. Anything named "The Devil's Cigarette Lighter" was fit for his attention. That the well was in the middle of the Algerian Sahara—and that the country was involved in what amounted to a civil war—simply added to the challenge.

Red put out the Devil's Cigarette Lighter on his first try, an operation as smooth as snapping down the lid on a Zippo. The publicity made him "the man they call first." Business took off like a blowout, and soon the company was averaging more than forty calls a year.

THE PERSIAN GULF GETS RED HOT

Deserts, jungles, swamps, subarctic barrens: over the years Red's been everywhere. Along the way he designed most of the equipment for his profession, always with an eye to standard pieces that could be customized onsite. In 1972 he formed a company solely to sell and lease his own firefighting equipment.

Red was 78 when he took three teams to Kuwait after Operation Desert Storm. Retreating Iraqi soldiers had left behind over 600 burning Kuwaiti oil wells. Right off the bat, Red's people put out 117 of them. An address to the Gulf Pollution Task Force and a chat with then-President Bush about logistics produced almost immediate results: within a month, equipment and resources started pouring into Kuwait, ultimately shortening a job that would have taken from three to five years down to nine months.

. . . AND RED ALL OVER

Among all the awards and honors he's received are some grassroots tributes. In Glasgow, Scotland, there's a rock band named Fighting Red Adair. Then there's the Red Adair cocktail: for a pitcher-sized batch, just mix six ounces of vodka, two cans of Red Bull (which is surprisingly *not* red in color), and cranberry juice for taste and redness. Just the thing to sip—or guzzle—while toasting its namesake, a true Texas hero.

Maynard Jackson, Jr., the first black mayor of Atlanta, GA (1973), was a Dallas native.

UNCLE JOHN'S TEXAS CLOTHES SHOPPER: THE HAT

Pulitzer Prize-winning novelist James Michener once said that the first step toward becoming a real Texan is: "That first big purchase of cowboy hat and boots . . . then you're on your way."

Old-time cowboy headgear didn't have a uniform shape or material for the longest time—any old army hat, fedora, or farming hat would do. But that changed around 1870, when the Stetson hat came into vogue. Oddly enough, the John B. Stetson Company was based in Philadelphia—not Texas or Missouri—and made all kinds of hats; not just the cowboy kind. But the wide-brimmed, felt models such as the "Hat of the West" or "Boss of the Plains" grew wildly popular in Texas and throughout the West, ultimately becoming a Texas fashion staple. Now, when you think of a cowboy hat, the shape you imagine is that of a Stetson.

WHERE TO BUY IT

You can buy straw or felt hats in just about every town in Texas, though it's best to stick to stores that specialize in Western wear because you'll have better luck when it comes to things like having your hat reshaped if it gets bent, buying hat bands, and stocking up on the rest of your wardrobe.

Although this is the electronic age, it's best not to buy your hat over the Internet. The hands-on approach, the feel, the smell, and the personal experience of buying the hat is not to be missed. It's a personal thing, you're going to want to try it on in person, plus it's easier to get someone to help you find a quality hat that's within your budget.

Austin inventor Gordon Matthews created the first voice mail system in the late 1970s.

PICK A HAT, ANY HAT?

On the inside of the hat you'll see a number with an "X" by it: 3X, 4X, 10X, etc. The more X's your hat is stamped with, the higher quality the hat. Two hats may look alike, but a 3X may cost you $75, while a 30X may cost $500. The difference is in the quality of manufacturing and the warranty. (A hat with a warranty? It must be good!) But take note that the system is not standardized—one company's 3X may be similar to another company's 100X. You'll be able to tell a better hat by holding it and trying it on. Typically, the higher quality the hat, the softer and more comfortable it'll be.

THE WAY TO WEAR YOUR HAT

Typically, a straw hat is worn in the warmer seasons and a felt one in the winter—though, take note, Mr. and Ms. Manners—straw hats are not appropriate for formal events, even in the summer. It's appropriate to take your hat off when being introduced to someone or when talking to your elders or dignitaries. Always remove your hat when you come inside. If it's an informal occasion, someplace like an airport or in a cramped situation where there's just no place to put it, you can always slip it back on once you're inside. And that thing better be off your head in a restaurant—even in a restaurant with a drive-thru window.

Tipping your hat as a gesture of courtesy to a lady is becoming less common, but it's still appreciated. When you tip your hat, do it by the brim if it's a straw hat and by the crown if it's a felt hat. If a man really wants to fawn over a gal, he'll remove his hat every time he sees her. Chicks dig that.

HOW TO CARE FOR YOUR HAT

Straw hats are somewhat disposable, but a good felt hat can last you a lifetime. You can keep 'em both looking good by treating them right. Keep your hat dry and cool—out of the rain, and not baking inside the 200-degree heat of a Texas pickup cab in August. Unless you live in Houston, where it can't be helped, keep your hat out of excess humidity—which can cause it to lose its shape. And keep it in a hatbox whenever possible to keep it from getting all dusted up.

If you're unlucky enough to spill beer on your baby, not that anyone reading this would do something like that, wash it with a little water and let it air dry. When in doubt, take it to a pro and have it cleaned.

IT'S NOT WHAT YOU THINK

Forget what you've heard about "Ten Gallon Hats," in terms of liquid gallons a hat might hold. No such thing! But there is such a thing as the old Spanish word *galon*, which refers to the decorative braids Spanish vaqueros have sported on the brims of their sombreros for centuries. A 10-gallon hat has 10 *galons*, or braids (often gold or silver), on the brim.

* * * * *

TUNEFUL TEXAS TOWNS

Texas has some great towns, so it's no surprise that there are bunch of songs about them. Can you match the artist with the song?

1. "Brownsville Girl"
2. "A**hole from El Paso"
3. "Who Do I Know in Dallas"
4. "(Is Anybody Going to) San Antone"
5. "Luckenbach, Texas (Back to the Basics)"
6. "El Paso"
7. "I'll Be Your San Antone Rose"
8. "Streets of Laredo"

A. Johnny Cash
B. Willie Nelson
C. Emmylou Harris
D. Charley Pride
E. The Grateful Dead
F. Bob Dylan
G. Waylon Jennings
H. Kinky Friedman

Turn to page 303 for Answers.

An outdoor drama, *Texas*, is staged in Palo Duro Canyon, near Amarillo.

JUST SAY NO

Martha McWhirter said God told her not to do it—and "it"
was marital relations of any sort.

MEET GEORGE AND MARTHA
By the time Martha McWhirter had settled in Belton, a
small Texas town about an hour from Austin, where her
husband, George, had opened a store in the late 1860s, she'd
already produced an even dozen kids. And she was done with it.
No more. Nada. The woman gave birth twelve times already! It's
tough to blame her.

THOSE WHO ARE WITHOUT SIN
Martha's pivotal moment came during a marathon of prayer and
fasting. She'd been concentrating on converting two of her daughters to Christianity, when a voice from nowhere started speaking
and told her to question everything her life had stood for so far.
She walked into the backyard where she was transformed or, as
John Wesley, the Methodist church founder and reigning evangel-
ist preacher of the time would say, she was "sanctified"— stripped
of all sins by a higher power.

KEEP YOUR HANDS TO YOURSELF, BUDDY
Wesley's teachings didn't demand it, but Martha took the transfor-
mation to mean that she should immediately become celibate. No
doubt her husband was taken aback by this news, ditto the other
husbands in town as Martha took on converts from the prominent
women of Belton society.

The rules were simple: the women could continue to live with
their husbands, but no physical relations and very little social contact of any kind would be allowed with the "unsanctified" males.

JOIN THE CLUB
The budding movement was welcomed not only by some Belton
women who were in physically and psychologically abusive

It's a musical romance and extravaganza that dramatizes the settling of the Texas Panhandle.

relationships, but also by those from quite happy homes who were just fed up with their submissive role in society.

Meanwhile, George went to live over his store while Martha crowded their home with her followers.

SISTERHOOD IS POWERFUL

By 1880, about 50 middle-class Protestant women had joined the Sanctified Sisters, and they proved themselves tough customers. When one husband called in the law to force the visiting women from his home, the policeman succeeded in evicting them, but came away with part of his ear gone and his nose smashed. Divorce and insanity trials overflowed the Belton courts; some husbands were crazy enough themselves to think that their wives must be crazy to refuse the "marital act."

WORKING GIRLS

The Sanctified Sisters supported themselves by collecting chicken eggs, chopping and selling firewood, doing laundry, and eventually opening one of the grandest hotels in downtown Belton on property owned by one of the sisters. The women pooled their resources and property and helped each other by learning trades ranging from dentistry to shoe cobbling.

SANCTIFIED BROTHERS?

The Sanctified Sisters shunned males as a point of principle. Boy children were welcomed into the communal lifestyle, but promptly handed back to their fathers at age eight.

When a pair of Scottish immigrant brothers sought to become sanctified themselves, neither the women nor the town looked on it kindly. The brothers were taken captive by the town's residents, beaten, and for a while committed to an insane asylum.

DREAMS AND SCHEMES

By the end of the 1880s, the Sanctified Sisters were grudgingly accepted in Belton. The hotel was a hit, and its small collection of books became so popular with locals that it was moved into another building and morphed into the city's first public library. The women were open-minded about all religious beliefs—they didn't attach themselves to any one denomination. Their separation from the rest of society led to some outlandish practices. Martha maintained a fascination with dream interpretation, believing God meant dreams as signs to be acted on literally. When one woman was committed to an asylum for turning down insurance money after her husband's death, Martha dreamed that she should contact the governor and ask for the woman's release. (It worked.)

MARTHA GOES TO WASHINGTON

Near the turn of the century, the sisters up and moved to Washington, D.C., where, as the Woman's Commonwealth, they could more vigorously pursue their activist beliefs, fighting particularly for equal rights for women.

Martha died in 1904 and the group's numbers dwindled. The last surviving Sanctified Sister, Martha Scheble, died in 1983 at age 101.

These days in Belton, the Sanctified Sisters are looked on as a quirky relic of the past, but with an entire section of the Bell County Museum dedicated to their memory.

* * * * *

FESTIVALS IN TEXAS

Texans celebrate just about everything. Here's just a sample of their festival fun!

Pioneers and Old Settlers Reunion	Alvarado
Old Fiddlers Reunion	Athens
Buccaneer Days	Corpus Christi
National Polka Festival	Ennis
East Texas Yamboree	Gilmer
Bluebonnet Days	Kenedy
Butterfield-Overland Stage Coach and Wagon Festival	Monahans
Prickly Pear Pachanga	Sanderson

A bicycle must be operated at a "reasonable speed" in Galveston.

TEXAS TEENS GO HOLLYWOOD

How does Hollywood depict the life of Texas teens and college students? We've got six movies that offer a lot of slackin', a little slashing, and of course—football.

SLACKER

One of the true classics of "Gen X" cinema and the debut film of scruffy Austin-born indie director Richard Linklater, who recently cashed in his indie chips to make the hit comedy *School of Rock*. His *Slacker* is arty all the way; the camera follows various college-age people as they rattle around the college town of Austin in the early 1990s, hanging out with each of them just long enough to give you a taste of their (usually odd) personalities before going on to someone new. Anyone who's spent time in college will recognize personality types they went to school with, and anyone who went to school in Austin will get a kick out the low-rent tour of their college town. But if you demand a plot with your movies, it's best to move along, possibly to the next film on our list.

DAZED AND CONFUSED

Here's Linklater again. He's still meandering, but this time he's also toying with the idea of a plot. It's the '70s, the last night of school for the kids of this Texas town, and the film follows them around as they try to figure out what the heck they're supposed to do with themselves from here. Linklater pegs the personalities of the kids just right—it's *That '70s Show* set in Texas and without a laugh track and a little more smarts. The film is also notable for Matthew McConaughey in one of his first roles, as the skanky 20-something stoner, Wooderson, who delivers the memorable line: "That's what I love about these high school girls, man. I get older, they stay the same age." And you just know that Wooderson is probably doing time at Huntsville right about now.

REALITY BITES

The Gen-X film with a difference—in that it was actually written by a Gen-Xer (Texas-born screenwriter Helen Childress was in college at the time she sold the script). Winona Ryder and Ethan Hawke star as Texans slacking through their first year out of college whose friendly relationship is complicated when Winona falls for a television producer, played by Ben Stiller (who also directs the film). Lots of snappy quasi-ironic dialogue, but the film is smart enough to realize that being sardonic only gets you so far: a key scene has Winona going for a job at a Houston area newspaper, which she doesn't get because she can't define "irony." Check out the excellent soundtrack.

VARSITY BLUES

What would Texas be without high school football? What would people do with themselves on Friday autumn nights? *Varsity Blues* focuses on the troubles of Mox (James Van Der Beek), a high school quarterback who chafes under the rule of his hard-assed coach (Jon Voight), who is gunning for yet another district championship and is not too picky about how to get it. The film reinforces the idea that football players are at the top of the high school food chain (especially in small West Texas towns), but also suggests that there may be something more to life than football.

TEXAS CHAINSAW MASSACRE

You know the drill: teenagers, hitchhikers, creepy house, Leatherface, the killing and the hurting and the screaming and the bloody gore thing. It comes in two flavors: The original, low-budget 1974 splatter-fest, which remains scary and creepy after all these years, and the 2003 version, which is every bit as bloody as the first version but a little more polished and missing that raw feel so omnipresent in the original. Maybe we need a *Massacre 3*: Leatherface of the first version could face off against Leatherface from the remake. *That* Texas match-up might be worth seeing!

THE FAR EAST IN THE SOUTHWEST

When you're in Texas, you're likely to think of chopped beef before you think of chopsticks. But—surprise, surprise—Asian culture is an important part of today's Texas.

CHINATOWN
Houston, Texas

Houston's Chinatown, near Beltway 8 and Bellaire, offers awesome Chinese shopping, dining, art, and even educational courses on topics from kung fu to Cantonese. Everything from street signs to storefront signs are written in Chinese. It's the real thing, folks. Pull $20 out of an ATM and even the statement comes out in Mandarin! Chinese-Americans live all over Houston, where the powerful and prosperous Chinese community is an integral part of the city. In fact, Houston has by far the largest Chinese-American population in Texas and the fourth largest in the nation.

FORBIDDEN GARDENS
Katy, Texas

Located in the Houston suburb of Katy, Forbidden Gardens is a striking outdoor museum that transports you not only to China, but also back in time to 300 BC. It's named for Beijing's original Forbidden City, which was home to the Chinese emperors and "forbidden" to the general populace. Only the royals and their associates were allowed inside for five hundred years. Among the main attractions is a one-third scale, 6,000-piece replica of the original Forbidden City's life-size terra cotta army that was buried with Emperor Qin and discovered by farmers in 1974. You can see a model of the entire Forbidden City and visit the Lodge of the Calming Heart—the replica of what might be called an Imperial Chinese day spa.

One of the few remaining colonies of prairie dogs in the U.S. is at Lubbock, Texas's Mackenzie Park.

KIMBELL ART MUSEUM
Fort Worth, Texas
The classiest spot in Cow Town, the Kimbell Art Museum is just off of Camp Bowie Boulevard. All the big names are here: Rembrandt, Cezanne, Picasso, to name a few. But the museum's Asian art collection takes the rice cake—jars that date back to the Chinese Neolithic period (the Stone Age, beginning around 10,000 BC), a figurine from Japan's Jomon Period (beginning in 10,500 BC), to the more modern Ming bowls and vases, and Tibetan mandalas (highly detailed diagrams used as aids in meditation). All housed in a stunning modern building designed by Louis Kahn, one of the foremost American architects of the twentieth century.

CHUNG MEI BUDDHIST TEMPLE
Stafford, Texas
On the south side of Houston's suburb of Stafford is a real-life living and breathing Texas-sized Buddhist temple. The Fo Guang Shan Chung-Mei Temple was founded in the late 1960s in Taiwan, and today its Houston location works to bring traditional Buddhism into the fast-paced lives of contemporary Texans. With large red-tiled roofs that arch outward and upward, the temple complex includes a library dedicated to Buddhist study, a shrine, a tearoom, and worship centers. In addition to religious instruction, the temple holds classes on vegetarian cooking, yoga, and tai chi.

* * * * *

RECORD SETTING
According to the *Texas Almanac*, the wettest year in Texas was 1941, with a total of 42.6 inches falling that year. The driest year for the entire state was 1917 when a little over 14 inches fell during the year. The most snow Texas has ever had in a season was in 1923–1924 (65 inches!).

Palo Duro Canyon, second only to the Grand Canyon in size, spans at least four geologic ages.

THE BLACK CAT OF TEXAS

Jack Johnson was the first African-American world heavyweight boxing champion. But not that many people know that he was also the first Texan world heavyweight boxing champion—black or white.

Boxing fans knew him as the Black Cat: fast on his feet, quick to strike—and bad luck to any boxer who crossed his path. From 1897 to 1928, Jack Johnson fought in 114 bouts, winning 80 of them, 45 by knockouts. Today's champions and contenders would do well to take a lesson from the fighter who also had to fight racism both in and out of the ring.

BLACK DAYS FOR BOXING

Perhaps in a bid to introduce some gentility to the rough-and-tumble Texas of the day, the state outlawed the sport of boxing in 1891. Luckily, most Texans thought their legislators were being a little overzealous. Locals looked the other way as promoters got sneakier so their boxers could keep boxing and the fans could keep watching them.

Arthur John "Jack" Johnson, born in Galveston on March 31, 1878, was a youngster when the law was passed. No matter. He'd still grow up to be one of the greatest boxers the world had ever seen. With the finesse of a Muhammad Ali and the ferocity of a Mike Tyson, Johnson made a name for himself in the Galveston area dispatching other boxers with remarkable ease.

A FIGHTING CHANCE

In those days, interracial *anything* was rare, including boxing matches. At the beginning, Jack fought mostly other African-Americans. But he wanted to take on *all* comers. He was big, proud, Texan, and exceptionally good at what he did. He wanted the recognition that was his due. What he got was something else.

In 1901 Jack got his first chance to fight a white boxer, one Joe Choynski, "The California Terror." Unfortunately, California beat Texas this time around—Choynski knocked out Johnson in

---

World's largest honky-tonk: Billy Bob's Texas, in Fort Worth, covers 100,000 square feet.

three rounds. After the fight, both men were arrested for "illegal boxing" and placed in jail together. Legend has it that while in jail, Choynski tutored Johnson in some important boxing tricks of the trade. After spending three weeks in jail, Jack decided to get out of Texas and go fight somewhere else. He kept on beating the best black fighters in the business: in 1903 he won the Colored Heavyweight Championship title. But he wanted more.

EYES ON THE PRIZE
In 1908, after chasing then-world champion Tommy Burns across Europe (where Burns was defending his title against all comers, provided they were white), Jack finally landed a title match with Burns. The date and the place were set: December 26, 1908, in Rushcutter's Bay, in Sydney, Australia, timed to coincide with the arrival of the American fleet in Sydney Harbor.

Beginning with a stiff uppercut, Jack quickly knocked Burns down once and then again twice in the first round. To his credit and ultimate misfortune, Burns got up and took a serious beating for nearly thirteen more rounds. During the fourteenth round, afraid that Burns would be killed, the police rushed into the ring and stopped the fight. The crowd was enraged; Jack was jubilant. He was the first black man (and Texan, as we may have mentioned) to hold the heavyweight boxing world championship.

THE GREAT WHITE HOPELESS
After Jack won the title, all the white boxers in the world wanted a piece of him. The term "Great White Hope" was coined to describe Jack's challengers. In 1907 he beat former world champ Bob Fitzsimmons; in 1909 it was the soon-to-be Hollywood actor Victor McLachlan (who had more luck in his later career, winning an Oscar for his performance in *The Informer*).

The fight that drew the most resentment against Johnson was in 1910, when undefeated former champion James J. Jeffries was persuaded out of retirement to deal with the Black Cat. As 22,000 people watched, Jack casually mauled the boxing icon for fifteen rounds before knocking him out. The outcome of the match sparked race riots that left twelve blacks dead. Several states banned showing films of the fight, and others extended the ban to include any fight in which Jack defeated a white boxer.

Up to 6,000 folks can cut loose in the Texas-size hall, or quench a thirst at any of the 40 bars.

A KINDER, GENTLER CAT
The tabloids of the day reported in detail on the way Johnson systematically beat up on his opponents, and how he stepped up the attack if an opponent happened to hurt him. For his part, Jack taunted the press, even admitting that he went easier on his black opponents. The media ate it up and reported every word.

NINE LIVES AND THEN SOME
Winning that heavyweight title in the first place opened America's racial wound; Johnson's behavior outside the ring rubbed salt in it. Between 1911 and 1924 he married three times, always to white women. He wore flashy clothes, drove fast cars, and had a mouth as big as Texas. Of course, all of this got him into the kind of bout he couldn't win.

In 1912 he took his fiancée for a vacation and just happened to cross a state line with her. He was quickly convicted on a trumped-up charge under the Mann Act (which forbids the transportation of women from one state to another for immoral purposes) and sentenced to a year in prison. Out on appeal, Jack fled the U.S. and continued to box mostly in Cuba and Mexico. He lost his title to a Great White Hope named Jess Willard in Havana in 1915. In 1920 he turned himself in to the law. After a year in Leavenworth, he was back in the ring.

THE LAST ROUND
Jack didn't hang up his gloves until he was sixty. He died eight years later in a car crash.

Jack is still ranked as one of the best boxers to ever put on the gloves. His big personality both inside and outside the ring guaranteed him a spot in history and his sheer ability made him an athletic legend. Like a true Texan, he came to fight and he came to win; and he did both exceedingly well.

Fort Worth's Stockyards Hotel once counted Bonnie Parker and Clyde Barrow among its guests.

MARFA'S NIGHT-LIGHTS

They've been sparkling mysteriously in the distant Big Bend sky for more than 100 years. But what the heck are they? Headlights? Aliens? Swamp gas? Or just good ol' Texas folklore?

The town of Marfa in southwest Texas was founded in 1881 as a water stop for the Texas and New Orleans Railroad. Today, the residents of the large ranges in the surrounding mountains visit little Marfa to stock up on supplies. But Marfa is better known for its mystery lights than its trading post.

BRIGHT LIGHTS, LITTLE CITY

Marfa's mystery lights put on a show for locals and tourists just about every night. Glowing orbs of yellow, red, green, but mostly white, dance across the sky, twist and turn and tumble, or just hover, flicker, and fade. They're erratic and fascinating—and there's no generally accepted explanation for their existence.

Most nights at dusk, people will drive about nine miles east of Marfa to the official viewing spot, pull up some lawn chairs, maybe pop open a beer or two, wait, and watch. If they're lucky, they'll spot the swirling lights off in the distance toward the Chinati Mountains, a good sixty miles to the southwest.

HISTORY OF THE MYSTERY

The first recorded sighting of the Marfa Lights was in 1883 when settler Robert Ellison and his wife spotted a strange glow during their second night in the area. Ellison thought it was the campfire of hostile Apaches, but discounted the idea when others told him they'd been seeing the lights for years.

Marfa served as a backdrop for filmmaker George Stevens's film *Giant*, the 1956 epic tale that starred Elizabeth Taylor, Rock Hudson, and James Dean. During the filming, even the movie stars fell under the spell of the Marfa Lights. James Dean was said to spend his evenings with his eyes glued to a telescope aimed at them.

Sea level is the lowest recorded elevation in Texas.

YOU LOOK "MARFA"LOUS . . .

Any number of explanations have been suggested. Some of the locals call them ghost lights, believing they're the spirit of Apache chief Alsalte, who's been haunting the mountains since his execution at the hands of the Rurales (the dreaded Mexican "rural police," a paramilitary group made up of ex-bandits) in the 1860s. Another legend is that the lights could lead to buried golden treasure, perhaps left there by Pancho Villa.

An old legend blames the lights on *brujas*, Mexican witches, who are having trouble learning how to pilot their brooms: when they twist and turn, they lose control and crash into mountains. Another theory is that the Marfa Lights are the ghosts of World War II bomber pilots who died during training in the area. And leave us not forget the inevitable UFO tie-in: the navigational lights of a flying saucer.

UP CLOSE AND PERSONAL

A twist on the legend is the reported "friendliness" of the lights. One famous account tells of a man who says the lights saved him from a blizzard by leading him to a cave to wait out the storm. Marfa Mayor Fritz Kahl swears years ago that he and a buddy were followed by a playful, basket-shaped light that almost dared them to chase it. Another story tells of a small airplane being surrounded by the lights. Other planes supposedly have tried to chase the lights only to have them disappear.

THE USUAL AND UNUSUAL SUSPECTS

Over the years, all kinds of semiplausible explanations have been offered for the sparkles in the night, but none have stuck. The most outrageous "scientific" theory is that the lights are jackrabbits with fur covered in glowworms. The less imaginative think it's swamp gas, glittery minerals in the ground, an electrostatic discharge, or—the most likely—a mirage caused when cold and warm layers of air collide and bend light so that it appears from a distance, but not up close.

A more mundane explanation is that the mysterious glowing orbs are just headlights from cars on highway 67, which runs between Marfa and the mountains. This reasoning fails to explain

---

At the Strand, Galveston's wharfside business zone, you can see the yacht that was once Mussolini's.

what the Apaches were looking at during the nineteenth century. There's a long-standing joke in Marfa that each of the 2,100 or so residents takes a turn at night, drives to the Chinati mountains, and turns on a few flashlights to entertain the tourists.

COME MARVEL AT MARFA

If you want to visit Marfa, consider Labor Day weekend when the annual Marfa Lights Festival is in full swing, featuring a street dance, local cuisine and crafts, plus a big main street parade. After you've eaten and drunk your fill at the fair, you can head up to the new (as of 2002) Marfa Mystery Lights Viewing Center. Located on eight acres, the center has a viewing deck, information on the Marfa Mystery Lights and local flora and fauna, and—Uncle John's favorite addition—renovated restrooms.

* * * * *

INSIDE OUT AND UPSIDE DOWN

Get inverted with these Texas roller coasters.

GREAT WHITE

Location: SeaWorld, San Antonio
Texas's first steel inverted roller coaster, this baby reaches speeds of almost 50 mph. First, the Great White drops 81 feet down and then goes upside down five times—two loops, two corkscrews, and Zero-G roll.

BOOMERANG

Location: Six Flags Fiesta Texas, San Antonio
Riders go through two inverted loops and a corkscrew at speeds up to 60 mph. But the fun's just begun. After the first time through, the train then climbs to the top of the second lift and the whole process is repeated, backwards.

SERIAL THRILLER

Location: Six Flags Astroworld, Houston
A suspended-looping coaster, the Serial Thriller reaches a top speed of 55 mph while it goes through its five inversions—a sidewinder half-loop, a corkscrew spiral, and a double spin. It's making us dizzy just writing about it.

The chachalaca is a popular turkeylike gamebird. Its hunting season in Texas is Nov. 1–Feb. 29.

WITHOUT A LEG
<u>TO STAND ON</u>

What's a plunge into Texas without a little Santa Anna to liven things up? We delved into Uncle John's Bathroom Reader Plunges into History *to dig up the dirt on Mexican leader Santa Anna. He had more than his share of ups and downs, but his leg—the real star of this story—had a life of its own.*

Antonio Lopez de Santa Anna was president of Mexico in the early 19th century. Actually, he was president more than once. Actually, he was president 11 times between 1833 and 1855. He was even dictator for a while. Between most of his presidencies, he was the most despised man in Mexico.

REMEMBER THE ALAMO?
Yes, we mean that Santa Anna, the one who led the charge on the Alamo and took no prisoners. Back then, Texas wasn't a U.S. state—it was still part of Mexico. In 1836, partly because Santa Anna had abolished the Mexican constitution, the citizens of Texas declared their independence. So General Santa Anna led his sizeable army across the Rio Grande, where he met with surprising resistance from a tiny contingent of Texas soldiers at the Alamo, an old Spanish mission. The general took the Alamo and massacred everyone in sight, so he probably deserved what happened to his leg—both the real one and the fake one.

EL PRESIDENTE
The first time Santa Anna was elected president of Mexico, he didn't even bother—ho-hum—to attend his own inauguration. He left the work of running the government to his vice-president, but when nobody liked the vice-president's reforms, Santa Anna and a group of conspirators pulled off a coup against his own government. Santa Anna took power again, this time, as supreme dictator of Mexico, a position he held from 1834–1836.

SIESTA TIME
Being supreme dictator gave Santa Anna supreme confidence, so during an ensuing battle at San Jacinto, he decided to take a siesta

without bothering to post guards. This pretty much guaranteed a victory to Texas hero Sam Houston and his troops (whose war cry, by the way, was "Remember the Alamo!"). Santa Anna was taken prisoner and delivered to President Andrew Jackson in Washington, where he signed a treaty agreeing to independence for Texas. But when Santa Anna went back home, Mexico repudiated the treaty he'd signed. Santa Anna was branded a traitor and fell into disgrace. But only for a while.

THE FRENCH PASTRY WAR
His next big chance to regain the favor of his people came in 1838, when a French baker in Mexico City sued the Mexican government for damages, claiming that some Mexican soldiers had looted his shop. This small incident led to the "Pastry War," in which Mexico took on the French army. They needed a general, so guess who was elected?

ENTER THE LEG
Santa Anna was only too happy to lead his troops against the French. At Vera Cruz, the general was so badly wounded that his leg had to be amputated from the knee down. Santa Anna milked this wound for every last drop of good press he could squeeze. He organized ceremonies, speeches, and even held a hero's funeral for the severed limb. The leg was buried with high military honors.

FIESTA TIME
Now sporting an artificial leg made out of cork and covered in leather, Santa Anna became president again. But he gave so many parties—mostly in honor of himself—and spent so much money outfitting his own private army that by 1842, he'd run through every peso in the Mexican treasury. He couldn't pay his troops, so they rose up against him. El Presidente headed for the hills—so far into the hills, in fact, that the Mexican people couldn't find him.

ATTACK . . . ON THE LEG
Since they couldn't take out their frustration on Santa Anna himself, they dug up his leg and tossed it around, then finally chopped it up into little pieces and scattered it to the four winds.

GOOD RIDDANCE!
When the Mexican government caught up with Santa Anna a couple of years later, the country was still peeved enough to exile

On view: the famous "Come and Take It" cannon, which fired that first shot.

him to Cuba. In 1846, when the Mexican-American War was about to break out, Santa Anna sensed an opportunity for another comeback. He wrote to U.S. president James Polk, promising to settle things without any further bloodshed. Polk fell for it. And as soon as Santa Anna hit Mexico, he went back on his promise. The general was back in business.

ON THE FRONT LINES
The war was underway. U.S. federal forces led by Captain Robert E. Lee (yes, the same Robert E. Lee who led Confederate forces in the Civil War) were closing in on Santa Anna. While they attacked the Mexican defense from the front, a volunteer force from the state of Illinois circled around to strike from behind.

SANTA ANNA LOSES HIS LEG—AGAIN
Meanwhile, Santa Anna was kicking back. He'd taken off his artificial leg and was about to enjoy a roast chicken dinner when the Illinois Volunteers came charging out of the woods, shouting and shooting. A Mexican cavalry soldier picked up the general and carried him to safety. But in his rush to get away, Santa Anna left his cork leg behind. The Illinois Volunteers ate the chicken and took the leg home as a war souvenir.

"THE LEG I LEFT BEHIND ME"
The American troops made up a song about Santa Anna's leg. (The words can be found among documents at the University of Kansas.) It goes to the tune of "The Girl I Left Behind Me." Here are a couple of verses:

> I am stumpless quite since from the shot
> Of Cerro Gordo peggin',
> I left behind, to pay Gen. Scott,
> My grub, and gave my leg in.
> I dare not turn to view the place
> Lest Yankee foes should find me,
> And mocking shake before my face
> The Leg I Left Behind Me.

Is it always rabbit season in Texas? Yup, there is no closed season for rabbits.

Should Gen. Taylor of my track get scent,
Or Gen. Scott beat up my quarters,
I may as well just be content
To go across the waters.

But should that my fortune be,
Fate has not quite resigned me
For in the museum I will see
The Leg I Left Behind Me

THE REST OF SANTA ANNA

Santa Anna was given one more chance to rule Mexico, this time
as military dictator. But after he sold some property to the
American government—30,000 square miles, now part of southern Arizona and New Mexico—a furious group of Mexican politicians drove him out of office and into exile again. He kept trying
to get back into Mexico, but it wasn't until 1874, when he was
considered too old to cause trouble, that he was allowed to return.
He immediately demanded a government pension for his past
services to the nation. The pension was refused, and Santa Anna
died at the age of 84—poor, nearly blind, and still one-legged.

WHERE IS SANTA ANNA'S LEG?

The wooden leg would seem to be a very valuable commodity. At
various times, the Mexican government, Santa Anna himself, and
the state of Texas tried to get it back from Illinois. In 1942, the
leg became a political issue in the United States. Chicago
Democrats introduced a bill to return it as a sign of friendship to
Mexico. Republicans refused, insisting that "the Democrats don't
have a leg to stand on." You can see the famous leg—if you want
to—today in the Illinois State Military Museum's collection at
Camp Lincoln, in Springfield, Illinois.

It's 814 miles from El Paso to Port Arthur. At 35 cents a mile, you'd be reimbursed $284.90.

MINE, ALL MINE

"A gold mine is a hole in the ground with a liar at the top."—Mark Twain

Some of Texas's most legendary treasures are the lost gold and silver mines that have teased treasure hunters for centuries.

LOST MINE PEAK
Chisos Mountains

The Chisos Mountains stand in southern Brewster County (which is 20 percent bigger than Connecticut—not that we're bragging) in Big Bend National Park. Covered in Douglas fir, maple, and aspen trees the Chisos Mountains' elevation rises to over 7,500 and stretches over 20 miles—plenty of room to hide a gold mine!

The mountains were named after the Chisos nation, and served as a hideout for the Mescalero Apaches, who made their living by staging raids into Mexico. Until the Spanish caught up with them. The legend goes that the Spanish, from their headquarters (and prison labor camp) at the Presidio San Vicente on the south side of the Rio Grande, started silver mining in the Chisos using the Mescaleros as slave labor. Eventually, the Mescaleros rebelled, killing every Spaniard in sight. Some say their ghosts still can be seen floating among the rocks.

The Spanish officially abandoned the Presidio in 1781 and the Mescaleros are said to have permanently sealed the entrance to the mine, as a final "good riddance" to their former enslavers. No one living today knows the exact whereabouts of the entrance, but the ruins of the old Presidio are still standing. The legend also says that if you stand at the Presidio entrance on Easter morning, you can see the sunlight reflect off the entrance to the lost mine. But from there, you still have to walk to it. (Sigh.) Getting rich quick has never been easy.

The state of Texas owns the water of every lake and natural stream, and the fish that live there.

THE LOST SUBLETT MINE
Guadalupe Mountains

"Old Ben" Sublett had a formidable case of gold fever and the only cure for him was to move to Odessa, Texas, in the late 1880s. Even though his family was penniless, he spent most of his time away from the hovel they called home to search the Guadalupe Mountains for gold. Old Ben scoured its 80,000 acres looking for the big strike that would make him rich. His family and friends begged him to stop this foolishness and get a real job, but did he listen?

One day, Ben—dressed in his usual oily rags—walked into Abe Williams's saloon and offered to buy everyone in the bar a drink. The patrons snorted and laughed, until Old Ben whipped out a big hunk of the purest gold anyone ever laid eyes on! A local appraiser said it was so pure that "a jeweler could just hammer it out from there." Old Ben remarked casually, "I could buy Texas and make a backyard for my children to play in." He finally found gold. But where had it come from, exactly?

Ben stayed as miserly as ever—dressing like a poor old prospector and saving his money like he might not eat the next day. But all through the 1880s and 1890s, Old Ben would disappear for a few days at a time, showing up days later with tens of thousands of dollars' worth of gold. Countless people tried to get the mine's location out of him, follow him, or figure it out somehow—but none ever did. Even his son, who remembers going there as a child, could only describe the site. Sublett wanted it that way, taking the secret of its exact location to his grave. He said simply, "If anyone wants my mine, let him go hunt for it like I did."

* * * * *

TURKEY, TEXAS

Up in the Texas Panhandle, you'll find the town of Turkey. With a population of 494, Turkey isn't a big burg, but attracts large crowds (10–15,000) during the Bob Wills Reunion, held on the last Saturday of April every year. A native son of Turkey, Wills also has a museum to honor him in his hometown. Memorabilia of the "King of Western Swing" and his Texas Playboys includes music, hats, boots, fiddles, and photos.

In LeFors, Texas, it is illegal to take more than three swallows of beer while standing.

GOODNIGHT, MR. GOODNIGHT, WHEREVER YOU ARE

*Cowboy, inventor, pioneer, and cattle baron,
Charlie Goodnight could do it all.*

Charlie Goodnight was the most famous cattleman in the Old West. During his life he did just about every job a man could do on the frontier. He was a cowboy, a Texas Ranger, a frontier scout, and a trailblazer in more ways than one, first opening new paths for settlers and then branching out to create the famous Goodnight-Loving Trail. It's no surprise that this forward-thinking man still lingers in the Texas imagination.

AT HOME ON THE RANGE
Goodnight was born in Illinois in 1836, but he was raised in Texas, near the Brazos River. As a young man he worked cattle and raised his own small herd. In fact, Goodnight was one of the few cattle barons who had actually worked in the saddle as a real cowboy. After the Civil War, he returned to ranching just as the boom years were starting. Texas cowboys drove huge herds of cattle to Kansas to be shipped east, but Goodnight realized there was a good market for beef in Colorado where there was a growing market of mines, forts, and reservations that couldn't be reached by rail lines. Of course, there were also hundreds of miles of badlands and tough Indian nations between central Texas and those hungry Coloradans, which was why no Texan had ever driven cattle up there.

DRIVE 'EM, COWBOY!
In 1866, Goodnight approached old-time cattleman, Oliver Loving, with an idea—what if they drove west across the inhospitable Llano Estacado (Staked Plains) into New Mexico (thus

To be elected in the state of Texas, one must believe in a Supreme Being.

avoiding the Comanche, Kiowa, and Cheyenne), and then struck north for Colorado? Loving thought it was a crazy idea to take a herd into the desertlike Llano, but he agreed to go along anyway. They started with 2,000 cattle and 18 cowboys. It took three days to cross the Llano Estacado, with nary a drop of water to be found. Hundreds of cattle dropped dead from thirst and exhaustion, and then a hundred more died when the herd stampeded to water at the end of the desert. Goodnight reached Colorado with a smaller herd, but nonetheless found a sweet payday at the end of the drive. Goodnight and Loving made more than $12,000 and started using the Goodnight-Loving Trail every year.

In 1867, Loving was shot by Comanches in New Mexico and died from infection. Goodnight was heartbroken, but honored his partner's dying wish to bring his body back to Texas for burial. The Goodnight-Loving trail would continue to be a heavily traveled cattle route from Texas to Colorado. And Goodnight continued to split the profits with Loving's family.

LAND GRAB

Years later, when Goodnight was itching for a new investment, he remembered the unclaimed land in the Texas Panhandle where in his youth he had fought Comanches with the Rangers. No Texan had dared to ranch that land, but the Comanche threat wasn't what it had been—the Comanche had been exiled to reservations by this time. The opportunistic Goodnight moved his herd up there in 1876. The following year, Goodnight teamed up with a wealthy English aristocrat named John Adair; the two bought a lot of land and both made a good amount on the investment. Goodnight's JA Ranch (the initials were Adair's, since he'd financed it) grew to more than a million acres (that's bigger than Rhode Island, not that we're braggin') and his herd numbered over 100,000 head.

Meanwhile Mrs. Charlie Goodnight, former schoolmarm Mary Ann (Molly) Dyer, became doctor, nurse, homemaker, spiritual comforter, sister, and mother to the hands who worked for her husband.

THE WAY TO A COWBOY'S HEART
Much to the delight of his cowboys, Charlie Goodnight invented the chuck wagon for use on cattle drives and roundups, and soon this restaurant on wheels was part of every ranch in the West. Goodnight was one of the first ranchers to use newfangled barbed wire to close off his vast ranges. He was also one of the first to improve his stock by mixing tough longhorns with shorthorn beef cattle. He even crossed cattle and buffalo to get a "cattalo."

GOODNIGHT, CHARLIE
After many years of being one of the most powerful men in the West, Goodnight sold off his land interests to try some new things. He continued to live in Goodnight, Texas, but tried his hand at investing in mining operations in Mexico and producing motion pictures. He died in 1929 at age 93. But he found new fame in the 1980s when Larry McMurty used his life as the model for Captain Woodrow Call in his popular novel, *Lonesome Dove.*

For more on cattle drives, see "Designated Drovers" on page 147.

For more on cattle drives, see "Designated Drovers" on page 147.

* * * * *

CLUB HOUSE

If you make it to Texarkana, be sure to see the Ace of Clubs House, one man's tribute to a lucky card in a poker game. Legend has is that entrepreneur James H. Draughon won a large sum of money when he drew the ace of clubs. To honor the lucky card, Draughon used the money to build his 22-sided house in the shape of that very playing card. When seen from above, the home takes on the shape of the lucky ace. Today the house is a museum and each room is decorated to represent a specific historical time.

BARBECUE BASICS

*For those of you already salivating in worship, here are just
a few ground rules.*

CARNECOPIA

Meat is the reason for the eating. "My father had a saying: 'It's not what you put on the meat, it's what you leave off,'" says Rick Schmidt of the Kreuz Market, a barbecue haven in Lockhart, Texas, where the meat is smokey and sweet.

DRY OR WET?

But, what about sauce? Some Texans, like those at the Kreuz Market, come down on the "dry" side of the "dry or wet?" barbecue question, meaning that meat is cooking so that it has a crust and is tender, but firm. But you'll find plenty of tasty variations at other Texas BBQ joints.

HOW SHALL I SMOKE THEE?

As far as Texan barbecue is concerned, there's only one way to smoke meat, and that's with wood. Several establishments will only use oak, but others use native varieties like pecan, mesquite, and hickory.

SIDE DISHES

You can get your sauce on the side, but often not much else. At Kreuz you can adorn your unsauced "beef clod" (shoulder) with bread or crackers, onion or jalapeno, or a slice of orange cheese—that's it. (And drinks run only to iced tea, beer, and the occasional Big Red soda, quaffed straight from the bottle.) At less orthodox restaurants, beans are usually on hand (almost always pintos), and sometimes potato salad and coleslaw, too. Macaroni and cheese, baked potatoes, and green beans are a bit highfalutin', but not unheard of—however, a green salad? You're in the wrong place!

Stephen Austin is known as the "Father of Texas."

'CUE ORIGINS

The question of from whence 'cue cometh may never be settled. Did Texas BBQ begin with *barbacoa*, the Mexican tradition of cooking meat in deep pits? Did it start with African-American spit-roasting imported from the Deep South? Or did it come from *Mitteleuropa* immigrants who smoked their leftover meats rather than waste them? No matter; it may be a big, delicious mystery, but those who hold Texas as the center of all that is BBQ are probably too busy eating to care!

For more on Texas barbecue, see "Hidden Barbecue Hot-Spots" on page 88 and "Food Feud" on page 232.

* * * * *

SOME PIG

Everyone knows the UT mascot is the longhorn, but did you know that the first University mascot was a dog named Pig? Yup, Pig came to campus in 1914 as the pet of the University's athletic director, Theo Bellmont. The tan-and-white mixed breed was named for Longhorn football center Gus "Pig" Dittmar. Pig had free run of the campus, attended classes with students, and sat on the sidelines of every football game, both home and away. Rumor has it that he would even growl at the mention of Texas A&M.

Sadly in 1923, a car struck Pig and severely injured him. He died a few days later. The University mourned the loss of their faithful friend and held a full funeral for him. His casket was decorated with orange and white ribbons; the Longhorn band led the funeral procession. The founder and then-dean of the College of Engineering delivered Pig's eulogy: "I do not know if there is a haven of rest to which good dogs go, but I know Pig will take his place by the side of the great dogs of the earth."

Today you can visit the Pig Bellmont Tree on the UT campus. A plaque has been placed there to mark the spot where he is buried. His epithet? "Pig's Dead . . . Dog Gone."

The first word spoken from the moon on July 20, 1969 was "Houston."

THE OTHER TEXANS

We dug up this little beauty from Uncle John's Supremely Satisfying
Bathroom Reader. *Texas politicians have quite a flair for the English
language. Read on for more fun from the Lone Star state.*

"It just makes good sense to put all your eggs in one basket."
—Rep. Joe Salem, *on an amendment requiring all revenues to go into
the state treasury*

"I want to thank each and every one of you for having extin-
guished yourselves this session."—Speaker Gib Lewis

"Lemme give ya' a hypothetic."—Rep. Renal Rosson

"Well, there never was a Bible in the room."
—Gov. Bill Clements, *on repeatedly lying about the SMU
football scandal*

"I am filled with humidity."—Speaker Gib Lewis

"It's the sediment of the House that we adjourn."
—Speaker Wayne Clayton

"This is unparalyzed in the state's history."—Speaker Gib Lewis

"Oh good. Now he'll be bi-ignorant."
—Ag. Commissioner Jim Hightower, *when told that Gov. Bill
Clements was studying Spanish*

"Let's do this in one foul sweep."—Speaker Wayne Clayton

"There's a lot of uncertainty that's not clear in my mind."
—Speaker Gib Lewis

"No thanks, once was enough."
—Gov. Bill Clements, *when asked if he had been born again*

"If it's dangerous to talk to yourself, it's probably even dicier
to listen."—Ag. Commissioner Jim Hightower

The Knights of Pythias building in downtown Fort Worth was the first such temple ever built.

OFFICIAL
<u>TEXAS CAPITALS</u>

If your Texas town is known for something, the Texas Legislature just might take time out of its busy schedule to pass a special Senate Resolution designating it the state capital of whatever. Check out some odd examples of their past handiwork.

ANAHUAC: THE ALLIGATOR CAPITAL OF TEXAS
Officially Capitalized in 1989
Alligators outnumber humans in Anahuac by almost three-to-one. It should come as no surprise, then, that the town is also home to the Texas Gatorfest, a two-day festival held (by the humans) every September in Fort Anahuac Park.

BAIRD: THE ANTIQUE CAPITAL OF TEXAS
Officially Capitalized in 1993
Twenty miles east of Abilene, dozens of antique malls and over 100 antique dealers make it easier to buy a grandfather clock than a double decaf latte at Starbucks. The town is named for Matthew Baird, the railroad director who drove the first stake on the Texas and Pacific Railroad in 1875.

BRECKENRIDGE: THE MURAL CAPITAL OF TEXAS
Officially Capitalized in 2001
An artist named Billy Ines painted the striking black-and-white murals that line Main Street. Inspired by the art of photographer and true Texas eccentric, Basil Clemons, these murals depict proud moments in town history from the days of the oil boom to a tribute to the Breckenridge championship football teams, called "The Spirit of the Buckaroos."

BROWNSVILLE: THE CHESS CAPITAL OF TEXAS
Officially Capitalized in 2003
In addition to being the southernmost city in Texas, Brownsville has the splendid honor of being Chess Capital because of local

---

Texas's Colorado River is not the same river as the one in Colorado, Utah, and Texas.

educators' and students' dedication to the game. Brownsville schools have won 16 state chess championships since 1988.

CALDWELL: THE KOLACHE CAPITAL OF TEXAS
Officially Capitalized in 1989
New Yorkers call it a "Danish" and Midwesterners call it a "sweet roll," but the kolache is important for this reason: it's the only Czech word that Texans have ever heard of. Caldwell's fantabulous annual Kolache festival has been discouraging other, less-ambitious, Texas towns from petitioning for Donut Capital status for over a decade now.

ELGIN: THE SAUSAGE CAPITAL OF TEXAS
Officially Capitalized in 1995
According to the Texas legislature, "In any given week, 65,000 pounds of sausage are produced by Elgin's three sausage plants, who together represent 188 years of sausage-producing experience." Locals are a little less than poetic; they refer to the sausages as "hot guts." No official word from the Senate on pending Cholesterol Capital title.

FREDERICKSBURG: THE POLKA CAPITAL OF TEXAS
Officially Capitalized in 1993
Not surprising. The town was named after Prince Frederick of Prussia, colonized by Germans, and designed like a village on the German Rhine River.

GATESVILLE: THE SPUR CAPITAL OF TEXAS
Officially Capitalized in 2001
Gatesville's Coryell Museum and Historical Center houses the largest assortment of antique spurs in the world. The Lloyd and Madge Mitchell collection owes its humble origins to a journey to Yellowstone National Park, where Lloyd Mitchell first found a single spur and has been looking for its match ever since.

GLEN ROSE: THE DINOSAUR CAPITAL OF TEXAS
Officially Capitalized in 1997
According to the Texas Parks and Wildlife Department, nearby

The Colorado River in Texas starts and ends within the state.

Dinosaur Valley State Park contains some of the best-preserved dinosaur tracks in the world. You can also see two fiberglass models of terrible Texas lizards: a 70-foot-tall apatosaurus and a 45-foot-tall tyrannosaurus rex.

HAWKINS: THE PANCAKE CAPITAL OF TEXAS
Officially Capitalized in 1995
The state legislature named Hawkins the Pancake Capital in honor of local resident Lillian Richard, born in 1893, who "worked for 37 years to promote the pancake industry for the Quaker Oats company." You might recognize Lillian as the face on the Aunt Jemima pancake syrup bottle.

HEARNE: THE SUNFLOWER CAPITAL OF TEXAS
Officially Capitalized in 1997
According to the Texas legislature, Hearne's glorious sunflowers' "display of color mirrors the positive attitude of the citizens of Hearne." You can catch these big beauties from late spring through autumn. In 2000, Texas production of sunflowers totaled 35 million pounds.

HUTTO: THE HIPPO CAPITAL OF TEXAS
Officially Capitalized in 2003
Uncle John's research team found no actual live hippos in Hutto, but legend has it that Hutto adopted the beast as its mascot back in 1915 when a hippo escaped from a circus train that had stopped in town. The city council has also decided that during its annual Olde Tyme Days festival held on the third weekend in October, Hutto can be officially called "Hippo."

ODESSA: THE JACKRABBIT-ROPING CAPITAL OF TEXAS
Officially Capitalized in 2001
It started as a publicity stunt at the Odessa Rodeo in 1932, and its participants have been rapidly multiplying ever since. The Texas legislature felt that Odessa deserved merit for bringing cowboys and jackrabbits together, even under such ridiculous circumstances: "two icons of the West . . . both of whom evoked the hardiness and adaptability required of all who made this rugged land their home."

STATE TREE AND STATE HEALTH NUT: THE PECAN

Chapter 97 (Senate Bill No. 317), 36th Legislature, Regular Session (1919)

Senate Concurrent Resolution No. 2, 77th Legislature, Regular Session (2001)

The Lone Star State produces more native pecans than any other state and ranks second only to Georgia when it comes to the orchard-grown variety. Many of today's trees are about 150 years old, but ancient fossilized pecans dating back to prehistoric times have also been found lying about in the Lone Star State. The word "pecan" is the Algonquin word, fittingly enough, for "hard-shelled nut."

WILD AND NUTTY
Wild pecan trees grow all over Texas, mostly near rivers and creeks. They normally reach 100 feet in height, but some have topped 150 feet with massive trunks that measure more than three feet across. The wood of the larger trees are used in furniture, flooring, and even baseball bats, and their shells are used as filler in plastic and veneer manufacturing.

AWWWWW, NUTS
But it's the nut that carries the biggest bang for the Texas buck. When the Lone Star State started exporting these nuggets in the mid-1800s, no one realized the pecan's real value; the trees were cut down and replaced with cotton. Finally, in 1910, Texas pecan production began in earnest when over five million pounds of the nut were harvested. In 1919, Senate Bill No. 317 recognized the pecan tree as the official state tree of Texas.

By 1945, there were over three million pecan trees Texas. The prosperous pecan was officially named Texas's state health nut in 2001.

Texas's 26 bonded wineries produce over a million gallons of wine per year.

IT'S OIL IN THE
WAY YOU SAY IT

*A glossary of oilfield slang, so if you're ever invited to the Petroleum
Club at any of its Texas locations, you can pretend to know what
they're talking about. (Don't forget: dinner is "Coat and Tie."
And "Ladies, please use your usual good taste!")*

Boll weevil
An oil field newbie. Experienced hands love to give the boll weevil a hard time—and the worst unskilled jobs.

Blowout
An uncontrollable eruption of reservoir fluids—oil, water, etc.—into the well and up to the surface, caused by natural gas. You'd think this was a good thing, but it's both dangerous and expensive.

Bulldog
A tool used to fetch broken pipe out of the hole. In a modern well, you don't have a solid drill like the kind you have in the tool shed. The drill bit is followed by lengths of pipe that control the flow of product and drill better.

Bullhead
To force fluids down the hole and back into the formation; often so that toxic gas doesn't reach the surface.

Christmas Tree
A vertical setup of valves, fittings, spools, gauges, and chokes that sits on the top of the well and controls fluids or production—it's tall and cluttery like a Christmas tree and often even painted green, hence the name.

Doghouse
A little shack at the drill site that typically doubles as an office, supply closet, and place to hang provocative calendars of girls in bikinis holding oilfield tools.

Doodlebug
A person or device (like a divining rod) supposedly able to sniff out oil, gas, or precious minerals—but without any apparent scientific method and more than a little guesswork. The term, and the methods, are rarely used today. (These days, "doodlebugger" is slang for a seismologist performing seismic field work.)

Dry hole
Just that. A well with no oil or gas in it whatsoever. Also known as a "duster."

Fracing
Pronounced "fracking," as in fracturing, this is a kind of "stimulation" that forces bigger openings in underground rock, using things like hydraulics, to get more oil and gas out of the ground.

Monkeyboard
The small oil rig platform a derrick hand stands on when handling pipe.

Mousehole
A hole in the rig floor through which drilling pipe is fed.

Pebble pup
The field geologist's assistant. Also a kid who collects rocks.

Rockhound
A field geologist. At one time, a rockhound would get out on the rig and tell you where to drill; now he or she most often sits in a Star Treklike room in Houston and tells people in seven countries where to drill at once.

Roughneck
Any member of a drilling crew, and sometimes a low-ranking one. Tough people who do hard, semiskilled labor for Herculean hours. Can also be a verb: "I roughnecked when I was a kid; wouldn't want to do that again."

Roustabout
Unskilled labor hired to make sure that the skilled hands on a rig aren't distracted by menial tasks. No fun, but a good entry into the drilling crew if you prove your salt.

Softline
Any rope not made of steel, such as nylon, cotton, or hemp.

Spud
Not a noun meaning "tater," but a verb meaning to start the whole drilling business by using the drill bit to go through rock and other material—right on down to your fortune!

Tight holer
An operator who keeps everything about his well a secret. A top-secret well is known as a tight hole.

Wildcatter
An independent oil man who explorers uncharted territory on his own, in parts of the world where nobody really knows what's down there. The opposite of your typical company oilman.

* * * * *

FROGGY GOES A COURTIN'

A young woman was out for a walk when she ran into her fairy godmother, who presented her with a frog. "What's this?" the woman asked. Her fairy godmother replied, "He's an enchanted talking frog."

The frog pipes up and says, "If you kiss me, I'll turn into a Texas oilman." As the frog puckers up, the woman takes a look at him and then puts him in her purse. "Aren't you going to kiss him?" asked her fairy godmother. "No," she replied. "Nowadays, a talking frog is worth a lot more than a Texas oilman."

BIG TEX

*Who wears size 70 cowboy boots and a 75-gallon cowboy hat?
The most famous cowboy in all of Texas.*

Tall, lanky, and friendly, Big Tex is the official greeter at the Texas State Fair and a symbol of all that is Texan. But he wasn't always lanky and clean-shaven—and he used to wear a red hat with a white pom-pom on it.

WHEN YOUR SANTAS GROW UP TO BE COWBOYS

The town of Kerens, in Navarro County, wanted to find a way to keep the locals in town to do their early Christmas shopping, so they built themselves a Santa Claus, almost 50 feet tall, to draw attention to the in-town retail stores.

Well, when R. L. Thornton, president of the State Fair of Texas, first laid eyes on this Santa, he had a vision. He wanted to start his own legend. So he bought the Santa components and used them to create a symbol of his state fair—the biggest cowboy in Texas.

With the help of an extremely talented crew, after about two years of labor Mr. Thornton gave birth to a 52-foot cowboy. Santa had been transformed into "Big Tex" by Charles Noland and a crew of seven people who used 4,200 steel rods for the body and papier-mâché for the head. Once Tex had been assembled, it took a crane to stand him upright to start greeting his first admirers— the attendees of the 1952 Texas State Fair.

SIZE MATTERS

The big Texan weighs 600 pounds, his 5-foot-tall hat is so big that you could pour 75 gallons of milk into it, and the Williamson-Dickie shirt that stretches across his 32-foot chest has a neckline of 100 inches and sleeves that measure 181 inches long. To possibly make it easier to picture this shirt in your mind, it's 600 times bigger than an average men's shirt. Every time it needs mending, it takes 8 people and 2 weeks to sew it perfectly. Then there's his belt, which could wrap around a smallish human being about 20

That doesn't seem to stop anyone. (Liquor stores are never very far.)

times; the buckle alone weighs 50 pounds. His pant size is 284 (inches) wide and 185 long.

And let's not forget about the famous boots—they're size 70 and taller than you, at approximately 7 feet tall.

MY STATUE CAN BEAT UP YOUR STATUE
Another upstart cowboy statue, one "Tex Randall" by name, has claimed to be the biggest Texan in the world, but Big Tex has him beat by far! Tex Randall has lived in the peaceful town of Canyon, Texas, since 1959. Like the original Santa, he was built to promote local shopping. His claim to be "Texas' biggest Texan" is hogwash. He only stands at 47 feet; Big Tex has him beat by 5 feet.

HE HAD US AT "HOWDY"
During the first year of his life, Big Tex was the tall, silent type. He stood on the fairgrounds and never said a word. But in 1953, Big Tex was heard to utter his first "Howdy" and he hasn't stopped talking since. Every hour on the hour, Big Tex welcomes everyone to the fair with a famous "Howdy, folks."

These days, he also tells fairgoers about what's going on at the fair that day, what kinds of shows there are, and when to catch them. Fans can even talk to Tex on the phone.

Like most aging celebrities, Big Tex has had a little work done to keep up his good looks. He's had numerous reconstructive surgeries over the years, especially on his eyes, nose, and teeth. But of all his improvements, the most dramatic change is Tex's ability to move. In the year 2000, Big Tex was able to actually wave to the millions of fairgoers for the first time. (Which sounds a little scary, doesn't it? Hope they don't teach him to walk.)

Lubbock, Texas, is known as "Hub City" because so many major highways meet there.

AIDS COMES TO TEXAS

Mark Spaeth had it all: good looks, money, a bright political future, and a TV-star wife. But he's remembered for something a lot less pleasant.

Mark Spaeth spent his life chasing the American dream. His father had come to the U.S. from Germany in the early 1930s to build the world's largest pipe organ for the Atlantic City, NJ, convention center and stayed to avoid Hitler's regime. He met and married the daughter of another German immigrant, after which the industrious Spaeths moved to Florida—where Mark was born—and started buying houses, fixing them up, and selling them at a profit.

THE FAMILY BUSINESS

Mark followed his parents' example. Even as a child he'd find little ways to make money—like renting out his mom's dusty lawn chairs to parade viewers in his hometown; at 16, he started in the real estate business. He dropped out of high school to join the Coast Guard (briefly), then worked as a desk clerk. Listening to the stories of traveling salesman made him realize that his true calling was his family's business after all. He went back into real estate sales, did a stint as a department store Santa on the side, and washed up in Austin.

Spaeth arrived in Texas in 1971 with $35,000, which by the mid-1980s he'd parlayed into more than $3.5 million in real estate holdings. This guy could charm the paint off the walls. He smooth-talked his new landlady into hiring him to sell her real estate holdings and he was off and running, plucking up and reselling prime real estate in the ritzy Tarrytown area, and worming his way into Austin high society.

LUCKY IN POLITICS

It took a couple of strokes of luck to spark Mark Spaeth's political career. An Austin city councilman lost his seat after he was arrested for shooting a gun inside the city limits (the councilman had fired at a garden hose that he thought was a snake, and when police arrived, they found cocaine in his house). It was the end of one political career, but opportunity of a lifetime for Spaeth.

The forty-something Spaeth was a dead ringer for Burt Reynolds, but his conservative Republican politics made him dead wrong for liberal Democratic Austin, plus he was a virtual unknown. But he had a patter that could sell ice cubes to Eskimos—and plenty of money—so in 1983 he decided to enter the race for City Council.

His $200,000 media campaign was greatly enhanced at no extra charge when his main opponent's campaign manager, as a prank, sent $50 in pizzas to Spaeth's headquarters, and then had Spaeth's phone lines cut. The media gobbled up the story, his opponent was publically shamed, and Spaeth was elected.

LUCKY IN LOVE

But it was Mrs. Mark Spaeth who made the councilman a real star, because she already was one. Amanda Blake, who'd played saloon owner Miss Kitty on *Gunsmoke* (the most popular TV show from 1957 to 1961), was yet another conquest for the ultimate salesman. She suddenly appeared on his arm after the 1983 election. By the next spring, Blake, in a $5,000 gown and holding a single pink rose was married to Spaeth, who was the picture of nattiness in his pinstriped suit.

His star was on the rise: people were talking Spaeth for mayor or even Spaeth for Congress. With Miss Kitty by his side, how could he lose?

NOT SO LUCKY AFTER ALL

Here's how. Unbeknownst to his new bride, Spaeth was deathly ill and getting worse. Rumors of his bisexuality began to circulate as the public began to notice his failing health.

Within months of the marriage, Spaeth was suffering from full-blown AIDS, a new illness that was rocking the gay community nationwide. Austin alone lost more than 1,500 people by the year 2001. Angered by her husband's deception, Blake filed for divorce and flew off to California.

Spaeth died in 1985 of what was initially reported as

pneumonia, but later revealed to be AIDS. Like a Texas version of Rock Hudson's death, Spaeth's passing brought lots of attention to the illness in Texas, including an undue amount of fear. The saddest part of the story is that Amanda Blake, who'd already battled cancer and won, succumbed to AIDS in 1989, the first female celebrity to die of the illness.

FROM REAL ESTATE KING TO REAL ESTATE PARIAH

The final irony came when real estate agents found his home almost impossible to sell because the public feared that AIDS dwelled in the very walls. In the 1980s, knowledge of AIDS and its transmission was limited; all anyone knew for certain was that the condition was fatal. The Texas legislature reflected the panicky feelings of the times and passed a law requiring real estate agents to reveal when someone had died of AIDS in a house.

* * * * *

MAMMOTH FIND

In 2004 a team of Texas A&M University students and the Brazosport Archaeological Society made quite a discovery. In Clute, Texas, they unearthed the first mammoth skull discovered on the Texas Gulf Coast. The remains are estimated to be 38,000 years old.

It all started when a backhoe operator, Joe Kimble, was working in a sand pit in November 2003. He came across a tusk, but the scientific community took little interest at first. When Kimble found another tusk about a week later, people started to take notice. Further excavation revealed more bones, some hair, and the skull.

The skull is believed to have belonged to a Columbian mammoth, a slightly larger and less-hairy cousin to the famous woolly mammoth.

FOOD FEUD

It's brother against sister in this torrid tale of Texas barbecue.

W ith all of this holy writ on barbecue, you'd think any disputes would center on sauce, sides, or smoke source—but no! Feuding families is the stuff of Texas 'cue conflict. Witness the sad tale of the Schmidts, and the tale of a market divided.

Lockhart, Texas, is a quaint town 30 miles south of Austin, the Caldwell County seat, and the legislation-proclaimed "Barbecue Capital of Texas." The original Kreuz Market (pronounced "Krites"), founded in 1900 by German immigrant Charles Kreuz, is one of the oldest in town. In 1948, Edgar "Smitty" Schmidt bought the meat market in 1948 from Alvin Kreuz. For years, the Kreuz Market was "the" place for barbecue. "If Texas is the holy land of barbecue," said the *Austin American-Statesman*, "then the Kreuz Market is its most hallowed shrine, beef shoulder its blessed sacrament."

HOUSES DIVIDED

Sadly, a BBQ war has split the family, pitting brother against sister. When pit master "Smitty" Schmidt of Kreuz Market died in 1990, he left the family business to his son, Rick—but the building that held that business to his daughter, Nina. Nina and Rick had a falling out over the rent in 1997. Rick claims he wanted to buy the building from Nina, and she just wanted to raise the rent.

Sibling rivalry resulted in an all-out war for control of the family business. Fifteen years later, the news is good for everyone: Nina held on to the original place and renamed it "Smitty's" in honor of her father, while Rick moved a couple of miles down the road into an all-new, larger Kreuz Market, laboriously transporting a tub full of burning embers from the original pit.

Competition remains fierce between the siblings. Even all these years later, Rick and Nina rarely speak. But the delicious barbecue tradition lives on in both Smitty's and the Market. Which one is better? Well, you best take your own "BBQ Challenge" to answer that one. Either way, you'll be in for some tasty meat, so everybody wins.

Texas has its own Mardi Gras, 12 days before Ash Wednesday in Galveston and Austin.

ZZ TOP: THE FIVE-SONG BIOGRAPHY

Find out what makes "That little ol' band from Texas" still rock and roll after four decades. In five songs!

Texas rock and boogie doesn't come any more authentic than ZZ Top. These three Texas natives (Guitarist Billy Gibbons from the well-off Houston suburb of Tanglewood, bassist Dusty Hill and drummer Frank Beard from Dallas) dug deep into the twin Texas traditions of rock and blues to come up with a sound that could only come from the Lone Star State—but which has been supple enough to stay in tune with its time over four decades. If you thought ZZ Top was just about long beards, cool cars, and vintage videos, it's time for a reappraisal.

BEFORE ZZ TOP: "99TH FLOOR"

Before ZZ Top became the rock monster it would be in the 1970s and 1980s, at least one member of the Texas trio had already had his first taste of fame. That would be Billy Gibbons, whose pre-ZZ Top band, the Moving Sidewalks, had a regional hit in the bluesy, psychedelic tune "99th Floor" in the late 1960s. Moving Sidewalks parlayed that fame into opening gigs for national bands that included The Doors and the Jimi Hendrix Experience. These artists came away wowed by the young Gibbons' fretwork; Jimi Hendrix declared on *The Tonight Show* that Gibbons was one of his favorite guitarists.

Moving Sidewalks busted up when some of Gibbons's band mates were drafted for service in the Vietnam War; the silver lining was that this allowed Gibbons to join with Dusty Hill and Frank Beard (themselves refugees from another Texas band, American Blues) to form a blues-rock trio which became ZZ Top—named after (depending on whose story you believe) two brands of cigarette papers, blues musician Z. Z. Hill, or a quickly glimpsed advertising sign.

Marfa, Texas, the second-highest town in the state, is a mecca for glider pilots.

EARLY CAREER:
"SOMEBODY ELSE HAS BEEN SHAKING YOUR TREE"

One of the remarkable things about ZZ Top has been the band's musical consistency: despite occasional nods to changing musical fashions, the band's core musical statement has almost always been the same: hard-driving rock saturated by Gibbons's Texas blues axe-work. As Gibbons told *Rolling Stone* in 2003, about the band's then-upcoming album *Mescalero*, "We've gone in some new directions . . . [but] it's still the same three guys playing the same three chords."

"Somebody Else Has Been Shaking Your Tree," the first song off 1970's cleverly titled *ZZ Top's First Album*, sets the pattern that the band would follow for the rest of its career, with a boot-stomping beat and mud-flecked guitar over raspy vocals belting out double-entendre-laden lyrics. But while the ZZ Top sound was there from the very first track of the very first album, it would take two more albums before the band would experience its first true wave of fame.

THE TOURING YEARS: "LA GRANGE"

That fame would come through the graces of "La Grange," inspired by the John Lee Hooker tune "Boogie Chillen," from the band's third album, *Tres Hombres*. Their popularity brought them the headlining slot at 1974's "Rompin' and Stompin' Barndance and Barbecue," a day-long concert with 80,000 fans that was at the time the largest concert ever held in Austin, Texas—and one of the rowdiest, as the fans totally trashed University of Texas's Memorial Stadium.

With that concert as a springboard, ZZ Top launched the Worldwide Texas Tour, a tour complete with cattle and haystacks that kept the band on the road for a year and a half promoting *Tres Hombres* and its follow-up *Fandango*. The tour made Gibbons, Hill, and Baker wealthy and famous, but it also wore them out; after the tour, the band went into hibernation for three years before releasing its next two albums, *Deguello* and *El Loco*.

I WANT MY MTV: "SHARP DRESSED MAN"

But as successful as ZZ Top had become, their greatest fame was

---

In Lubbock: Buddy Holly's grave is in the Lubbock Cemetery, at the east end of 31st Street.

yet to come through the graces of MTV. For the band's 1983 release, *Eliminator*, the previously TV-shy band hit upon a simple formula for its videos: hot chicks and a cherry red 1933 Ford coupe, repeat as necessary. It didn't hurt that the long-bearded band members (except, ironically, chin-baring drummer Beard) and their muscular American blues-rock were an iconoclastic change from the usual big-haired, mascara-wearing musicians who were MTV's mainstays in the early days. Through its videos for "Legs" and "Sharp Dressed Man," ZZ Top became one of the most popular bands on earth.

This popularity lasted through the next album *Afterburner*, even though by that time the video shtick was beginning to affect the music. When the members of ZZ Top danced their way through the video for "Velcro Fly" (a song that heavily features synthesizers) long-standing fans of that little ol' band from Texas couldn't be blamed for wondering what the heck was going on with their favorite rockers.

ZZ TOP COMES BACK TO EARTH: "MESCALERO"
Time took care of much of their concerns; starting in 1994, with a switch in music labels and the release of *Antenna*, ZZ Top began to swing back toward its original Texas sound but still kept an ear tuned into contemporary tastes. The title track from 2003's *Mescalero* shows where the band is today: the song's got a lot of modern touches, including a chunky, grungy guitar sound and Mexican xylophones, but it's still recognizably the same band who was "shaking the tree" in 1970. Indeed, ZZ Top is one of the longest-lasting bands in rock history, without a single personnel change from its first record through its most recent.

That sort of longevity—and consistency—is its own reward; still it's also nice when someone else notices. Which is why fans celebrated when the band was inducted into the Rock and Roll Hall of Fame in its class of 2004, along with Prince, George Harrison, and Bob Seger. The Texas trio was more than ready for the ceremony. After all, its members are famously "Sharp Dressed Men."

The headstone spelling "Buddy Holley" preserves the singer's birth name.

YET ANOTHER WHITE MEAT

Rattlers, rattlers everywhere! What's a Texan to do?

Throughout the state, resourceful Texans have devised numerous events that capitalize on the public's fascination with rattlesnakes. There are festivals, safaris, roundups, and competitions. Many of these events undoubtedly grew out of a need to rid potential real estate developments of the dangerous predators. But now they've grown into big business.

AN ENDLESS SOURCE OF AMUSEMENT

The Sweetwater Rattlesnake Roundup, introduced in 1958, is billed as the world's largest. It features parades, demonstrations, and a cook-off. The Sweetwater Jaycees, who sponsor the event, estimate that 123 tons of western diamondbacks have been rounded up so far. This translates to about 20,000 snakes per year.

The Jaycees of Taylor, Texas, also host an annual rattlesnake event. The main attraction here is a contest to see who can bag the most live rattlesnakes in a given amount of time. The rules include a penalty for harming the snakes. And there's a five-second penalty for being bitten!

The town of Freer holds an annual rattlesnake roundup that features a contest to see who can capture the longest, heaviest, and shortest of the "critters." According to their publicity, the festival includes stagecoach rides, a carnival, a petting zoo (we kid you not!), and an appearance by Miss Texas. Freer even boasts the "World's Largest Rattlesnake" (not a real one) guarding the entrance to its chamber of commerce building.

Not to be outdone in the whimsy category, San Patricio, Texas holds annual World Championship Rattlesnake Races every year on St. Patrick's Day to commemorate the anniversary of the snakes being driven out of Ireland. Competitors "thump" the ground near their snakes to make them move along marked lanes. Contestants are invited to bring their own rattlers, but you can rent one for $20.

ON THE OTHER HAND

The Humane Society of the United States (HSUS) has called for a halt to the staging of rattlesnake roundups. Citing the Freer roundup specifically, the society criticizes the roundups for the treatment of the snakes. Because these events tend to be attended by families, the HSUS maintains that roundups teach youngsters a flagrant disregard for living creatures. Not only do these shows expose the public to the risk of venomous snake bites, but killing rattlesnakes in such great numbers threatens the ecological balance of the areas; rattlesnakes prey on rodents and other disease-carrying pests. Disrupting the ecosystem could have dangerous repercussions.

In their defense, the roundup promoters claim they're performing a valuable service in milking captured snakes for their venom, from which antivenin, the antitoxin to the rattlesnake venom, can be produced. But the Humane Society points out that the venom is seldom acquired under sterile conditions and is therefore unusable for pharmaceutical purposes. These demonstrations, the society asserts, are only meant for entertainment, not for scientific benefit. No kiddin'.

WHAT DOES HE DO FOR AN ENCORE?

A popular performer at many roundups and festivals is Jackie Bibby, who calls himself "The Texas Snakeman." According to his website, he holds four world records:

- National Rattlesnake Sacking Champion: sacking ten rattlesnakes in 17.11 seconds
- Bathtub Sitting: Sitting in a bathtub with 75 rattlesnakes
- Sleeping Bag: Getting in a sleeping bag with 109 rattlesnakes
- Rattlesnakes in the Mouth: holding 8 rattlesnakes in his mouth

There is no indication whether he had any competition in these feats—or indeed, what may have happened to any of his rivals.

IF LIFE HANDS YOU A RATTLESNAKE, MAKE CHILI

With tons and tons of rattlesnakes being rounded up every year, it didn't take long for Texans to develop a distinctive cuisine based on rattler meat. Recipes abound for rattlers pan-fried, deep-fried, breaded and fried (is there a pattern here?), roasted, broiled, steamed, or boiled. Some intrepid Texans have been known to eat freshly killed snake gallbladders raw!

But it is with chili, that quintessential Texan dish, that rattlesnake has made a perfect culinary marriage. There are almost as many rattlesnake chili recipes as there are Texans.

BUT HOW DOES IT TASTE?
You won't be surprised to learn that it tastes a little like chicken (though it's a bit gamier and somewhat stringy). Some folks think it tastes more like pork. And not to worry: there doesn't appear to be any danger from venom in the meat. Just make sure you heed the warnings in most rattlesnake recipes: "Before skinning and gutting the snake, make sure it is dead!"

DEEP FRIED
Texas Agricultural Extension Services of Texas A&M University offers this tasty method for preparing rattlesnake meat:

> Rattlesnake may be cooked in a manner similar to rabbit or chicken. It should be soaked in brine overnight before cooking. It may be fried, baked or served as a stew or soup. It is tasty fried with breadcrumbs.

> Use only large healthy rattlesnakes (3 to 5 pounds live weight preferred). Decapitate with an ax about six inches behind head. Remove the skin and viscera and cut the remaining body sections diagonally into 1-inch steaks. Soak 5 pounds of steak in vinegar for 10 minutes, remove and sprinkle with hot sauce, salt and pepper, and roll in flour. Fry in deep fat. Serve immediately. Serves six.

Now sit back and enjoy your supper. Bon appetit!

KING OF THE ROAD

To Lance Armstrong, cancer was just another opponent to beat.

BORN TO RIDE

Born in Plano, Texas, in 1971, Lance Armstrong spent his childhood without a father. Which turned out not to matter all that much because his mother, Linda Mooneyham, who was only 17 when he was born, was enough mother and father for any child, instilling in her son such valuable qualities as the determination to "make every obstacle an opportunity."

While studying for her college degree, Mom worked two part-time jobs: at the local Kentucky Fried Chicken and at the corner convenience store. Whatever it took, she was going to raise her son right.

THE ROAD ROOKIE

The sport of choice in most Texas towns is football, but Lance liked cycling. He rode his bike everywhere, including 20-mile round-trips for swimming practice. When he got bored he'd ride as far as Dallas (a 40-mile round-trip). And when he got *really* bored he rode all the way to the Texas-Oklahoma border (and called his mom to come pick him up).

IRON BOY

Those swimming lessons came in handy when, at 13, he won the Iron Kids triathlon (cycling, running, and swimming). He turned professional as a triathlete at 16, but soon centered his attention on cycling. By the time he was a senior in high school, he had a Rolodex full of potential cycling sponsors.

UPHILL CLIMB

When he was a senior in high school, he qualified to train with the U.S. Olympic developmental team; the grueling schedule almost cost him his diploma. And qualifying for the 1989 junior world championships in Moscow gave him his first chance to see the world outside Plano, Texas, and the U.S.

After finishing fourteenth at the 1992 Olympics in Barcelona, and finishing last in the 1993 Classico San Sebastian, Armstrong didn't know how strong he would have to be to compete on the world stage. He dug down deep and found the strength and determination to stage an amazing comeback, winning 10 titles in a year, including his first Tour de France stage victory.

Meanwhile, he'd been making a name for himself on the circuit. His aggressive style and healthy ego earned him the name "Toro de Texas," or "Texas Bull." He lived the life of an international cyclist: eight months a year in Europe on the racing circuit, and the rest of the time at home in Austin, away from the glare of publicity.

In 1996 he was the number-one-ranked cyclist in the world. And he was diagnosed with cancer.

HIS WORTHIEST OPPONENT

It was testicular cancer, the most common form of cancer to strike men from ages 15 to 35. But it had spread to his lungs and there were even traces of it in his brain. Told he had only a 20 percent survival rate, Lance underwent two surgeries, one to remove the cancerous testicle, the other to remove what had spread upward to his brain. He put himself on an aggressive form of chemotherapy that wiped him out physically. Determined as ever, Lance kept his mental focus and five months after the diagnosis, he started riding and training again.

He'd treated the cancer like another challenge, as if it were just another competitor who had "picked the wrong guy to mess with." Lance beat the odds and the disease.

THE COMEBACK KID

His complete recovery surprised most people, but his return to cycling astounded the world. He rode and trained like there was no tomorrow. This was his second chance at life and he was not going to pass it up. He rebuilt his strength and by May 1998 he was racing in the Tour de France. With five straight Tour de France victories (1999, 2000, 2001, 2002, and 2003), Lance has shown the world what Texas toughness can do.

Lynn "Nolan" Ryan, baseball's all-time strikeout king, was born Jan. 31, 1947, in Refugio, Texas.

"IT'S NOT ABOUT THE BIKE"

Getting cancer was " . . . the best thing that ever happened to me," Armstrong has said. After lying on what could have been his deathbed, he developed a newfound appreciation for life. He's since become actively involved in the search for a cancer cure; to that end, he's created the Lance Armstrong Foundation.

He's also found time to write two books: *It's Not About the Bike* and *Every Second Counts*. Both deal with his struggles as a cancer survivor and detail the persistence, perseverance, and dedication that helped him beat the odds to become one of the most admired athletes of this era. Lance Armstrong has truly "made every obstacle an opportunity."

* * * * *

FIDDLE DEE DEE

You don't have to go to Tara to enjoy a little *Gone with the Wind*. Scarlett O'Hardy's *Gone with the Wind* Museum in Jefferson, Texas hosts one of the largest private collections of memorabilia related to the epic tale. Bobbie and Randy Hardy, the museum's purveyors, chose historic Jefferson as an ideal site for their collection. You can see rare movie posters, a signed first edition of the novel, a full-scale reproduction of Scarlett's green-velvet-curtain dress, and a pair of original seats from Loew's Grand Theatre in Atlanta, site of *Gone With the Wind's* 1939 world premiere.

Notorious gunslinger John Wesley Hardin was killed in El Paso by John Selman in 1895.

THE SNIPER
IN THE TOWER

*Charles Whitman was an Eagle Scout, an all-American kid,
and a product of his environment.*

He looked like a regular, clean-cut guy. Born in Lake Worth, Florida, in 1941 to a well-off family, Charles Whitman went to Catholic schools, excelled at piano playing and became an Eagle Scout at age 12. But all was not perfect within the family home. His father, called C.A., abused his wife and wasn't much nicer to his kids. Even when Charles was 18, his father continued to beat him for what he saw as transgressions.

GOOD CONDUCT
If anybody needed a new start in life, it was Charles. He enlisted in the Marines in July 1959. He proved himself a model Marine who excelled at following orders and soon earned a good conduct medal, a sharpshooter's badge, and the praise of observers who noted that he was an expert at long-distance shooting, particularly when his targets were moving.

A TASTE OF FREEDOM
When offered the opportunity to study engineering in an officer training program, Whitman enrolled at the University of Texas at Austin. But he was in over his head and struggled with his studies. After years of rigid discipline at home and in the Marines, he didn't quite know what to do with himself. He met his wife Kathleen there and the two married, but that didn't settle him down. He bounced in and out of the university over the next few years; at one point he was ordered back to military service due to poor college grades.

In 1963, Whitman was court-martialed after threatening another soldier to whom he'd loaned money. He was sentenced to 30 days behind bars and 90 days of hard labor, and stripped of his rank as well; he was a lowly private again. Miserable, he turned to his hated father to pull some strings to reduce his enlistment period. His father succeeded, and Charlie was discharged in December 1964.

Multiple Grammy winner Beyonce Knowles was born in Houston on Sept. 4, 1981.

TAKE TWO VALIUM AND CALL ME IN THE MORNING

Charles returned to Austin and tried to get his life back on track with little success. His mother had left his father and moved to Austin to be near her boy. But Charles was depressed and anxious about his inability to live up to his own standards. Kathleen urged him to get professional help. He visited the university's health center in March and gave two clear messages to the attending doctor: he felt like a failure and he despised his father.

He also mentioned fantasizing about "going up on the Tower with a deer rifle and shooting people." The doctor didn't take him seriously and prescribed Valium to calm his nerves.

THE SCENE OF THE CRIME

The University of Texas Tower rises 307 feet into the sky. On evenings after a Longhorn win it's bathed in orange light and can be seen for miles in every direction. Whitman first visited the Tower on July 22, 1966, to stake it out.

Shortly before noon on August 1, Charles Whitman arrived on campus with his old Marine footlocker stuffed with food, water, a radio, and an arsenal of guns and rifles and talked his way into the Tower. On the 28th floor observation deck, he took his place and picked up his scoped 6mm rifle. Within about 90 minutes, he'd killed 14 people and injured 31 more. Almost two hours after he'd had entered the Tower, police officers finally made their way to the deck and shot him dead.

THE NOTE HE WROTE

Later, the police would find that, before going to the Tower, Whitman had killed his mother in her apartment and his wife in their home. He left a note in his home that read, "I truly do not consider the world worth living in, and am prepared to die, and I do not want to leave her to suffer alone in it . . . similar reasons provoked me to take my mother's life also."

NEW AND IMPROVED

The university kept the Tower open for several years and spent $5,000 to repair the bullet holes. But several suicides from the observation deck convinced the school to close it in 1976. The observation deck was reopened in 1999 in a gesture toward restoring the Tower to its rightful place as a positive symbol for Texas. Only now, visitors have to pass through a metal detector to enter.

Eighty-three percent of trees harvested in Texas are pine.

WASTE NOT . . .

Everybody has junk, and getting rid of it can be a challenge.
Meet a few Texans who've found innovative uses for theirs.

ONE MAN'S JUNK IS ANOTHER MAN'S CATHEDRAL

On a quiet street in a suburban neighborhood of Austin, a young man has given form to his unique vision—a shrine to junk—right in his own backyard. His monument to American consumerism has been dubbed a "Cathedral of Junk."

Even though he's become something of a celebrity around Austin, Vince Hannemann, the innovative genius behind the shrine, doesn't take himself too seriously. He doesn't claim any special significance for the work that has consumed decades of his life; what he did, he maintains, he did purely for his own enjoyment.

BUILT TO LAST

It all started in 1988, when Hannemann was in his twenties. He started organizing junk he had lying around his yard into a structure of sorts. The results pleased him, so he just kept adding to it. Before you know it, his neighbors and friends started bringing him some of their own castoffs, and the project took off.

Hannemann's structure contains over an estimated 60 tons of unwanted stuff and now resembles the biggest backyard fort you've ever seen. It consists of three 30-foot-tall towers that are organized into interior spaces and linked by passageways, ladders, and stairs. Hannemann didn't stint on the creature comforts: the cathedral is electrified, replete with clocks, lights, and neon signs. And he didn't ignore safety issues, either. "This has been built to withstand Texas storms," he says proudly.

THERE'S JUNK, AND THERE'S JUNK

So just what kind of junk makes it into the shrine of trash? Not just any old run-of-the-mill junk. Each piece, be it a baby carriage, bicycle wheel, or rusty car bumper, needs to strike his fancy. It must be something with that indefinable quality that only he

---

The Tigua Indians have the smallest of the three Indian reservations in Texas.

recognizes when he sees it. Overall, Hannemann's Cathedral has a very organic feel to it—totally unpredictable and unplanned.

True to its name, the Cathedral served as backdrop to Vince Hannemann's own wedding to Jo Rabern on May 30, 1999. Visitors are welcome every Sunday, free to wander in and explore the Cathedral and its towers.

WHERE DO OLD CADILLACS GO TO DIE?
Texans love their cars. But could one man have gone just a bit too far?

In a bleak desert landscape just outside of Amarillo, an unsuspecting visitor might chance upon a scene that's sure to make him think he's seeing a mirage. How else to explain the sight of ten vintage Cadillac rear ends sticking out of the desert sand? All ten are precisely lined up in a row and half-buried, nose down, with their vintage fins a'waving in the air. Unknowingly, our hypothetical visitor has stumbled upon the Texas Cadillac Ranch.

WHO YOU CALLIN' ECCENTRIC?
The ranch has been a part of the local "cultural scene" since 1974. That was the year that Stanley Marsh III, a helium millionaire (there are such things in Texas) and grandson of Stanley Marsh, an early Texas oil millionaire, assembled a collection of ten classic finned Cadillacs and had them partly buried in a wheat field. A man who literally got rich off hot air, Marsh, with the help of an art collective from San Francisco, put together this installment as a tribute to the "Golden Age" of American automobiles.

To heighten the surrealism of the scene, the cars are covered in graffiti, a distinctly modern touch. Stanley Marsh III seems undisturbed by the somewhat haphazard artistic embellishment. As a result, the exhibit is ever changing. Visitors to the Cadillac Ranch are encouraged, 24 hours a day, seven days a week.

Their 66 acres are in Ysleta, a suburb of El Paso.

O. HENRY'S DAZE IN AUSTIN

*The city of Austin gets credit for transforming
William Sydney Porter into O. Henry the writer—all it took was
putting him behind bars for embezzlement.*

It started with a bad cough that might have been the first sign of tuberculosis. William Sydney Porter was 20 in 1882 and an apprentice pharmacist in his hometown of Greensboro, North Carolina, when a doctor suggested he go to La Salle County, Texas, for a curative: the country air would do him good.

Porter was soon living the cowpoke life, well, actually the sheep-poke life, since those were the critters he helped to raise. In his spare time, he studied the dictionary, looking to improve on the education that formally had ended when he was 15. And the wild tales he soaked up about outlaws and Texas Rangers was fodder for later short stories like the ones in his 1907 collection *The Heart of the West.*

WELCOME TO AUSTIN AND DRINK UP!
Porter moved to Austin in 1884 and worked as a pharmacist, a bookkeeper, clerk, and bank teller. He joined a quartet, and discovered the saloon, where he began a lifelong infatuation with the bottle. (Scotch, to be specific.)

He fell in love with Athol Estes, an artistic high school student, and married her. Athol contracted tuberculosis early in their marriage, and had a baby, Margaret. To support them, Porter started publishing *The Rolling Stone* humor magazine (which had to be considered a hit, with 1,000 readers in the then tiny town of 11,000) but had to pull the plug after only a year because the magazine was losing money.

SPEAKING OF LOSING MONEY . . .
Porter took a $100-a-month job as a teller at the First National Bank, which was known for its shoddy bookkeeping. When bank examiners couldn't account for a missing $4,000, the bank blamed

Porter and fired him, even though the whole matter was likely an accounting error. Porter left his wife and daughter and fled to Houston, where he wrote a column for the local paper, but got antsy when it looked like an embezzlement trial was about to start. He took off again—first to New Orleans, then to Honduras where he hoped to hide out.

MEANWHILE, BACK IN AUSTIN
But Athol's health was deteriorating and Porter's need to be with his ailing wife was stronger than his need to hide from the law. He came home to face the music. Athol died in 1897 and Porter was sentenced to prison a few months later. He left Texas for the federal penitentiary in Columbus, Ohio. And he would never return.

O. HENRY IS BORN
While in jail, Porter published the first of his short stories signed "O. Henry"—*Whistling Dick's Christmas Stocking* (1899)—in *McClure's Magazine*.

There are three possible explanations for the pen name. Some say it honors a friendly prison guard named Orrin Henry; others think it harks back to his single days in Austin living in the Harrell family's guest house and calling out to their cat, "Oh, Henry!" Literary experts suspect it's an abbreviation of the name of a French pharmacist, Etienne-Ossian Henry, the author of a reference work that Porter used when he worked as a prison pharmacist. Whatever the source, by the time of his release three years later, O. Henry was on his way to being famous.

NEW YORK STORIES
O. Henry moved to New York, where he published more than 300 stories and became the country's most recognized short story writer. His most famous stories, "Ransom of Red Chief" and "The Gift of the Magi," relied on irony and surprise endings, which came to be known as "O. Henry endings."

O. Henry drew on his Texas days for inspiration in stories like "The Reformation of Calliope," "The Caballero's Way," and "The Hiding of Black Bill." He briefly remarried, this time to a childhood sweetheart, but she couldn't replace Athol and it ended quickly.

THE O. HENRY ENDING

The lifelong habit he'd picked up in Austin finally did him in; he died of cirrhosis of the liver at 47, with hardly a penny to his name. His last words were reportedly, "Turn up the lights—I don't want to go home in the dark." His daughter, Margaret, died 17 years later and was buried next to her father in Asheville, North Carolina.

AUSTIN REMEMBERS

Back in Texas, they honor the famous author, not the (probably wrongly) convicted embezzler. Two middle schools are named for him—one as O. Henry, the other as William Sydney Porter. And every spring since 1978, people have gathered at Porter's former Austin home, now the O. Henry Museum, to celebrate the man's way with words at the O. Henry Pun-Off, where the common weather forecast is "mostly punny with a chance of blunder."

* * * * *

THE PUBLICATIONS OF O. HENRY

1904	*Cabbages and Kings*
1906	*The Four Million*
1907	*The Trimmed Lamp*
1907	*The Heart of the West*
1908	*The Gentle Grafter*
1908	*The Voice of the City*
1909	*Options*
1909	*Roads of Destiny*
1910	*Strictly Business*
1910	*The Two Women*
1910	*Whirligigs*
1910	*Let Me Feel Your Pulse*
1911	*Sixes and Sevens*
1912	*Rolling Stones*
1917	*Waifs and Strays*

THE SINGING
COWBOY

*Clint Eastwood he was not. But Gene Autry was the
perfect picture of a cowboy in the first half of the 20th century: his
manners were impeccable, he never had a trace of trail dust on him,
and he always got his man.*

Orvon Gene Autry was born in Tioga, Texas, on September 29, 1907, to parents Delbert and Elnora. He grew up with music and even played the saxophone as a kid. He saved up to buy his first guitar (from the Sears Roebuck catalog) when he was twelve.

MR. ROGERS COMES TO VISIT
When he grew up he got a job as a telegraph operator—but he just couldn't keep from singing. When fate walked into the telegraph office one day, in the person of cowboy-humorist Will Rogers, Autry's future was sealed. Rogers told him he should be singing professionally, and that was all young Autry needed to hear. He started singing on a local radio station, and within three years had his own show and made his first recording.

KING OF THE COWBOYS
His popularity blossomed like a Texas bluebonnet. Soon he was starring in his own B-movie Westerns for Republic Pictures. He shot to the top of the popularity polls of Western stars, and in 1940 was voted the fourth biggest box office attraction in all of Hollywood, right behind Mickey Rooney, Clark Gable, and Spencer Tracy. He was one hot cowboy.

His movies were packed with action but short on romance. He never once kissed a girl (on-screen, that is), but had some very cozy scenes with his horse, Champion.

His recordings sold by the millions: "Back in the Saddle Again" (his theme song), "Here Comes Santa Claus," "Frosty the Snowman," and his most famous reindeer . . . oops . . . recording of all, "Rudolph the Red-Nosed Reindeer" (which is the second all-time best-selling Christmas single, after "White Christmas."

Shortest highway: Loop 168 in downtown Tenaha in Shelby County is .074 miles long, or 391 feet.

ANOTHER GUY NAMED ROGERS

Again fate stepped in, this time in the form of World War II.
Autry went off to join the Air Transport Command as a flight officer, and while he was gone a young whippersnapper named Roy
Rogers filled Autry's cowboy boots. By the time our hero got back
home, Republic Pictures and the fickle American public had
crowned Roy Rogers the new "King of the Cowboys."

Like any cowboy worth his salt, Autry was undaunted. He
made a lateral move to Columbia Pictures, and later formed his
own production company. And through it all, he stood fast by his
principles: besides never kissing the girl, his character never
smoked, never drank, and never fired his gun first.

RENAISSANCE COWBOY

When television arrived, Autry was one of the first movie stars to
try his hand at the small screen. *The Gene Autry Show* had a successful run during the 1950s. As a result, Autry is the only entertainer with five stars on Hollywood's Walk of Fame—one each for
radio, recording, movies, television, and live performance.

In addition to his five stars, Autry was inducted into both the
Country Music Hall of Fame and the National Cowboy Hall of
Fame. In 1988, he achieved his greatest dream of all when he
opened the Gene Autry Western Heritage Museum in Los
Angeles, his way of preserving the lifestyle he loved and showcas-
ing the unique contributions of the American West.

TAKING CARE OF BUSINESS

He retired from show biz in 1964, after having made almost a
hundred movies and over 600 records. He invested widely: in real
estate, radio, and television. He'd bought into the California
Angels (now the Anaheim Angels) baseball team in 1960. When
he died, his estimated wealth was over $300 million.

GET CLEAN WITH GENE

Gene Autry lived his life by "The Cowboy Code," a set of rules
that little cowboys and cowgirls learned while huddled up close to
their 7-inch black-and-white TV screens: a real cowboy was always
honest, gentle, and respectful; he worked hard, helped those in
need, and always kept his word. And a real cowboy was a patriot.

It was a tall Texas order, but the original Singing Cowboy sure
filled the bill.

THE TEXAS PHRASE BOOK

Texans have all sorts of colorful ways of describing their neighbors.

About someone who isn't very generous:
"He's tighter than bark on a tree."

About someone who's conceited:
"She thinks the sun comes up just to hear her crow."

About someone you've met briefly:
"We howdied, but we ain't shook yet."

About someone who's "been around":
"This ain't his first rodeo."

About a couple who are "living in sin":
"They ate supper before they said grace."

About someone who isn't very attractive:
"She looks like she been hit with the ugly stick."
"He looks like the dog's been keepin' him under the porch."
"She's nothin' I'd wanna send my saddle over."

About someone who isn't very smart:
"The engine's runnin' but ain't nobody driving."
"He ain't the sharpest crayon in the box."
"She's dumber than a can o' rocks."
"He couldn't pour rain out of a boot with a hole in the toe and directions on the heel."
"Her cornbread ain't quite cooked in the middle."

About somone who's all talk and no action:
"Big hat, no cattle."

About someone who's doing very well:
"He's ridin' the gravy train with biscuit wheels."

About someone who's staggering drunk:
"He couldn't hit a bull in the butt with a banjo."

The Rio Grande separates Texas from Mexico for 1,270 miles

MAKING RAIN ON THE PLAINS

Post, Texas was built by Charles William Post, a 19th-Century Texanized Yankee born in Illinois. But what this real estate developer and the cereal baron (he invented Grape Nuts cereal) hungered for was the power to make it rain.

THE BEST WAY TO START THE DAY

1854-born Charles Post, or "C.W." as he was called, was a highly-strung man. His overwhelming ambition drove him to great fortune, but some say it also drove him crazy. In 1891 at the age of 37, C.W. suffered his second nervous breakdown. For treatment, he traveled all the way from Fort Worth, Texas, to a sanitarium in Battle Creek, Michigan. There he fell under the care of Dr. John Kellogg, future breakfast baron and future Post competitor. The doctor's prognosis was pretty grim. He felt that C.W. was too depressed to recover.

But C.W. did get better. Through his devotion to the idea that good health begins in the stomach, he rallied and eventually created a series of breakfast foods based on this idea. His first three products—Postum (a coffee substitute—C.W. believed coffee to be poisonous!) Grape Nuts cereal, and Post Toasties cereal—were smashing successes and built Post a huge fortune.

Flush with his new cereal dollars, Post decided to pursue a dream and build his own town. He pictured it as a Utopia for self-sufficient, well-nourished farmers. So Post bought some land in West Texas and, little by little, built a growing farm community in the middle of nowhere—complete with an ample supply of breakfast cereal.

RAIN, RAIN, FALL I SAY

What is today Post, Texas, 42 miles southeast of Lubbock, averages only a meager .58 inches of rain in its driest month. C.W. knew that to make a go of his farming community, it would need reliable rainfall; he thought if he could make the skies over Post City rain whenever he wanted, the city would really thrive. At the time it seemed possible.

Number of bridges in the Texas highway system: 30,000.

During C.W.'s life there was a school of thought, dating back centuries, which believed one could make it rain through use of explosives. In an 1871 book called *War and Weather* by Edward Powers, it was observed that it often rained after battles during the Civil War. Similar claims were made on Napoleon's battlefields. In some ambiguous way it seemed to make sense to people, so much so that the government sprung a few thousand bucks for some formal experiments.

General R. G. Dryenforth, an ex-patent attorney and somewhat of a swindler, was the leader in the rainmaking movement. Through a combination of meteorological coincidence and salesmanship, Congress had granted Dryenforth a small budget to blow things up in an attempt to summon up some showers.

Based in Midland, Texas, about 150 miles southwest of Lubbock, Dryenforth managed to convince the nation in 1891 that he could make rain—no longer would Western immigrants eke out dry existences in dusty, unproductive, fields. "They Made It Rain!" read the headline of Denver's *Rocky Mountain News*. *The Washington Post* reported that the science behind it was "exhaustive." But of course, it was a sky full of snake oil. None of these reporters had even bothered to send a correspondent to observe the experiments.

If they had, they'd have seen a series of random explosions, mostly detonated near ground level. The ruse finally came to an end in San Antonio at a major demonstration of the technology. Dryenforth and his buddies, hoping to get more money from Congress, blew things up for days, including trees and the windows of a hotel, with no meteorological result. He and his experiments were ridiculed thereafter and he became known as "Dryhenceforth."

THE POST EXPERIMENTS

But Post remained a Dryenforth believer. And by 1910, when his town was dry and water management had become a hard and hoary problem, he decided to bring out the big guns in the war on drought. Post chose 15 strategic spots around his town, storing an expensive cache of dynamite in each. Each time the humidity reached above 75 percent, he let 'em rip. He'd fire four-pound dynamite charges every four minutes for hours at a time!

Post called these locations his battle stations, and referred to each series of explosions as his battles. He was sure the blasts would force the humid air to higher altitudes, where it would condense into rain. But all he managed to do was scare the prairie dogs, even though he claimed a success rate in 1912 of seven showers for every thirteen tries. It must have helped that his experiments tended to fall in the rainy season, so those numbers don't mean very much. At the end of his venture, he had blown up $50,000 in a vain attempt to rein in Mother Nature. C.W. died in 1914 from unexplained causes. Some say that the pressure to make it rain was just too much for him.

Years later, during World War I, the city leaders of Post were concerned about the 24,000 pounds of dynamite lying around town. They were remnants from Post's battle stations that locals worried that German spies and saboteurs could use to make mischief. So the Post locals decided to blow it all up. And it didn't rain a drop after they did.

* * * * *

CLOSE ENCOUNTERS

The year is 1897, the place Aurora, Texas. A mysterious airship flew over the small town before the craft crashed into a windmill. When townspeople searched the debris, they supposedly found the small body of the pilot who appeared to be "not of this world." A newspaper account in the *Dallas Morning News* reported the incident and that the townsfolk gave the alien pilot a proper burial in the Aurora cemetery.

The story persisted for almost 100 years. In 1973, a team of scientists and UFO buffs went to Aurora to check out the story. Some locals claimed to remember the incident while others insisted that it was all a publicity stunt. The incident still remains a mystery since a district court blocked an effort to exhume the grave where the alien pilot is supposed to lie.

FIT FOR THE KING RANCH

Bigger than a breadbox, and built for raising beef,
the King Ranch is a Texas legend.

The King Ranch, cradle of American cattle ranching, occupies a stretch of south Texas larger than the state of Rhode Island (1,300 miles). From its sheer size, to its ranching innovations, this Kingsville-based agricultural Gotham has earned its place in the handbook of all things Texas-sized.

HOW BIG IS IT?
Today, the King Ranch measures in at 825,000 acres (it used to be bigger, at 1,250,000 acres!) and sprawls into four Texas counties. Founded in 1903, Kingsville is the town that King built, nurtured by the ranch's prosperity and the St. Louis, Brownsville & Mexico Railway. It currently boasts a population of 25,000 people. The Ranch's web site proudly claims that 10,000 rattlesnakes were eliminated to make room for those humans! In spite of running off those rattlers, rumor has it that the King Ranch's brand, the "Running W," may or may not be based on one of these many diamondback rattlesnakes. The brand itself is a distinctive and distinguished design that visitors now love to tote home on items from the King Ranch Museum Gift Shop.

KING'S DOMINION
The King Ranch came to be in 1853, when one Captain Richard King traveled north from Brownsville, Texas, to attend the Lone Star Fair in Corpus Christi. En route, in the midst of the Wild Horse Desert, he found the Santa Gertrudis Creek, the first live water he had seen for over a hundred miles. The mesquite-shaded oasis seemed like the perfect place to found a farm, so King and his partner, Texas Ranger Captain Gideon K. "Legs" Lewis, formed a partnership to purchase the 15,500-acre Mexican land grant called Rincon de Santa Gertrudis.

Graceta de Tejas, the first newspaper in Texas, began publishing in 1813.

King himself didn't move in until 1860, when he brought bride Henrietta, the tough daughter of a Presbyterian minister, to their new home. (She must have been quite a woman; at one point, she stood fast against Union forces that held her, her family, and the Ranch workers hostage while trying to find her husband, an ardent Confederate.) After her husband's death in 1885, Mrs. King doubled the size of the ranch—overseeing its operations even through an 1880s drought so severe it was known as "The Great Die." (Henrietta King herself did not die until 1920; due to disputes among heirs, the Ranch is settled into a series of 10 different trusts.)

ALL IN THE FAMILY
However, the real secret to King's success was figuring out early on that he and his would need help, and plenty of it, in order to get *really* big. After buying all the cattle from a Mexican village and realizing he might have destroyed these people's livelihood, he rode back and invited them all to come work on his ranch. To be one of the "*Kineños*," as descendants of the workers from that village, now in the seventh generation, are known, you must be born, raised, and employed on the King Ranch. *Kineños* live on the ranch, which has its own school district—and a high school at Texas A&M University.

Since the King Ranch is one of America's oldest continuously run family businesses (number 67 on the list), it's no surprise that their workers have formed a family, too. Today, over 150 years after Captain King's founding of the ranch, his family still owns and operates all of it.

MONKEY FATHERS CATTLE?
The King and *Kineño* family trees have long roots, but the Kingsville family tree with the broadest branches belongs to the distinctive red cattle, the *Santa Gertrudis* breed, recognized as "America's Original Beef Breed." The sturdy, hardy, and adaptable breed was the culmination of crossbreeding between Shorthorn, Hereford, and Brahman cattle. The first sire came to be in 1920 when Monkey, the perfect bull calf was born. All of today's Santa Gertrudis cattle trace their beginnings back to Monkey, whose

The word "maverick" came into common use to refer to unbranded cattle in 1845.

sturdy stock has become one of world's leading producers of beef—and more importantly, from a rancher's perspective, one of the world's most efficient producers of beef, as well.

Longer calving seasons for the females, lower birth weights for the calves, ability to withstand arid climates, and calmer dispositions for the bulls that result in better mating means that these steers produced a profit—at first, just for the King Ranch; today, and since 1934, for many other U.S. cattle ranches as well. In 1994, the King Ranch Santa Cruz breed was introduced, as well.

A RENAISSANCE RANCH

While cattle may be the bread and butter of the King Ranch, the owners were wise and diversified their business interests. The King Ranch and its livestock have been involved in any number of agricultural and husbandry innovations, from the early tick-dipping vat to net wire fencing to modern micronutrition studies. With 1,000 registered Santa Gertrudis cattle in breeding, 23,000 commercial cattle, and scores of working horses (the first quarter horse registered by the American Quarter Horse Association was theirs), the whole operation is bigger than what most people can take in—and it's involved in all kinds of other operations, including "Rancher's Renaissance," a group supplying cattle for a beef brand marketed in a major grocery chain.

Besides cattle ranching, the Kings are involved in hunting (the ranch stocks quail, deer, turkey, and Nilgai antelope), citrus production (they own 50 percent of a partnership that controls Minute Maid acreage in Florida), and crops like cotton, sugarcane, and wildflowers. Its primary "exports" to the world include cotton, grain, sugarcane, and sod. Today, the King Ranch remains one of the largest privately held corporations in the United States.

* * * * *

Edna Ferber's novel *Giant* and the movie based on it (which starred James Dean, Elizabeth Taylor, and Rock Hudson) was inspired by the King Ranch.

Assault, the 1946 Triple Crown champion, was a King Ranch-bred racehorse. Over his career, he had eighteen victories.

AHOY, Y'ALL!
IT'S THE TEXAS NAVY!

*"The Texas Navy . . . it is no exaggeration to say that without it . . .
the State of Texas would still be a part of Mexico."*
—Theodore Roosevelt, 1936

Between 1836 and 1845, Texas was an independent nation—complete with its own navy. Still steamed after losing so much land to the Texan up-starts, Mexico loomed as a constant threat to the fledgling Lone Star Republic. If not for the Texas Navy, the Mexican forces could have simply sailed in, seized the land, and removed those trouble-making Texan tenants before the afternoon siesta. A strong naval solution was the answer.

AYE, AYE FOR THE REGULAR GUY

At first, Texas had no ships (a navy must–have). To kick start naval efforts, the Texas government issued "letters of marque," allowing private ships to fight on the Texas government's behalf. So men who normally shipped lumber or fished for red snapper could now spend their time capturing foreign trading vessels stocked with guns or supplies—they even got to keep some of the loot! Unfortunately, Mexico's two biggest sea trade partners were England and the U.S.—both nations' navies kicked sea salt in the face of Texas's puny naval numbers. On many occasions, the do-it-yourself Texans were declared to be pirates by these other nations who engaged them with both court orders and cannon fire.

While the Mexican Navy employed professional naval officers, the Texas Navy had to oftentimes settle for tough Texas frontiersmen. Texas's sailors cut an interesting figure in their wide-brimmed straw hats, red bandanas, and Colt pistols. And they carried cutlass swords just like the sailors of Britain or France. Their grit and guns came in handy for the hard life of fighting, sunburn, scurvy, malaria, lousy food, tropical storms, and the loneliness that comes with months at sea. The work was hard, but the Texans were up to the challenge.

The scene of a cowboy contest in 1883, Pecos today touts itself as "Home of the World's First Rodeo."

FIGHTING DIRTY!

Texas sailors liked to win, and they weren't above a little deception to protect their native land. Once, the Texas ship *Invincible* spotted two Mexican vessels: a warship and a merchant ship whose rudder had been torn loose by a reef. The Texan commander, William Brown, immediately hoisted a U.S. flag. He dressed a sailor in an American uniform and sent him to the Mexican warship to give his best impression of a concerned, clean-cut American. Tricking the Mexican captain into coming aboard the Texan ship, the Texas sailors immediately threw him in the brig and began blasting the Mexican ship into firewood.

On another occasion, a Texan ship had been justifiably seized for smuggling by a Mexican warship. Texan sailors found a tough American captain in port and convinced him that their captured Texan ship was actually American. The enraged American captain fell for it—hook, line, and sinker. He called his ship into action and attacked the Mexican warship, chasing it into harbor and affecting the return of the Texas ship to its crew.

THREE TIMES A NAVY

The Texas Navy tanked completely in 1837, all the ships having been sunk, surrendered, or sold. Another fleet was bought in 1839, but after years of outstanding service, Sam Houston authorized the sale of the second navy in 1843. Over 100 years later, a third Texas Navy was chartered in the 1970s—a nonprofit dedicated to assuring that the rich naval history of Texas is never flushed for good.

* * * * *

TEXAS TOWNS

Bronte (population 1,076) was established in 1887 and named for famed British novelist, Charlotte Bronte.

Flatonia (population 1,344) was founded by the Southern Pacific Railroad in 1873 and named after a pioneer merchant, F. W. Flato.

Katy (population 11,775) was first settled in 1872 and named for the Missouri, Kansas, and Texas Railroad.

Tomball (population 9,089) was named for Thomas H. Ball, a successful Houston lawyer and U.S. Congressman in the early 20th century.

The meteor crater in Odessa is the second largest in the U.S. and sixth largest in the world.

SHOOT ME SOME SUGAR!

Texas is covered with bakeries and candy shops that serve up enough sugar to buy your dentist a Texas-sized Cadillac. So when you've got a hankering for desert, try these Lone Star sweet spots.

COLLIN STREET BAKERY
Corsicana, Texas

The Collin Street Bakery in Corsicana, 50 miles south of Dallas, makes a fruitcake that's actually good. Baker Gus Wiedmann brought the recipe from Wiesbaden, Germany, over 100 years ago, and the Original DeLuxe Fruitcake has been selling solid ever since. Corsicana may be a small town, but its clientele make it world-famous: the fruitcake has been shipped to the likes of Princess Caroline of Monaco, Vanna White, and Madison Square Garden.

THE CHOCOLATE BAR
Houston, Texas

As candy store and ice cream shop, The Chocolate Bar could go head-to-head with the best Belgian and Swiss sweet shops. Don't think brown, prepackaged squares. Think premium blends of chocolate lovingly teased into the shape of chocolate toothbrushes and cell phones, or exotic ice creams such as Orange Sunrise (made from Valencia oranges, rind and all). The culinary wizard behind the bar is Gilbert Johnson. And Candylicious, the store next door, has an impressive collection of retro candy favorites.

BLUE BELL CREAMERY
Brenham, Texas

The Brenham Creamery Company built its business making butter only when it opened in 1907. But by 1911, it was making a couple of gallons of ice cream a day and delivering it by horse and buggy. They've since changed their name to Blue Bell Creamery, but the excellent ice cream hasn't changed a bit. They now get 100,000

Actor-dancer Patrick Swayze (*Ghost, Dirty Dancing*) was born in Houston on Aug. 18, 1952.

takers a year for the creamery's 40-minute tour. Blue Bell sells over 50 flavors, but their Homemade Vanilla is Texas's favorite. Blue Bell is only available in 14 states in the South and Southwest.

TEXAS HERITAGE PROVISIONS COMPANY
Jasper, Texas
The name is nondescript, but you'd be a fool to pass this provisioner by. Jasper pie maker "Texas Charlie" offers autographed pictures of himself—which sounds pretty egotistical, until you taste one of his apple pies. Charlie doesn't even share the recipe with family, but . . . about a dozen apples, secret spices (of course), and enough butter to choke several arteries go into a pie that weighs around six pounds before it's baked. The *Houston Chronicle* noted that one of Charlie's pies "looked like Jiffy Pop popcorn right before the tin foil explodes."

WALKER HONEY COMPANY
Rogers, Texas
For a more natural rush, try some good ol' Texas honey. The Walker Honey Company packages up to 150,000 pounds of honey a year in everything from an 8-ounce jar to a 55-gallon drum. They make 60 percent of their own honey and buy the rest from apiaries around the state. Make a reservation to take a tour, or just drop by to pick up a jar of pecan honey butter. And save some for Uncle John.

SUSIE'S SOUTH FORTY CONFECTIONS
Midland, Texas
According to *The Guinness Book of World Records*, Susie's has the distinction of making the Largest Texas Pecan Toffee (it weighed in at almost 3,000 pounds). Proprietor Susie Hitchcock-Hall rustles up true Texas treats from pecan pralines to fudge to toffee—in beverage form or in nifty Lone Star tins and baskets. And that's not all. Try her Barbaritas—Mexican key lime cookies—or buy some business gifts such as the "Oil Field Trash" Praline Crunch.

SHIRLEY'S BURNT BISCUIT BAKERY
Marathon, Texas
Anyone who's seen the TV show *King of the Hill* knows how
Texans love a good fried pie. And 40 miles north of Big Bend
National Park lives Shirley Rooney, the Fried Pie Queen. Up
before 5 AM every day to start her daily grind, Shirley is as hard
working as she is in demand. The bakery is an adorable little old
place, and her pies have been praised by every major publication
in Texas worth its HDL.

MARTA'S DESSERTS
Austin, Texas
With $150 and her mother's killer recipe for homemade flan,
Marta Guzman started a flan business in 1988 from her home. Her
flan was soon in huge demand, and not just the traditional vanilla
flavor; Marta laces her flan with exotic flavors like coconut,
pumpkin, or coffee liqueur. Now she's much more than flan; she
bakes a variety of sweets (meringue kisses, anyone?) and ships her
confections to pretty much anywhere. Marta is regularly featured
in cooking publications and on *The Food Network*.

* * * * *

BACK TO THE BASICS
Willie Nelson and Waylon Jennings made Luckenbach, Texas
famous with world over with their renditions of the song of the
same name. Originally settled in 1850, the town (population 25)
remained pretty obscure until the 1970s.

Luckenbach still has just one general store that also doubles
as a beer tavern and dance hall. One writer commented on its
magical atmosphere by saying Luckenbach "is like Brigadoon;
you're almost afraid to go back because it might not be there
again." If you do go looking for Luckenbach, don't count on
seeing any signs. Souvenir hounds swipe them almost as fast as
they're put up.

Wink was a dull West Texas town until rock music star Roy Orbison put the city on the map.

MONUMENTAL TEXAS TRIVIA

*Texas has dozens and dozens of larger-than-life monuments—
each well worth a day trip.*

THE SAN JACINTO MONUMENT
Deer Park, Texas
Built between 1936 and 1939, this 570-foot shaft topped by a 34-foot star marks the location of the final battle in the Texas Revolution, where Sam Houston's underdog force defeated Santa Anna's Mexican army.

- The San Jacinto Monument is 15 feet taller than the Washington Monument.

- During the 57 hours it took to pour the Monument's foundation, workers consumed 3,800 sandwiches and 5,700 cups of coffee.

- The star on top of the monument weighs 220 tons (as heavy as 20 of the *Titanic's* anchors or 132 Honda Accords) and was designed to be seen as a five-point star no matter from which direction it's viewed.

- Only 35 of the 150 men who built the monument had any construction experience, yet not a single life was lost (despite the rumors, there really isn't anyone buried in the concrete—your grandfather was just messing with you).

- There is a museum at the base of the monument. One floor below it, in the basement, lays a secret cache of Texas antiquities. One floor above it, a library with thousands of rare books.

"Oh, Pretty Woman" singer Roy Orbison attended North Texas State University with Pat Boone.

SAM HOUSTON STATUE:
Huntsville, Texas

This 76-foot-tall statue on a 10-foot-high base is a tribute to the early Texas political leader and war hero who was the president of Texas during the Republic period.

- The official name of the statue, which was dedicated in 1994, is not "Big Sam" (which is its nickname), but "A Tribute to Courage."

- "Big Sam" is the largest statue of an American hero in the world.

- The statue's designer, David Adickes, saved the rubber mold he used for Big Sam's face—"just in case."

FANNIN SQUARE MONUMENT
Goliad, Texas

Another (ahem) tall, upright monument, this one memorializes James W. Fannin and his troops, who were executed while prisoners of war after an uprising against the Mexican government.

- The man who started the Fannin Monument Association was not a historian or civic administrator, but an actual survivor of the Goliad Massacre.

- The cannon near the monument is not just a period piece, but an actual cannon that was used by Fannin's forces.

STEPHEN F. AUSTIN MONUMENT
Austin, Texas

The monument marks the grave of the "Father of Texas," who first arranged the Anglo colonization of Mexican Texas in the early 1800s.

- Austin's grave is in Texas State Cemetery, Texas's version of the Arlington Cemetery in Washington. Other Texas digni taries buried there include Bigfoot Wallace, General Albert Sidney Johnston, and James and Miriam Ferguson—Texas's only husband-and-wife governors.

• The monument was built by Italian-born Pompeo Coppini. Raised in Florence, Italy, Coppini created 36 American monuments and was for a time head of the art department at San Antonio's Trinity University.

• The statue was designed with Austin's arm extended, as if pointing at something. That's because it was supposed to be placed on Austin's Congress Avenue, overlooking the Colorado River, with his hand showing off the biggest street of "his" city. Instead, it wound up in the cemetery.

THE ALAMO MONUMENTS
Austin and San Antonio, Texas
Three Texas monuments have been erected in honor of the Battle of the Alamo.

• The first Alamo monument in Austin, a ten-foot high pyramid designed by Englishman William B. Nangle, was constructed of stones from the Alamo. It initially had no home, but toured Texas and Louisiana like a circus act. It was ruined during a fire in the Texas Capitol building in 1881.

• A replacement monument—35 feet tall and made of Texas granite—includes a statue of a typical soldier of early Texas. It was commissioned by the legislature in 1881 and still stands, just to the right of the entrance to the Capitol building, but over 40 of its inscribed names are incorrect.

• The Alamo Cenotaph (a cenotaph is a memorial not directly over the remains of those it honors) stands 60 feet tall on Alamo Plaza in front of the Alamo itself. It was dedicated in 1939, designed by the architectural firm of Adams and Adams, who also designed the ranch house at the King Ranch.

Longest sand castle, two miles long, was built on South Padre Island by kids on spring break in 1987.

STATE VEGETABLE: THE SWEET ONION

House Concurrent Resolution No. 148, 75th Legislature,
Regular Session (1997)

*Like everything else in Texas, the onions are big! Only the Lone Star
state could have created the 1015. And yes, that is the sweet onion's
real name. Honest.*

HOW SWEET IT IS
Sweet onions came from a single packet of seeds shipped to
South Texas in 1898 from the Canary Islands. Planted near
Catulla, Texas, the seeds yielded a crop of what were then called
"Bermuda" onions. They were an instant hit when they were sent
North in 1899. The onions proved so popular that more were planted
the next year. By 1904, Texas's onion fields blossomed to nearly 500
acres and four years later, Bermuda onion production doubled.

Eventually, the Canary Islands couldn't keep up with the
demand for seeds. In 1933, the Texas Agricultural Experiment
Station partnered up with the Department of Agriculture in the
hopes of developing their own varieties and hybrids. That team
came up with the mild-tasting Texas Early Grano 502. Next, came
the yellow Granex, a cross between the Bermuda onion and the
Grano. The Granex, however, found its way to Vidalia, Georgia,
where it's tasty reputation flourished.

IT'S 1015, DO YOU KNOW WHERE YOUR ONIONS ARE?
Researchers developed more hybrids, but it wasn't until the 1980s
that they came up with the very popular Texas Grano 1015Y.
Grown in southern Texas's Rio Grande Valley, the sweetest of
onions measures three to four inches in diameter and weighs up to
one pound. Thin-skinned and mild, the 1015 is different from
most of its onion-cousins because of its reduced levels of pyru-
vate—the chemical that not only gives most onions their taste,
but also makes us cry. But why call it a 1015? Because October 15
is considered the ideal day for planting. Honest.

San Antonio's Sea World is largest of all the Sea World parks, and home to Shamu the killer whale.

UNCLE JOHN'S TEXAS CLOTHES SHOPPER: THE BOOTS

"And he can take a look at the boots you wear
And know a whole lot about you, man"
—from "Charlie Dunn," by Jerry Jeff Walker

The "cowboy boot" we know today comes from the Spanish *vaqueros* of the old days, who used its narrower toe to place their feet quickly and firmly into the stirrups of horses. Theirs were strictly durable work leather, though—much more utilitarian than today's glitzy footwear, which can be made from cows, bulls, calves, ostriches, alligators, crocodiles, goats, snakes, iguanas, stingrays, elephants, eels, camels, or even anteaters. But the *vaqueros* were far from the first to prefer "well-heeled" protective footwear. Horsemen from the Mongols to the Moors insisted on big, boot-type footwear to help them do their job and stand out in the crowd. Contrary to popular myth, the pointed toe on a cowboy boot is a relatively new invention, added to the design around 1940.

WHERE TO BUY THEM

You can get a great pair of boots at any major Western wear specialty store, like the ubiquitous Boot Town, which has 25 stores in major cities across Texas and carries dozens of different brands and a gazillion different styles and price ranges. But if money is no object, consider having a pair custom-made; they start at $500 or $600 and range as much as the cost of a small house in the suburbs.

Boot makers like Paul Wheeler or Jesse Guevera of Houston, Ramon Navarro of Austin, or Jose L. and Norma Sanchez of El Paso have the tools and talent to make exactly the boots you want. If you go this route, it helps to bring or send a picture of an existing boot to get the communication started, especially if you have in mind some porcelain white boots decorated with little engraved rolls of toilet paper.

Star Trek creator Gene Roddenberry was born in El Paso, Texas, on Aug. 19, 1921.

HOW TO CHOOSE

If you go the off-the-rack route, don't even think of buying a pair of boots until you've tried on at least five different pairs. Style, material, and construction varies so widely that, like your hat, they're the kind of thing you really need to try on before you buy. Consider your environment and what you'll be using 'em for. Fashionable or functional? City or country? Muddy or dusty? Suede or snakeskin boots don't stand up as well in rough, outdoor wear as more durable bull hide. On the other hand, bull hide might not be the best choice for an awards ceremony or formal dinner. When you get a feel for the style you want, be sure you're getting a quality boot—avoid leathers that are scarred or pitted. Check the stitching to see that it's not frayed or uneven and look for stray bit of glue, which can be an indicator of poor quality. You'll know the right pair when you put 'em on.

HOW TO WEAR YOUR BOOTS

Tucking your jeans into your boots, unless you're five, is a great way to look like a Yankee in most Texas towns. It just plain looks stupid. But other than that, there aren't many ways to mess up wearing a cowboy boot. Although, if you have a habit of dragging your feet when you walk, a boot's loud heel will make the habit apparent and annoying to others—especially someplace quiet, so don't go to the library.

If you wear spurs, you'd better look like the kind of guy who's just finished using them. If you did just finish using them, take them off when you're done working. Spurs that jingle-jangle don't do much good; they just scratch things up. Don't try to drive anything but a horse with them on.

HOW TO CARE FOR YOUR BOOTS

The best thing you can do to take care of your cowboy boots is to attend to damage or cleaning as soon as it's required and not put it off until later. As soon as you buy your little booties, locate a shoe hospital or Western wear store that restores and repairs boots so you know where to go to care for the suckers. When plain old cowhide boots get muddy, wipe them with a damp cloth and let them drip-dry. You can use a toothbrush to get in between the

Morgan Fairchild, born Patsy Ann McClenny, was born Feb. 3, 1950, in Dallas.

cracks. Don't let suede boots get wet. When dusting snakeskin boots, brush *against* the scales, not with them. Use an appropriate conditioner, depending on boot's material, for regular cleaning.

WHAT AM I BID?

In December 2003, Leland's, the New York sports auction house, sold the white cowboy boots and tuxedo worn by John Travolta in the 1980 Texas movie classic *Urban Cowboy*. The boot heels were covered up with white tape for a total white-out effect. The entire set sold for $1,641 despite a mysterious stain on the pants of the tuxedo. Maybe someone got a little too scared on that mechanical bull ride?

* * * * *

HOT ENOUGH FOR YOU?

A Texan dies one night and goes to Hell, where it's awfully hot. But the heat doesn't seem to both the Texan. The Devil looks over and says, "Hot enough for you?" The Texan replies, "Nope. Just like a spring day in Amarillo."

So the Devil turns the heat way up. Again, the Texan seems fine with it. "Hot enough for you?" asks the Devil. "Nope," says the Texan. "It's just like a summer day in Laredo."

So the Devil decides if he can't cook this Texan's goose, then he'll just freeze it. The Devil turns the temperature way down and now everyone and everything is freezing over. The Texan, happy as a clam, starts laughing. "I don't get it," says the Devil. "Doesn't the cold bother you either?" The Texan smiles and says, "Nope. The way I figure it, the Rangers must have won the World Series!"

AUDIE MURPHY'S RESUME

Get familiar with the accomplishments of this American hero from Texas.

Name: Audie Murphy
Date of Birth: June 20, 1924
Original Home Address: Sharecropper's shack near Kingston, Texas
Present Address: Arlington National Cemetery, Virginia

1928–1942: COTTON CHOPPER, HEAD OF HOUSEHOLD

Hit the fields—picking cotton barefoot at age five. Great Depression in full swing. Shot rabbits and squirrels and other small game to feed family. Good at school, but didn't go much; needed at home to keep everyone else fed and such. Worked hard, often went to bed hungry.

1942: U.S. MARINES

Got sent home. Said I was too young at 17; and too short at five feet, seven inches.

1942: ARMY PARATROOPERS

Sent home the first day. Same reason as the Marines.

1942–1945: REGULAR ARMY INFANTRY

Successfully enlisted in Greenville, Texas, when I turned 18. Got off to a shaky start. Passed out during my first Basic Training close-quarters drill at Camp Wolter. Superiors didn't want to send me overseas; didn't think I could handle it. But I finally talked them into it.

Highlights:
• Received advanced training at Fort Meade, Maryland.
• Fought for assignment to North Africa.
(Company B, Fifteenth Infantry Regiment, Third Infantry Division)

It takes up to six gallons of peanut oil to deep-fry a turkey Texas style.

- Killed a total of 240 enemy soldiers single-handedly throughout service.

- Received battlefield promotion to second lieutenant.

- Became the most decorated combat soldier of World War II. Won every single medal that the United States could give a soldier for valor, including: Distinguished Service Cross, Silver Star, Legion of Merit, Bronze Star, Purple Heart, U.S. Army Outstanding Service Medal, Good Conduct Medal, Distinguished Unit Emblem, American Campaign Medal, European-African-Middle Eastern Campaign Medal, and World War II Victory Medal.

- Received five medals from France and Belgium: French Croix de Guerre with Palm, French Croix de Guerre With Silver Star, French Fourragere (In Colors of the Croix de Guerre), French Legion of Honor (Grade of Chevalier), and Belgian Croix de Guerre (1940 Palm).

- Awarded the Congressional Medal of Honor for fighting near Holtzwihr, France. Wounded in action, but managed to kill or wound 50 German soldiers in less than 30 minutes. It was called a "one-man stand." The French erected a small memorial to me as the soldier who best exemplified the courage, valor, and sacrifice that Americans soldiers had made there.

1945–1949: STRUGGLING ACTOR, WRITER
James Cagney saw my picture in *Life Magazine*; invited me to Hollywood. Moved out there, went to audition after audition. After a few years, landed some bit parts. In 1949 got a starring role in a movie called *Bad Boy*, a juvenile delinquent drama.

While waiting for my big break, I wrote *To Hell and Back*, the story of my own personal war experience. Also wrote poetry and song lyrics.

1950–1969: HOLLYWOOD STAR
Made 45 films, mostly Westerns: played Billy the Kid in *The Kid from Texas*, Jesse James in *Kansas Raiders*, Tom Destry in *Destry* (a remake of *Destry Rides Again*).
In 1955, starred as myself in the movie version of *To Hell and Back*, Universal Studio's highest-grossing film until *Jaws* was released 20 years later.

Actor Barry Corbin was born Oct. 16, 1940, in Lamesa, Texas.

In 1958, played "The American" in *The Quiet American*.

In 1960, was third-billed (after Burt Lancaster and Audrey Hepburn) in *The Unforgiven*.

Came full circle in 1969; played Jesse James again in my last film, *A Time for Dying*.

1959–1971: BUSINESSMAN, GAMBLER

Made over $3 million making movies; invested a lot of it. Owned ranches, bought thoroughbred horses, played high-stakes poker. In 1971 on a business trip, my private plane crashed into a mountain. I was 46.

POSTHUMOUS HONORS

1973

Of the many memorials to me in Texas, the citizens of Farmesville, Texas, dedicated one right in the middle of town. The inscription reads:

In Memory Of
Audie L. Murphy
1924–1971

And all American men and women of all races and creeds—military and civilians--who have loyally and proudly served this nation in times of war and peace. To their courageous sacrifices and their unselfish devotion to duty without regard to personal preference or safety, we owe our liberty and our right to the pursuit of happiness.

"Greater love hath no man than this that a man lay down his life for his friends." St. John 15:13

1999

George W. Bush proclaimed June 20th "Audie Murphy Day" in Texas.

Rock singer Meat Loaf (Marvin Lee Aday) was born Sept. 27, 1947, in Dallas.

OIL IN THE FAMILY

Ever wonder what all that Texas tea is fer?

A little less than half (47 percent) of the petroleum produced in the U.S. is used to make gasoline. Around 23 percent is used for heating oil, 10 percent for jet fuel, 4 percent for propane, and 3 percent to make asphalt. So what does the rest make? You'll be amazed at how far a little petroleum can go.

STUFF FOR YOUR BODY

Band-Aids
Casts
Catheters
Chap Stick
Combs
Deodorants
Eyeglasses
Face masks
Hair brushes

Hair colorings
Heart valves
Hospital blankets
Laxatives
Lipsticks
Mascaras
Pepto-Bismol
Perfumes
Prosthetic limbs

Shampoos
Shaving creams
Skin moisturizer
Soft contact lenses
Sunglasses
Surgical drapes
Toothbrushes
Wound dressings

STUFF FOR YOUR CLOSET

Beads
Bras
Dresses
Earrings
Faux furs

Flip-flops
Gym bags
Imitation leathers
Pantyhose
Polyester

Ribbons
Swimsuits
Sweaters
Shoelaces

STUFF FOR FUN

Athletic shoes
Boats
Bowling balls
Cameras
CD "jewel boxes"
Fishing rods and lures
Football helmets
Frisbees

Golf balls
Hot tubs
Ice chests
Music albums
Roller-blades
Shotgun shells
Sleeping bags
Snorkels

Soccer balls
Soda bottles
Tennis rackets
Tents
Water bottles
Waterproof jackets

Sam Houston described his first son, Sam, Jr., as "a hearty brat, robust and hearty as a Yorkshire pit."

STUFF FOR YOUR HOUSE

Bug spray
Candles
Carpet
Composite wood
   furniture
Dishwashing liquid
Drinking straws
Duct Tape
Egg cartons
Fake Christmas trees

Fertilizers
Freezer bags
Garbage bags
Garden hoses
Home sidings
Insulation
Kitchen containers
Lawn chairs
Linoleum
Measuring cups

Panels
Pillows
Plastic wraps
Power tools
Shower curtains
Telephones
Thermometers
Toilet seats
Weatherproofing

STUFF FOR THE KIDS

Action figures
Baby aspirin
Baby lotions
Baby oil
Baby-proof cabinets
Baby shoes
Balloons
Bike and skate
   helmets

Car seats
Child-proof bottles
Crayons
Disposable diapers
Dolls
Etch A Sketch
High chairs
Milk jugs
Model cars

Mr. Potato Head
Outlet covers
Pacifiers
Rattles
Rubber duckies
Silly Putty
Toy robots
Video cassettes
Video games

STUFF FOR WORK

Bubble wrap
Calculators
Coffee makers
Computer cabinets
Computers
Copy machines
Correction fluid

Extension cords
Floor cleaners
Magic markers
Measuring tape
Mobile phones
Name tags
Packing "peanuts"

Paint brushes
Ring binders
Transparent tape
Staplers
Trash cans
Venetian blinds
Writing pens

STUFF FOR YOUR CAR

Air bags
Bumpers
Dashboards
Doors
Engine belts
Fenders
Floor mats
Gaskets
Gauges

Hoses
Inside panels
Knobs and controls
Motor oils
Outside panels
Road signs
Safety flares
Safety windshields
Seatbelts

Seats
Spoilers
Steering wheels
Stereo speakers
Tires
Water seals
Windows
Wiring

THE TRAGEDY OF ISAAC CLINE

"You don't need a weatherman to know which way the wind blows."—Bob Dylan

D**ON'T BE ABSURD!**
Galveston meteorologist Isaac M. Cline assured his fellow citizens that a terrible tropical storm—which so commonly thrashed other Gulf Coast towns—could never strike their fair city. He was sure that the gradual slope of the coast between Galveston and the Gulf of Mexico's deeper waters would protect the little island from violent storm surges and other floodwaters. In an article he published in 1891, Cline said that: "It would be impossible for any cyclone to create a storm wave which could materially injure the city." In his not-so-humble opinion, anyone who disagreed was the victim of "absurd delusion." Such was the state of meteorology in the late nineteenth century.

THE NATURE OF THINGS TO COME
It was a time in American history when human arrogance and technological progress made it seem like man could do anything. Nature, it was believed, could be controlled and contained just like other nations—as a ship's captain makes unquestioned demands of her crew. Little did man know that Nature was waiting right around the corner in ambush.

THOSE CRAZY CUBANS
Weather officials knew that a "cyclone" had departed Cuba that week and was expected to turn north. Cuban weather gurus, who knew a dangerous storm when they saw one, tried to convince their American weather counterparts that this was one volatile *mamacita* of a storm. But the Americans thought the Cubans were being alarmists.

Country star George Strait was born May 18, 1952, in Poteet, Texas.

NEXT STOP, GALVESTON

The morning of September 8, 1900, Cline hoisted the conventional storm warning flag at Galveston's observation center. But the storm, which was growing exponentially more violent, wouldn't be anywhere near conventional. As soon as it left the Cuban coast, it headed toward Texas, barreling straight for Galveston. Low, black storm clouds were soon pounding the city with rain, and toads (yes, toads) were hopping all over the streets, sidewalks, and lowlands that weren't already flooded.

BLOWN AWAY!

At first, the locals were amused, but soon realized they were in jeopardy. Cline's office had downplayed the danger and now there was no time to evacuate. By the time people thought to leave the island, the bridges to the mainland had all washed out. Homes, offices, and trains began to flood, and then were simply washed or blown away.

The 20-foot storm surge put the island completely underwater, destroying everything in its path and killing 12,000 people—more than any other natural disaster in America. The barometer reached 28.53 inches, one of the lowest readings ever recorded up to that time. Property damage costs were nearing $100 million dollars (in today's dollars); over 2,600 houses and 1,500 acres of shoreline were destroyed.

WEATHERING THE STORM OF BAD PUBLICITY

You'd think this would have ruined Cline professionally, but that wasn't the case. He must have had some politician in his blood: he pointed out the lives he saved when he finally did give the order to evacuate, and played up his record and reputation. His reputation survived somehow, but his house and his pregnant wife didn't. Therein lies the tragedy.

As to his career, you know how bureaucracies work: Cline was given a *promotion* for his "example of courage and fidelity to duty," not to mention a transfer to the cobblestone streets of New Orleans. He continued his "distinguished" life of service and even today is revered as a pioneering meteorologist.

"Barometer, n.: An ingenious instrument which indicates what kind of weather we are having."—Ambrose Bierce

Thirty-two species of bat are found in Texas—more than any other state!

EAT IT OR WEAR IT?

Musician "Mambo" John Treanor made a unique reputation for himself in Austin—but not just for his abilities as a drummer.

GROWING UP (AND GROWING WEED)

Born in 1953, John Treanor grew up listening to his mother sing in the church choir and showed he had an ear for music at a young age. He was indispensable as his high school's marching band and jazz band drummer, and by the mid-1970s was leading a jazz group that shared the bill (albeit in smaller letters) with the likes of Frank Zappa and Stevie Ray Vaughan. Around this time, Treanor made a joke about wanting to be a street musician and told people, "You can call me Mambo Johnny." The name stuck and Mambo John was born. During the 1980s, Treanor played gigs all around Austin, but he failed to keep one important thing secret: the fact that he sold marijuana.

In 1989, just as his musical career was picking up, it came to an unhappy end. Mambo John was arrested for growing 796 marijuana plants. He was packed off to Federal Prison Camp in El Reno, Oklahoma, where he was put on landscape detail, which he found ironic since he'd been put in prison for cultivating a greenhouse.

STUFFED ANIMALS

Actually, landscape detail in large part consisted of picking up garbage along the highways. Which was where Treanor got his brilliant idea. Instead of just chucking the roadkill he found, he started collecting it. He taught himself taxidermy and asked the prison powers-that-be for supplies so he could tan the hides.

Over the next couple of years, Mambo John collected, and made hats out of raccoons, jackrabbits, and skunks. The prison warden got into the act, too, occasionally putting Mambo and his hats on display.

Music critic Michael Corcoran of the *Austin American Statesman* said, "He [Treanor] saw his curbside furrier activity as a metaphor for how the discarded could be compassionately, skillfully reformed into something useful and creative." As explained in John's self-published book of prison essays, *The Power of Love*

CBS anchor Dan Rather was born October 31, 1931, in Wharton, Texas.

and the Life of Dead Animals, he viewed his collection of roadkill as
"something beautiful to keep the soul of the animal alive,
admired, and honored long after the body was gone."

MUSICIAN AND HAT-WEARER AROUND TOWN
After his release in 1993, Treanor went straight back to his music
with a fire he hadn't felt before. His roadkill hats became his
trademark, and soon most of the population of Austin knew who
he was. His drumming skills rose to legendary status. He picked up
a new instrument—the washboard—and made it onto four *Austin
City Limits* shows as a percussionist.

THE LEGEND LIVES ON
After being diagnosed with cancer in his lymph glands in 1999, he
went through surgery after surgery, but continued playing shows.
"He'll walk in looking too frail to play, but when he sits behind
the drums, everything changes," said longtime band-mate Robert
"Beto" Skiles, "Whatever ignites him comes from somewhere
other than his body. It's a total mystery, but to be in the presence
of that kind of energy is what all musicians want."

When Treanor died of cancer in August 2001, his mother
donated his roadkill hats to a local museum for musicians. Now a
skunk hat sits atop a statue of John's head for people to remember
the trademark of a wonderfully talented drummer who uniquely
distinguished himself in a city of many musicians.

* * * * *

GET THE VOTE OUT!
Texas is the only state that permits residents to cast absentee
ballots from space so all those working astronauts can have vote
for governor and the legislature.

Texas Governors serve a four-year term. James S. Hogg was the
first Governor to be born in Texas. Miriam Ferguson was the first
female Governor of Texas.

The Texas Legislature has 181 members. Each of the 31 state
Senators serves a four-year term while each of the 150
Representatives serves only two years.

HORSE, COW, AND THE HOOSEGOW

At one time, Huntsville's Texan Prison Rodeo was the place to be for the state's wildest rodeo action.

In 1894, Marshall Lee Simmons was about to graduate from the University of Texas and enter his brother's law firm when he was arrested for shooting a man who'd bad-mouthed one of his relatives. It was the first major role he got to play within the legal system, but not the last. The shooting was ruled self-defense and Simmons went on to become a respectable businessman, banker, sheriff, and eventually general manager of the state prison system. It was in this capacity that he first came up with the idea of having a rodeo for prisoners. He billed it as the "fastest and wildest rodeo" and, while Marshall Lee Simmons retired in 1936, his rodeo would ride on for another 50 years.

JAILHOUSE RODEO

The Texas Prison Rodeo started out as a way for the inmates, staff, and family members to have a little fun during a time when, even outside the gates of Huntsville, life could feel oppressive. The Great Depression created a longing for escape and excitement, and bull-riding, calf-roping and bronco-busting seemed the perfect way for everyone Texan to cut loose.

On Sunday afternoons in a field near the Walls Unit (Huntsville's Death Row) inmates from all of the area prisons gathered to watch or participate. At first, the participating inmates had to know what they were doing. But a few years into it, any inmate who kept his—or her—nose clean for a year was eligible. One hundred slots were offered, and inmates were paid (modestly) for their time. The handful of outside spectators thought it was small-town entertainment at its finest.

HUSTLE AND BUSTLE

The audience grew consistently, often doubling from year to year. Soon the prison needed to build wooden benches to hold them all. When the rodeo rolled, Sundays in the city of Huntsville had

---

Lyle Lovett graduated from Texas A&M with degrees in journalism and German.

an unusual, electric bustle; retail shops and restaurants stayed open, serving barbecue, pumping gas, and giving directions to people from Houston, Dallas, and San Antonio.

The guards were paid for overtime, and the prisoners got to see the fruits of their labor—not just all that rodeo practice, but the planning and preparation work as well. The wild cattle the farm prisoners had rounded up for the event were finally put to work; the uniforms sewn by women prisoners stretched across the hard backs of the bull riders, and a midway full of prison-made arts and crafts would finally find their market.

BIG TIME IN THE BIG HOUSE

And as word caught on about the rodeo—so much so that people had to be turned away at the gate—the wooden bleachers were replaced by a concrete mega-structure. Over the years, the rodeo had invented its own unusual tongue-in-cheek events, like "Hard Money," where convicts in red shirts tried removing a sack of cash from between a bull's horns, or the greased pig contest where female prisoners tried to put greased pigs in a sack. By the mid-1980s, the event was grossing almost half a million dollars, all of which was used to help run the prison.

The lineup included exhibitions by the top rodeo stars from around the country and entertainment courtesy of the likes of Willie Nelson and Loretta Lynn. The rodeo was attracting 100,000 people a year.

ADIOS, COWBOYS!

The Texas Prison Rodeo had become wildly popular all right—but *too* popular. In 1986, engineers declared the prison's rodeo facility unfit to hold the massive crowds safely. The prison couldn't afford to pay for the necessary reconstructions, and so the Texas Prison Rodeo was closed up for good.

Lots of Texans have lobbied to bring it back, but as Dan Beto, director of the Sam Houston State University Correctional Management Institute of Texas told the *Houston Chronicle*: ". . . when we had a prison rodeo, we had a lot of inmates who had some agricultural background . . . Most of the inmates who come to the prison system now are from major metropolitan areas. You're dealing with a different kind of inmate, a different culture, a different time."

Actor Matthew McConaughey (*A Time to Kill*) was born Nov. 4, 1969, in Uvalde, Texas.

BELLE WAS A STARR

"When the legend becomes fact, print the legend."
—The Man Who Shot Liberty Valence *(1962)*

The Wild West had its share of lawless legends, but the overwhelming majority of them were men. Perhaps that's why in 1889—shortly after her death—tales of Belle Starr and her outlaw ways entranced a nation. Reporter Richard Fox published *Belle Starr, the Bandit Queen, or the Female Jesse James*, an account which purported to tell the tale of the gunslingin', horse-rustlin', man-eatin' adventures of the roughest, toughest, shootingist female that ever did live. A female outlaw! How novel!

The problem is—of course—that there's not a whole lot of truth to the Belle Starr legend. Yes, there was a Belle Starr, and yes, she did spend a lot of her time on the shady side of the law. She even served nine months in prison for rustling horses. But when it comes right down to it, most of her adventures—from saloon shootouts to bank robberies to all the men she was supposed to have "known"—were nothing more than the inventions of pulp writers looking to thrill an audience.

SOUTHERN BELLE

Belle's real name was Myra Maybelle Shirley. She was born in 1848 in Missouri to well-to-do parents John and Eliza Shirley. Her parents brought her up as a proper young woman; but that didn't stop little Myra from learning how to ride horses and handle guns from her older brother Bud. During the Civil War, the Shirleys took the side of the Confederacy. Bud joined a band of bushwhackers where he met Frank and Jesse James as well as a man named Cole Younger. Belle is thought to have passed on information collected at social gatherings to her brother during these times. Bud was killed by Union troops in 1864. Some accounts have Belle taking to her guns to avenge brother Bud's death, but historians don't find that too likely.

BELLE GETS HITCHED

Other parts of the Belle Starr legend pair her off with Cole Younger at this time in her life. Not only were the two supposed

---

The Prude Ranch is a guest ranch and working cattle ranch six miles west of Fort Davis.

to be an item but also she bore him their love child. Chances are this colorful story isn't true either. Younger himself claims to have met Belle once in 1864 and then to have not seen her again until 1868 after she had married another man and was pregnant with his child.

So after the Civil War, the Shirleys had moved to Texas and there Belle met her first husband, Jim Reed. Legend has it that Belle's parents objected to their pairing, so Belle and Reed got married on horseback as they ran away, with the rites performed by a member of Reed's gang. In fact, the parents were fine with the match and the two got married by a minister pretty much like anyone else. And the two settled at Belle's parents' farm, which suggests family tensions weren't too high.

First Reed tried being a farmer and a salesman, but he felt his true calling in the life of an outlaw. Reed hooked up with the gang of Tom Starr, a Cherokee outlaw of some infamy. During this spell with Starr, Reed shot a man and then took Belle, their daughter Pearl, and himself to California in 1869 until things cooled off in Texas.

But Reed had problems staying on the right side of the California law as well. He got into trouble with some counterfeiting and then moved the family back to Texas after the birth of his son in 1871. Reed continued his life of crime in Texas, but there's little record that Belle was interested in joining him to be an outlaw. She left him. Belle's first husband died in 1874, shot while trying to escape arrest.

BELLE GETS HITCHED AGAIN

During the six years between Reed's death and Belle's second marriage in 1880, not too much is known about Belle's whereabouts. This is gray period of time is where Belle's "biographers" would pepper her history with wild tales of her life of crime. Belle burns down buildings, elopes with law enforcement officials to spring herself from jail, busts up poker games with gunplay, and rewards members of her gang with her favors. The real explanation is probably much more pedestrian; she more likely spent time with her mother in Texas and the Reed family.

In 1880, Belle married Sam Starr, the son of Tom Starr who her first husband had run with in a gang. She robbed the cradle the second time around as Sam was nearly a decade younger than she. The two settled in Indian Territory near Arkansas in a place they called Younger's Bend.

BELLE STEALS HORSES

It seems that Belle's notorious life of crime primarily consisted of horse thievery. One of her first actual, verified events of lawful malfeasance happened in 1882 when both Sam and Belle were charged with larceny for stealing horses. They were convicted and sentenced in 1883 to a year in the pokey. The two were out in nine months, partially due to Belle's making nice with the warden. Just call it good behavior.

Over the next few years, Belle and Sam were suspected in a string of horse thefts and other thievery, but Belle always managed to beat the rap. Sam Starr started spending a lot of time away from home. Lucky for Belle she met John Middleton, with whom it is very likely she had an affair. Middleton died not long after Belle purchased a horse for him; turned out the horse had been stolen, and Belle was charged with larceny (again). Luckily she beat the rap at her trial.

BELLE TAKES HUSBAND NUMBER THREE

Sam was killed at a Christmas party in 1886 after he drew a gun on an old enemy. Belle then had a short dalliance with a bad guy named Jack Spaniard (short because Spaniard would soon be swinging from a gallows for his crimes). Belle married her third and final husband: Bill July, the adopted son of Tom Starr and thereby, her late second husband's brother (Who knew the old West was like a soap opera?). This marriage was not especially happy; rumor had it that Belle's new husband had found a young Cherokee woman on the side.

BELLE IS MURDERED

Belle's children were none too fond of mother either. Her daughter Pearl became pregnant out of wedlock, causing Belle to boot her out of the house and break up her romance. Belle's son Ed hated Bill July. Belle also wasn't making friends with neighbors—she reneged on an agreement to let neighbor Edgar Watson rent

---

Texas has more churches than any state in the union—16,961 according to one web site.

her land for farming. She made the mistake of slipping into their conversation that she knew Watson was wanted for murder in Florida and chided him about what a shame it would be if the authorities found out.

And so Watson, Ed, Pearl, *and* Bill were all suspected in Belle's murder in 1889, when she was blasted out of the saddle with a shotgun while she was on the way home from visiting friends. The prime suspect was Watson, who had motive and opportunity (the shooting occurred near his home) and who, of course, had done this sort of thing before. But officially the murder was never solved.

In the end, there was no denying Starr's life was eventful, just not in the highly romantic, female-cowboy-outlaw way. Given the choice, which would Belle Starr have preferred to live? A quote from her gives a hint: "I am a friend to any brave and gallant outlaw." One suspects she would have been happy with her fictional life.

* * * * *

TEXAS SALLY

With a name like Sally Scull, she had to be tough. Born Sarah Jane Newman in 1817 and raised in Texas, Sally was famous for her five marriages, her salty language, and her abilities with a gun. She developed a reputation as a desperado who could play with the big boys when it came to poker playing and horse trading. When the Civil War broke out, Sally quit trading livestock to haul Confederate cotton to Mexico. Nobody is quite sure how Sally died. Rumor has it her last husband killed her for her gold.

Model and Mick Jagger's ex-wife, Jerri Hall was born in Mesquite, Texas.

THE LAW AND THE LILLY

In the age before teenage fan clubs, Judge Roy Bean did all he could to bring the Lilly to town.

Roy was born in Kentucky in the mid-1830s as Phantly Roy Bean (he wisely dropped the Phantly before he headed out West). After several escapades in California, Roy and his other brother, Sam, first moved to Texas during the Civil War to support the Confederacy. Roy would spend much of his life in Texas and created quite a legend for himself. He was known as "The Law West of the Pecos."

THE JUDGE AND THE ACTRESS

In 1882, Roy moved west of the Pecos River where the Southern Pacific Railroad was laying track. He had been named by the Pecos County Commissioners as Justice of the Peace and had also managed to open a small tent saloon. So Roy alternated between selling whiskey to workers and then fining them for public drunkenness. No matter which hat he wore, lawman or barkeep, it was a convenient arrangement either way.

Nobody is really sure how the town of Langtry got its name. Some claim that the town had been renamed Langtry in honor of a railboss who had laid track there for the Southern Pacific railroad. But Roy Bean liked to say it was named for a famous beauty of the day, actress Lillie Langtry, or "The Jersey Lilly" as she was also known.

THE JERSEY LILLY

In 1853, Emilie Charlotte "Lillie" Langtry was born on the Isle of Jersey in the Channel Islands. She grew up to be a famous society beauty, posing for artists, going to parties, and being admired by many rich and powerful men. Among her admirers was King Edward VII of England. In 1881, Langtry became an actress and won international fame for her performances. She toured the provinces and the United States. As her fame grew, she became known far and wide as "The Jersey Lilly."

In 1860s Fort Worth, hunters usually received one dollar for a buffalo hide.

LILLIE'S NUMBER ONE FAN

Across the pond in Texas, Judge Roy Bean was worshipping at Lillie's shrine. He desparately wanted the actress to come to his town of Langtry. So when Roy built his saloon, he named it "The Jersey Lilly," in her honor. His big dreams of luring the British beauty to Texas to perform would not be thwarted. It's rumored that Roy struck up a correspondence with the actress to entreat her further to come to Texas. When he built a house across the street from the saloon, he called it "The Opera House" because he wanted Lillie Langtry to perform there.

LILLIE TOURS THE STATES

Lillie the actress toured the United States and in 1888 a transcontinental tour took her across the Southwest. She made stops in Galveston, Austin, Houston, Fort Worth, and San Antonio, but not Langtry. Judge Bean may have caught her act in San Antonio, but it is unlikely that the two ever met in person. Sadly, Lillie's biggest American fan would die before she made it to Langtry, Texas. Roy passed away in 1903.

Ten months later on another tour across the Southwest, Lillie Langtry did make a stop in the town named for her. The Judge had left her his six-shooter, a gift that was presented to her upon that visit. Lillie bequeathed the gun to the isle of Jersey. It is on exhibit with many of her personal items in the Jersey Museum at St. Helier.

* * * * *

A LITTLE MORE BEAN

Judge Roy Bean certainly was a memorable man.

Judge Roy Bean once fined a corpse $40.00 for carrying a concealed weapon.

"Dear Governor:
You run things up in Austin and I'll run 'em down here."
—*Bean's response to criticism from Governor Jim Hogg*

Judge Roy Bean
Justice of the Peace
Law West of the Pecos
—*Inscription on Bean's headstone*

The ghostly Lady of Dallas's White Rock Lake will hitch a ride and leave your back seat wet.

SCANDALOUS STARS

*Can you match the famous Texan on the left with
his or her criminal arrest?*

1. Gary Busey, Actor

2. Colby Donaldson, Runner-up from *Survivor: The Australian Outback*

3. Jamie Foxx, Comedian

4. Woody Harrelson, Actor

5. Waylon Jennings, Singer-songwriter

6. Janis Joplin, Singer

7. Matthew McConaughey, Actor

8. Willie Nelson, Singer-songwriter

9. Anna Nicole Smith, Model

10. Barry Switzer, Former Dallas Cowboys' coach

A. Spousal abuse with second wife. 2000

B. Possession of a loaded, illegal revolver at Dallas-Fort Worth airport. 1997

C. Possession of cocaine with intent to distribute. 1977

D. Disorderly conduct, "bad mouthing" a police officer. 1969

E. Suspicion of criminal damage to a London taxi. 2002

F. Disturbing peace, battery, resisting arrest at a casino. 2003

G. Public intoxication. Found lying face-down in San Angelo. 1999

H. Drug charge (marijuana) found in ashtray of car. 1994

I. Playing bongos at night outside wearing only a University of Texas bandana and a smile. 1999

J. Public nudity, Bahamas. 1995

Answer on page 305.

Turns out she drowned in the lake. Her legend has many variations.

HOWDY, GUV!

A passel of Texas governors is hidden in the Lone Star. Wordsearch puzzles not being as big as Texas, a few guvs had to be left behind. But we've got this funny feeling that somebody really important has been left out, too. Maybe once you've found all 28 of the capitalized last names in the grid—reading across, down, and diagonally—the leftover letters will clue you in as to who's missing.

James V. ALLRED
Dolph BRISCOE
Edward CLARK
William P. CLEMENTS
Oscar Branch COLQUITT
John CONNALLY
Charles A. CULBERSON
Price DANIEL
Edmund J. DAVIS
Andrew J. HAMILTON
J. Pinckney and James W.
    HENDERSON
Sam HOUSTON
Richard B. HUBBARD
John IRELAND
S.W.T. LANHAM

Francis R. LUBBOCK
Pendleton MURRAH
W. Lee O'DANIEL
Ann RICHARDS
Oran M. ROBERTS
Lawrence Sullivan ROSS
Hardin R. RUNNELS
Joseph D. SAYERS
Allan SHIVERS
Preston SMITH
Ross S. STERLING
James W.
    THROCKMORTON
George T. WOOD

Answer on page 306.

```
                    T   H
                    E   G
                    T   S
                    H   D
                    R   R
                  U O A V
                  S C H W
                S D K C E F
                E O M I H R
S R E V I H S T R E B O R O D A N I E L H E G O
  S T N E M E L C H A R R U M T G T H A O O M
    E C O L Q U I T T N S T I N T M C O
      A N N W I D O S T P R I I S
        R M O O C N E O U M L I
        A K S O O A N S T R
        H C S R D N L O B E
        N O S R E D N E H T
      I A B A L K B A A R S S
      D L B S R       L V L I R
      E N B U A       U I L E T
      G U E L         C S Y O
      H R C           G A E
    W B U             S S H
```

SAGACIOUS
SPORTING TEXANS

Words of wisdom from wise athletes from Texas.

"No one wants to quit when he's losing and no one wants to quit when he's winning."—Richard Petty, *race car driver*

"Study the rules so that you won't beat yourself by not knowing something."—Babe Didrikson Zaharias, *pro-golfer*

"You can't win them all—but you can try."
—Babe Didrikson Zaharias

"Enjoying success requires the ability to adapt. Only by being open to change will you have a true opportunity to get the most from your talent."—Nolan Ryan, *Texas Rangers*

"Spectacular achievements come from unspectacular preparation."
—Roger Staubach, *Dallas Cowboys*

"No matter how far life pushes you down, no matter how much you hurt, you can always bounce back."
—Sheryl Swoopes, *Houston Comets*

"I have always believed that anybody with a little guts and the desire to apply himself can make it, can make anything he wants to make of himself."—Willie Shoemaker, *jockey*

"I think sleeping was my problem in school. If school had started at 4:00 in the afternoon, I'd be a college graduate today."
—George Foreman, *boxer*

"When you want to win a game, you have to teach. When you lose a game, you have to learn." —Tom Landry, *Dallas Cowboys*

In 1844 Dallas consisted of "two small log cabins, and two families of ten to twelve souls."

THE UNCONVENTIONAL PROFESSOR

Intellectuals used to be viewed with suspicion in Texas. How could anyone who wrote poetry and read books be a real he-man? Just ask James Frank Dobie.

James Frank Dobie became an internationally famous folklorist by collecting and preserving the folk tales and legends of Texas. These are the unique cultural assets of the Southwest. But Dobie was more than that. He was a tireless crusader who fought against the erosion of the human spirit in an increasingly regimented and mechanized world. He campaigned for labor unions, academic freedom, and shocked racially segregated Texas by demanding that blacks be given the right to vote. By standing up to the system and playing by his own rules, Dobie's take-no-prisoners approach to his studies made him one of the true symbol of Texas.

He battled any form of censorship. "I have come to value liberated minds as the supreme good of life on earth," he wrote. His targets were bragging Texans, state politicians, and any dogmatic religious organization that impeded freedom of thought. Discussing political systems with his students, Dobie said: "When I get ready to explain homemade fascism in America, I can take my example from the state capital of Texas."

A REAL LIVE ONE

Dobie's independent streak grew from his own childhood. Born on a ranch in Live Oak County on September 26, 1888 he left home at 16 to continue his education. He lived with his maternal grandparents in Alice, Texas until he graduated high school. Four years of college at Southwestern University in Georgetown followed. He graduated with a BA Degree in English in 1910 then added a Masters from Columbia in 1913.

For a few years, Dobie pursued two careers. He was a schoolteacher but worked as a newspaper reporter during summer vacations. In 1914, he joined the faculty of the English Department of the University of Texas at Austin. Two years later, Dobie had married Bertha McKee, a girl he had met in college. It was a long and happy union that lasted until his death 48 years later. Dobie's relationship with the university would not run so smoothly. The prickly, uneasy alliance between the brilliant, liberal professor and the conservative university regents would continue, with intermittent breaks, until 1947 when Dobie resigned over a policy dispute. The unrepentant Dobie characterized the board as "unctuous elaborators of the obvious."

His first break with the university lasted for two years, 1917–19, when Dobie enlisted in the Army. Returning to Austin in 1919, he stayed only a year at the University then left to manage "El Rancho de los Olmos" (The Ranch of the Elms), his uncle's ranch in south Texas.

TRUE CALLING

The year spent at Los Olmos was the turning point in his life. Listening to the tales and legends being told by Mexican *vaqueros* (cowboys), J. Frank Dobie found his true calling. "It came to me that I could collect and tell the legendary tales of Texas," Dobie recalled. "I thought that if collected so as to show the background out of which they had come, they might have high value." Collecting these tales became his life work and his obsession; it would keep him from taking the time to earn a PhD, which Dobie felt would be too time-consuming of a project and take him away from what he now saw as his life's work. Time was of the essence, especially since many of Dobie's sources were elderly. "The average PhD thesis is nothing but the transference of bones from one graveyard to another," he raged.

Dobie returned to the university after a year on the ranch and began a lifelong association with the Texas Folklore Society. He served as Secretary-Editor for 21 years. The Society published the first book he edited, *Legends of Texas* in 1924, but his ongoing conflict with the university continued. Dobie was denied promotion because he did not have a PhD. To his wife he once confessed, "At the university I am a wild man, in the wilds I am a scholar and poet."

He left UT to accept the position of Chairman of the English Department of Oklahoma A&M College, 1923–1925. Soon the UT Board of Regents saw the error of their ways and backed down.

Gen. William J. Worth is little known historically, but he gave Fort Worth its name.

Dobie was reinstated and promoted, becoming the first non-PhD holder to be given a full professorship at the University of Texas.

DOBIE TAKES ON THE BOARD, AGAIN

Despite Dobie's fine reputation as a scholar and an author (he won the national Literary Guild Award for his masterpiece *Coronado's Children*), he clashed with the regents again in 1941. Over the protests of university president Homer P. Rainey, the board fired a non-tenured English instructor who had dared to put John dos Passo's *USA* on the sophomore's reading list. They claimed the book was "subversive and perverted." Dobie sided with his friend to fight for academic freedom. The regents fired Dobie again, but then quickly reversed the decision. The obstreperous Professor Dobie had brought honor and acclaim to the university and they could bet their boots that his firing wouldn't play well in the public. Dobie's class "Life and Literature of the Southwest" was the most popular on the curriculum and had been adopted at dozens of colleges in the Southwest. So the Board had to give in, reinstate Dobie, and reinstate the instructor as well. After the battle, Dobie chastised some timid faculty members who had avoided the fight. He branded them "dull, well meaning, cunning climbers (and) quellers of those who refuse to knuckle under."

THE BOARD STRIKES BACK

In 1943 J. Frank left for a two-year assignment as Visiting Professor of American History at England's Cambridge University. Controversy followed him. In November 1944, the Board of Regents fired President Rainey. Some faculty members asked Governor Coke Stevenson to intervene. Stevenson replied that he was "too experienced an old cowhand to burn his lips on such a hot coffee pot." From Cambridge, Dobie commented that he had a front row seat in a war that had come about because other leaders had adopted that same attitude. Reacting to Dobie's criticism, Stevenson grumbled that Dobie was "a troublemaker and should be replaced." Eight thousand university students went on strike to protest Rainey's dismissal, but the regents won. Rainey lost his job anyway. Dobie responded in the school newspaper, the *Daily Texan*: "When the Board of Regents acted behind the closed door . . . they tried a man without a public hearing. When they convicted that

---

Dale Evans, aka Mrs. Roy Rogers, was born Oct. 31, 1912, in Uvalde, Texas.

man of charges they will not list, the Board of Regents sentenced a great University to an infamy that makes meaningless its past and futile its future."

Dobie returned to the Austin campus in 1945. Two years later several European universities requested he return for another tour as Visiting Professor. Dobie's request for another leave of absence was rejected. The Board of Regents passed a rule that no professor could be absent for more than two years. Since then, this rule has been known as "the Dobie Law." The Board and Dobie would continue to clash. In 1956, Dobie had this to say when the regents attempted to censor the *Daily Texan*: "The Board of Regents of the University of Texas are as much concerned with free intellectual enterprise as a Razorback sow would be with Keats' 'Ode on a Grecian Urn.'" Ouch.

HIS LEGACY

Despite differences with the university, Dobie continued to write and lecture until his death on September 18, 1964. Four days earlier, President Lyndon Baines Johnson, another ranch-bred Texan who had started his professional life as a schoolteacher, had awarded him the nation's highest civilian honor, the Medal of Freedom. He was laid to rest in the state cemetery in Austin.

Dobie published sixteen books in his lifetime, and his legacy also lives on in the Dobie-Piasano Foundation. He deeded his Piasano Ranch to the University of Texas and left funds for a stipend to support artists and writers for six months on the ranch in the hills above Austin, so they can work on their projects free of any distractions.

* * * * *

BOOKS BY J. FRANK DOBIE

1929 *A Vaquero of the Brush Country*	1947 *Tongues of the Monte*
1931 *Coronado's Children*	1949 *The Voice of the Coyote*
1931 *On the Open Range*	1950 *The Ben Lilly Legend*
1936 *Tales of the Mustang*	1955 *A Texan in England*
1936 *The Flavor of Texas*	1955 *Up the Trail From Texas*
1939 *Apache Gold and Yaqui Silver*	1955 *Tales of Old-Time Texas*
1941 *The Longhorns*	1960 *I'll Tell You a Tale*
1942 *Guide to Literature of the Southwest*	1964 *Cow People*
	1965 *Rattlesnakes* (Posthumously)

Kermit, Texas, was named for the son of President Theodore Roosevelt.

URBAN LEGENDS
<u>TEXAS STYLE</u>

Two famous urban legends got their start deep in the heart of Texas.

Urban myths have long been a mainstay of modern life, but the Internet is certainly giving them a life of their own. But did you know that two of the most famous legends of all time got their start in Texas? The University of Texas and Neiman Marcus are both the sources for two old favorites.

LOOK MA, NO KIDNEYS!
You may have heard this one before. According to legend, it all happened at the University of Texas at Austin during something called Texas Premier (more on that later). So the story goes that a guy goes to a party, has a grand time, drinks a bit too much, and is invited by a dazzling beauty to follow her to another bash. Once there it all gets hazy . . .

He wakes up naked and shivering in a bathtub full of ice. There's a telephone next to the tub and written on his chest is "Call 911 or you will die!" He calls and the operator tells him to look in the mirror and check for bodily damage. He finds nine-inch incisions along his back. His kidneys were stolen and sold on the black market for $10,000 each! The poor student is left on life support in the hospital awaiting a spare kidney. Help him now, the newspaper story allegedly read. Only it didn't. The *Daily Texan* never ran any story resembling a true tale of kidney theft.

SOMEONE STOLE THE TRUTH!
Of course, the only true victim was the *Daily Texan*. According to Internet hoax experts at Snopes.com, an administrative assistant at the university received the kidney-napping story in an email; she forwarded it on to her friends. As it made the rounds of cyberspace, the assistant suddenly morphed into the *Daily Texan*'s editor and the newspaper, not a chain email, became the source of the original story. Her email address stayed in the message header, which only fueled the fire.

Novelist-screenwriter Terry Southern (*Candy, Dr. Strangelove*) was born in Alvarado, Texas.

For years, the *Daily Texan* has fought the perception that they reported the story. For a few years, it ran a blurb on its Web site announcing that the story was all a hoax and there is not an event called "Texas Premier."

THEM COOKIES IS TASTY!

The kidney tale pales in comparison to the saga of expensive baked goods that hounds swanky Texas department store Neiman Marcus to this day. The legend is a woman was eating at the store with her daughter and tried the Neiman Marcus Cookie. It was the best cookie she'd ever tasted! She asked the woman behind the counter for the recipe and was told she had to pay "two-fifty" for it. "No problem," the happy cookie lover said and handed over her credit card. Two dollars and fifty cents was a steal! Weeks later, her credit card bill arrived with a charge for $250 for "cookie recipe." Incensed, she called Neiman-Marcus to complain. Nope, that was the charge, she was told.

So, she seeks revenge. In an email you've probably received yourself, she tells her story and then includes the pricey cookie recipe. The email closes with a plea for you to forward it to all your friends and stick it to the evil Neiman Marcus! Revenge is oh-so-sweet.

YES, THERE ARE FREE COOKIE RECIPES

Only it isn't revenge at all. Like most urban myths, this incident never happened. The expensive cookie legend goes back perhaps 50 years, with Neiman Marcus as just the latest victim. Mrs. Fields Cookies has been a victim prior to Neiman Marcus's rise to evil corporate cookiedom.

You can get your mitts on the cookie recipe for free. Just go to Neiman Marcus's web site and you'll find it for free next to a note explaining that the whole thing never happened. Or you can ask for the recipe at the store and get if for free. Of course, Neiman Marcus came up with a recipe only after the Internet legend started.

FORT HOOD
LOOMS LARGE

In April 2002, Late Night With David Letterman's "Top 10 List" was "Top 10 Responses to 'How big is your Army base?'" Ten soldiers stationed at Fort Hood, Texas answered that question. Number Four got the biggest laugh when SFC Alec Fry, a First Cavalry Division tank commander said: "Let's just say, big enough."

Fort Hood is just plain big (it's not the biggest military installation in the United States—that honor belongs to Florida's Eglin Air Force Base). It's the largest armored installation, meaning it's got the most tanks, trucks, and HumVees—anything on wheels. No wonder the Fort Hood-based Fourth Infantry Division's motto is "Hell On Wheels!" Thousands of vehicles, hundreds of motor pools, and acre after acre of parched training area are laid out smack in the middle of Texas.

OPERATION LONGHORN

Construction on what was originally known at Camp Hood near Killeen, Texas, began in 1942. In 1951 Fort Hood was designated a permanent military installation. Named for Confederate General John Bell Hood (while post-Civil War Americans might not realize it, several Army posts are named after Confederate generals, including Fort Lee, Virginia and Fort Jackson, South Carolina), Fort Hood is the only post in the United States capable of stationing and training two Armored Divisions, a headquarters group (III Corps), the 3rd Personnel Group, the 3rd Signal Brigade, the 3rd Air Support Operations Group, the 21st CAV Brigade, the 89th Military Police Brigade, the 504th Military Intelligence Brigade, and many other units and tenant organizations. The post's primary mission is to maintain armored units in a state of readiness for combat missions.

Today Fort Hood comprises 214,570 acres, about 335 square miles! Yep, as troops began arriving on Camp Hood in 1942, some 300 farming and ranching families had to give up their land on very, very short notice from the federal government; in the

Its arboreal deficiency has been remedied somewhat since the town was founded in 1946.

mid-1950s, during "Operation Longhorn," the government leased even more acres of ranchland in order to conduct the world's largest-to-date exercise involving paratroopers.

WHERE THE BOMBS WERE

While Fort Hood's large-scale exercises were making contemporary headlines, its large-scale role as a Cold War storage facility was a closely guarded secret. Site Baker (also known as Killeen Base), a part of Fort Hood, was next to Gray Air Force Base, one of three National Stockpile Sites where nuclear weapons were stored, assembled, and maintained

The 7,000-acre Site Baker was constructed from 1947–1948 and owned by the Air Force until 1952. It was placed to the west of then-Camp Hood, and its construction was shrouded in secrecy. Warrens of 20-foot wide and 30-foot high concrete tunnels were carved out of solid rock down to 80 feet below a mountain and reinforced with steel. From 1952–1969 it was owned and operated by the Army, the only one of seven such sites nationwide to be under the Army's control.

In 1969 the Defense Atomic Support Agency redesignated Site Baker as part of Fort Hood. Now it became part of the army's testing directorate, because its low-lying, cool tunnels were ideal for research and development of all manner of military gear, including weapons, uniforms, and vehicle components. Site Baker is now known as West Fort Hood—and fittingly, that's where the 504th Military Intelligence Brigade is stationed.

THE CAISSONS GO ROLLING ALONG . . .

Of the 71,580 folks on post at Fort Hood on any given day, 40,672 are military personnel assigned to duties that include maneuvers on training area of 335 square miles, or 136,094 acres, involving 2,619 tracked vehicles and 11,932 wheeled vehicles.

BUT NEVER OVER THE SONGBIRDS . . .

Despite all of the road-chomping, foot-stomping military activity at Fort Hood, the locale serves as an essential nesting habitat for two endangered neotropical migratory songbirds: the golden-cheeked warbler and the black-capped vireo. Fort Hood partners

---

NASCAR's new Texas Motor Speedway in Fort Worth is America's second largest sports facility.

with the U.S. Fish and Wildlife Service to manage 25 percent of the base (about 66,000 acres) as recovery area for these two species.

OR THE BURIAL MOUNDS . . .

In 1973 skeletal remains of forty-five Indians were reinterred at Fort Hood, where there are more than 2,000 archaeological sites dating from the Ice Age, including more than 1,000 sites of hunting and gathering people from all major time periods in Texas's pre-history and in the nineteenth and early twentieth centuries. Descendants of the reinterred Indians are the only people allowed access to that land.

From military might to animal rights, Fort Hood's size is about more than just acreage: it plays roles in many different areas. However, the post's primary duty is to maintain the readiness of its armored units—something the American people and Fort Hood's own soldiers deployed to the Middle East won't soon forget.

* * * * *

THE LAST WORDS

"Texas: It's Like a Whole Other Country"
—*Slogan from the Texas State Travel Guide*

"Texans don't lie. We just think bigger."
—A *Solid Explanation*

"Don't Mess With Texas"
—Good Advice *(also an antilittering slogan)*

A young man asked his grandfather, "What would you be if you weren't a Texan?"
His grandfather answered, "Ashamed."

ANSWERS

SOLUTION TO "TEXAS BASICS" FROM PAGE 3.

1 – A Austin

2 – B Houston has over 1.9 million people.

3 – D Boone County

4 – D The Colorado River in Texas is different from the other Colorado River that makes its way through the Grand Canyon.

5 – C Sixteen. Three species of copperheads, eleven rattlers, one kind of cotton mouth, and the Texas coral snake.

6 – A The mercury rose to 120 degrees F twice, in 1936 and again in 1994. It fell to -23 twice as well, once in 1899 and again in 1933.

7 – C Yes, there really is a town called "Tolette" and no town called "Whatchamacallit."

8 – A There were 14 million cattle accounted for in 2003—a value of $8.4 billion.

9 – B Smokey is sure to be on your tail if you're over 70 mph.

10 – D 20 million people call the Lone Star state home.

SOLUTION TO "PICK-UP TRUCK POP QUIZ" FROM PAGE 101.

1 – A The 1994 Chevrolet C1500 4x2. In a 2003 study of most popular stolen vehicles, pickup trucks took the top 11 spots in Texas. By contrast, the number one stolen vehicles in their respective states include the 1989 Toyota Camry in California, the 2000 Honda Civic Si in New York, and the 1994 Honda Accord LX in Florida.

2 – D Porsche was a professor at the time he developed his La Toujours Contente (Always Satisfies), over 100 years before the Porsche company mass-produced the Porsche Cayenne—its modern 450 horsepower uber-SUV.

3 – C   Street and Racing Technology. This street bully was
fashioned with the chassis and body of a Dodge Ram
1500 and the power plant from a Dodge Viper: a 500
horsepower, 505 cubic inch V-10 monster that tops out
around 150 mph. It comes with a Hurst shift linkage,
Dana 60 rear axle, Pirelli tires, Bilstein shocks, custom-
designed power hop damper, and brakes from a Ram
Heavy Duty work truck.

4 – B   In 2004, the 250-acre General Motors plant in Arlington
celebrated its fiftieth anniversary. The facility has been
expanded seven times over the years and currently
produces such popular models as the GMC Yukon,
Chevrolet Suburban, Chevrolet Tahoe, and Cadillac
Escalade. The 27 GM plants in Texas have about a
$4 billion economic impact on the state.

5 – D   Go between two- and four-wheel drive while moving. In
the old days, when you wanted to go off-roading in your
four-wheel drive, you had to stop the truck, get out and.
"lock-in" the two front wheel hubs manually.

6 – D   The Scout. Heavy machinery manufacturer International
Harvester started the Scout line of trucks in 1961 and
quickly gained traction as the truck of choice for serious
off-road connoisseurs. By the 1970s the truck was a leg
end. But then came the days of the gas line; the pressure
to make more fuel-efficient cars just didn't jibe with beasts
that swapped parts with huge, industrial vehicles. The
whole product line was scrapped in 1980. Scouts can still
be seen from Lubbock to Plano—towing more popular
road-warrior wanna-bes out of the mud and into the
realization that not all four-wheel drives were created equal.

7 – B   At the beach. It's a defense to prosecution under this
statute if you're legally driving on the beach. It's also legal,
if not always advisable, to tote your kids in the back
during a parade, emergency, hayride, or from one farm
field to another for work purposes. But unless you have a

good excuse, the Texas Department of Public Safety can slap you with a misdemeanor that carries up to a $200 fine.

8 – D Nunn, a Brownfield native (who's also famous for "That's What I Like about Texas" and "London Homesick Blues"), sang the Texas classic in which he warns: "Slow down, slow down, we're all movin' too fast, slow down, slow down, in pickup truck Texas, slow down . . . " But Rick Cardwell wrote the tune.

SOLUTION TO "TEXAS MOVIE QUIZ" FROM PAGE 82.

1. Mac Davis
2. New Orleans
3. Frank Sinatra and Dean Martin
4. Wim Wenders
5. Gilley's
6. *Midnight Run*
7. Matthew McConaughey
8. Fandango
9. John Wayne
10. Joe Don Baker

SOLUTION TO "TUNEFUL TEXAS TOWNS" FROM PAGE 194.

1. F, Bob Dylan
2. H, Kinky Friedman
3. B, Willie Nelson
4. D, Charley Pride
5. G, Waylon Jennings
6. E, The Grateful Dead
7. C, Emmylou Harris
8. A, Johnny Cash

SOLUTION TO "TRAIPSING THROUGH TEXAS" FROM PAGE 28.

The leftover letters spell: Some other cities are Brownfield, Brownsville, and Brownwood.

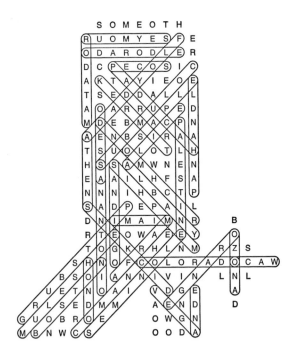

SOLUTION TO "TEXANS IN TERRIBLE TROUBLE" FROM PAGE 150.

1 – C Joe Ball
2 – E T. Cullen Davis
3 – A Robert Durst
4 – O John Wesley Hardin
5 – J Clara Harris
6 – D Genene Jones
7 – M Ronald Clark O'Bryan
8 – G Walker Railey
9 – B Charles Reynolds
10 – H Darlie Routier
11 – K Jeff Skilling
12 – F Karla Faye Tucker
13 – L David Waters
14 – I Charles "Tex" Watson
15 – N Andrea Yates

SOLUTION TO "SCANDALOUS STARS" FROM PAGE 287.

1 – A Gary Busey
2 – G Colby Donaldson
3 – F Jamie Foxx
4 – E Woody Harrelson
5 – C Waylon Jennings
6 – D Janis Joplin
7 – I Matthew McConaughey
8 – H Willie Nelson
9 – J Anna Nicole Smith
10 – B Barry Switzer

SOLUTION TO "HOWDY GUV!" FROM PAGE 288.

The leftover letters spell: The guv we forgot to mention is
President George W. Bush.

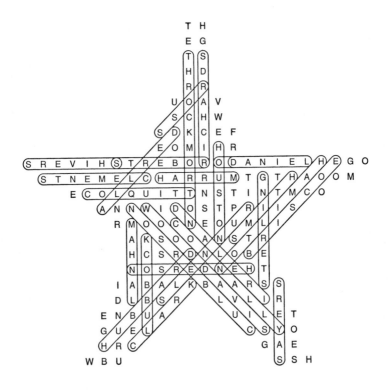

TO ORDER

Contact:
Bathroom Readers' Press
P.O. Box 1117,
Ashland, OR 97520
Phone: 541-488-4642
Fax: 541-482-6159
brorders@mind.net
www.bathroomreader.com

Shipping & Handling Rates:
- 1 book: $3.50
- 2 – 3 books: $4.50
- 4 – 5 books: $5.50
- 5 + books: $1.00/ book

Priority shipping also
available.
We accept checks &
credit card orders.
Order online, or by fax, mail,
e-mail, or phone.

Wholesale Distributor
Publishers Group West (U.S.):
800-788-3123
Raincoast Books (Canada):
800-663-5714

THE LAST PAGE

Uncle John's new Readers are already in the works!

Keep your eyes out for:

- *Uncle John's Slightly Irregular Bathroom Reader*—the biggest and best! (Nov. 04)
- *Uncle John's Plunges into the Presidency* (Aug. 04)
- *Uncle John's Plunges into History Again!* (Sept. 04)
- *Uncle John's Colossal Collection of Quotable Quotes* (Oct. 04)
- *Uncle John's Plunges into Michigan* (Dec. 04)
- *Uncle John's for Kids Only: Big Book of Fun* (Aug. 04)

For more information on what's new with Uncle John and to keep abreast of any new developments, why not become a member of the Bathroom Readers' Institute? You'll receive an:

- Official membership card,
- A permanent spot on the BRI honor role, *and*
- Issues of the BRI e-mail newsletter, filled with special offers on our books and other Uncle John's merchandise.

Just send a self-addressed, stamped envelope to:

Bathroom Readers' Institute
P.O. Box 1117
Ashland, Oregon 97520

Or sign up when you visit our web site:

www.bathroomreader.com.

As always, we thank you for your support and look forward to your thoughts and comments.

Enjoy!